Gifted Books, Gifted Readers

Literature Activities to Excite Young Minds

Nancy J. Polette

2000
Libraries Unlimited, Inc.
Englewood, Colorado

Libraries Unlimited, Inc.
P.O. Box 6633
Englewood, CO 80155-6633
1-800-237-6124
www.lu.com

Library of Congress Cataloging-in-Publication Data

Polette, Nancy.
    Gifted books, gifted readers : literature activities to excite young minds / Nancy J. Polette.
        p. cm.
    Includes bibliographical references and index.
    ISBN 1-56308-822-3
    1. Literature--Study and teaching (Elementary)--United States. 2. Reading (Elementary)--United States. 3. Gifted children--Education (Elementary)--United States.
    4. Gifted children--United States--Books and reading. I. Title.

LB1575.5.U5 P64 2000
371.95--dc21   00-023257

Gifted Books,
Gifted Readers

Contents

Acknowledgments

The author is grateful to the following educators who have contributed literature units for inclusion in this book:

Joan Ebbesmeyer: "The Classics and Poetry." Reprinted from *Literature Classics for Children* (Book Lures, Inc., 1995). With permission of Book Lures, Inc.

Edmund Staude: *Snow Treasure* unit

Karen Machens: *James and the Giant Peach* unit

Laura Abbott: *Mr. Lincoln's Drummer Boy* unit

Esther V. Murray: *Jericho's Journey* unit

Kathy Miller and Stacie Critchlow: *My Brother Sam Is Dead* unit

Literature for the Gifted
A Gateway to Greatness

We are living today in a sea of words. Our children are bombarded from the day of their birth by radio, television, computers, cereal boxes, signs, and billboards. Children who are identified as gifted can hardly keep from becoming "letterate" unless pressures from home or classroom have built a wall of resistance to printed symbols. Many educators feel that when released from scholastic pressures gifted children would learn to read on their own, effortlessly. So the question arises, are we doing enough to build a society of individuals who are "literate" in the full sense of the word? When one considers the number of classroom hours spent on phonics, sight drills, basal texts, and other reading skills, in contrast to the number of true readers in our society, it becomes evident that "literacy" is a rather singular accomplishment, or soon will be.

But we are not helpless; writers with profound messages and artistic brilliance are focusing their creative talents in books particularly appropriate for gifted children. Although we cannot, however dedicated we are and no matter how hard we try, be in tune with all of the active mental meanderings and discoveries our gifted students are experiencing, we can lure gifted children to meet gifted writers. We can introduce them to those who through the centuries have spoken through the pages of literature to the greatness within those who are listening. Lively, creative minds are writing today as well, and we need but to get their works into children's hands.

There are those who would ask, "Do the gifted really need a literature program? Surely, children who started reading early and are already fluent in written language can find their own way." Those of us who have gone down a rabbit hole, climbed the mast of a plunging schooner with a pirate hot on our tails, learned to breathe underwater on a Martian moon: Those of us who have done these things realize how narrow and bleak our lives would have been if untouched by these mind-stretching adventures. Beyond the skill of learning to read lies a land of vision and enchantment. A child who is never pointed in that direction may grow to adulthood literate in only the "letters" sense of the word, and with a sadly undernourished spirit.

A literature program can do much to enrich the lives of gifted children who might otherwise have no stimulus to strive for excellence. Competition in an average classroom can be suffocating or demanding to the sleeping intellectual.

Reading itself is not as great a problem as what to read after either letteracy or literacy has been achieved. The information overload stuns us all. The gifted student cannot learn everything there is to know (even in any one subject) during his or her lifetime. It is said that the mark of an educated man is his ability not to be overwhelmed by the freight train of knowledge hitting him. So perhaps selectivity is the most essential skill to be learned today. Children need to develop it in their reading as well as in all other areas of choice. Especially in literature, it is surely better for the gifted reader to savor beauty and meaning, to assimilate luxuriously at his or her own pace, than to gulp frantically and forget.

Great books do help to shape great minds. Understanding real humanity, nobility of character, and the vitality of love through books of quality rather than through counterfeit, superficial, remote, and plastic mannequins of the media world helps one to live life deeply. Real writers know that love and life are inseparable. Isaac Bashevis Singer, the talented Yiddish storyteller, admitted, "Kindness, I've discovered, is everything in life."[1] Humor and subtlety, as well as kindness, radiate from his rich tales for children.

IMAGINATION ILLUMINATES REALITY

Our schools have tended to overemphasize the "steam shovel" approach to learning. The "how to" or "first book" of atoms, magnets, automobiles, and pumpkin pies abounds in classrooms and school libraries. In learning the construction of a bird's wings, we must not allow gifted children to lose the awe that it does take flight. In our absorption with practicality, we can't let building freeways overshadow building bridges to one another's hearts. The great Russian writer for and about children, Kornei Chukovsky, warned against those who look upon every children's book as something that must immediately produce some visible, touchable, beneficial effect, as if a book were a nail or a yoke.[2]

Many young children are placed at computer keyboards before they can read. They are taken to engine rooms, factories, and offices, use telephones and computers with frequency and amazing dexterity. Are we spending as much time emphasizing the quality of imagination that can grasp the unseen, the intangible? Chukovsky has also cautioned that the present belongs to the sober, the cautious, the routine-prone, but the future belongs to those who do not rein in their imaginations. He has also told us that without imaginative fantasy there would be complete stagnation in both physics and chemistry.[3] It is interesting to note how many of those working in our space program were avid readers of science fiction in their growing-up years!

One of the world's great thinkers, Albert Einstein, has written, "The fairest thing we can experience is the mysterious. It is the fundamental emotion which stands at the cradle of true art and true science. He who knows it not, who can no longer wonder, can no longer feel amazement is as good as dead—a snuffed out candle."[4] He would be saddened, no doubt, to know that some critics say that many academically talented youngsters who are placed in gifted programs either cannot or are afraid to comprehend a dragon. Our gifted children need to be given the opportunity through books to develop an elasticity of mind. Many dragons face us all in life today, and fortunate is the child who has tilted with many on his or her path and emerged victorious. Fortunate, too, is the child who has won dragons to his or her side through gentleness and understanding. The child will need both skills in the years ahead. What better skill sharpener than exposure to meaningful books, for all great books, including (or especially) fantasies, teach us about life.

INSPIRED WRITERS

Gifted children today are privileged indeed that so many of the most talented and creative thinkers in the literary world are speaking to them. It is interesting to read how many authors who write the very best juvenile fiction do not consider themselves "writers for children." They speak from the heart and unselfconscious children respond. William Armstrong didn't know his book

Sounder was a juvenile book until after it was published. He had a story to tell about human beings who care for one another and the publisher decided who would listen.

Madeleine L'Engle writes in *A Circle of Quiet,* an autobiographical work that shines with quality like all her books: "If I have something to say that is too difficult for adults to swallow, than I will write it in a book for children. … Children still haven't closed themselves off with fear of the unknown, fear of revolution or the scramble for security."[5]

All children, including the gifted, should have the opportunity to wonder. Gifted students are so easily catapulted into the world of pure academia, a world of fact and figures and reason. But without the wonder, the humanness of compassion, charity and empathy, where is the link to bind all people together? We must keep on the alert not to bypass those sharp perceivers who will help the world to find answers to living together in harmony. Enlightened authors with lucid minds and fresh styles for communicating ideas will help us.

A six-year-old who was reading at the ninth-grade level entered a private school. He was unable to tie his shoes, skip, or relate to the other children. His teachers were conscious of his need for growth in awareness of others, but his parents were dedicated to his intellect, feeding him a steady and heavy diet of fact books: astronomy, biology, and paleontology. Will he grow into an adult recluse, or will someone reach him with mythology and folklore to help his humanity keep stride with his academic genius? It will take dedicated teachers to help balance his exploding intellect with an understanding of the needs of his neighbors. A literature program will help his heart to sing along with his mind.

It is the authors who do not blunt their pens when they write for children who lift us all to a clearer view of ourselves and our reason for being, whose words ignite us. We are blessed by many dedicated and gifted writers who are leaving, or have left, messages that continue to change and live and perhaps ultimately save mankind: J. R. R. Tolkien, C. S. Lewis, Ursula LeGuin, Mary Norton, Natalie Babbitt, and E. B. White are among many. If some eyebrows are still raised at the notion that the substance of fantasy could be considered a world saver, just call it a sanity saver.

BOOKS TO ADD ZEST

Gifted children need not only mystery, awe, and wonder in their lives, but also laughter and joy and delight. When we can laugh at ourselves, it clears the air so we can do better after the next tumble. When a nation can recognize its shortcomings, chuckle over its foibles, and regroup to plunge ahead with lightened heart, surely the chances for success are more secure. Even if the concerted effort of all the creative thinkers who write and read is not enough to turn the tide of human events, surely laughter can enhance the struggle. How many gifted children continue to ask for another book like *The True Story of The Three Little Pigs* by Jon Scieszka and Lane Smith or Barbara Robinson's *The Best (Worst) School Year Ever?* Even an "I-Can-Read" book laced with enough humor can be a best-circulator. Note the Amelia Bedelia series books, which are in danger of being torn asunder as children fight over who gets which one next. One child confessed to his teacher, "I don't know whether it's *Winnie the Pooh* which is so funny or the way you read it." The teacher's enjoyment had spilled over into her voice, doubling the shared pleasure.

Even if all the reading of the great books and great authors had no effect on the lives absorbing them, we still have the matter of language. It is impossible for gifted readers to continue to read challenging books without expanding their vocabularies. How much more rewarding for the child than memorizing vocabulary lists! When words are confronted again and again in various ways, with all their subtleties implied, the gifted child is deepening not only his or her means of communicating but the ability to handle ideas as well. Concepts are difficult to wrestle with when we have no means of communicating them. Even within, we seem to need words to clarify our thoughts. A child who is deprived of the richness of language is deprived of the greatest tool he or she has been given to tackle the future. Language is the key to all of life, to all ideas, all thinking, all sharing.

Gifted children often have a natural affinity and delight with words. One pre-schooler came dancing downstairs for breakfast singing, "Fee, fi, fo, fum, I smell the blood of an English muffin!" From the earliest experiences with *Mother Goose* to the "punny" *Nose Drops* by Larry Schles (where a nose lost from its face wants to achieve greatness, like Dr. Hypotenose or Julius Sneezer), language fascinates and lures them. The lyrical language of Bill Martin, Jr.'s "Listen to the Rain" inspired a group of sixth graders in a Michigan gifted program to create their own "Listen to the Sea" poems with lines such as "Listen to the sea, the roaring of the sea, the stomping, moving matter, the clang and clash and clatter, the mournful sound, the roaring of the sea."

Many gifted children are natural poets, and when exposed to the fluid beauty of genuine poetry, as well as nonsense verse, they respond with ever keener adeptness in their own communications. Still in tune with the living poetry in wind, sea, and sky, they share with us such awakenings as, "Ice is water which has gone to sleep." Or after hearing waves breaking on a beach one twilight: "Does the ocean clear its throat all night?" And who could forget that perfect expression of disappointment, uttered thus: "I fell down inside."

Young gifted children can be intensely literal when the world of words is fresh and new. When asked to help "pick up the living room" before going to bed, one tike responded, "I can't. It's attached to the house." Another offered, "You always say the water is running. Why can't it walk?" Then there was the timid toddler, squealing in fear over a beetle crossing the floor, who was admonished to love it and it wouldn't hurt her. She remarked in exasperation, "You can't love a bug, it hasn't any neck."

BOOKS AS EXPERIENCE

Words, of course, are not substitutes for life. Nor are books substitutes for experience: They *are* experience. Gifted children seek more than the commonplace in their language and in their lives. Books can and do provide interesting, stimulating, ever-fresh experiences. Good books release new energies in the minds that absorb them. This energy radiates out in an ever-widening circle.

Everything gifted children read or experience is enhanced by everything else they have read or experienced. We could liken the consciousness of the gifted child to a giant jigsaw puzzle, with pieces missing here and there. Each literary experience can perhaps fit a missing piece of understanding into the whole, until a world view is achieved that is solid and beautiful.

There are diversities of gifts, but in this book the focus is on those children whose talents currently lie in the intellectual realm. How many geniuses have drifted through school unrecognized, or as failures? The list goes beyond Einstein and Edison. It includes Isaac Newton, Leo Tolstoy, Louis Pasteur, Walt Disney, Louisa May Alcott, and Winston Churchill. The invasion of mediocrity into classrooms produces an incalculable loss; the tyranny of modern thought sets limits on mental powers and obscures potential excellence.

Gifted literature can lure excellence to the surface. Literature can help us to identify those with a quickened heart and mind. Watch for the child who bursts out with sudden laughter at subtle humor or irony when you are reading aloud in a classroom. Watch for the brimming of tears when a deep source of compassion for the human condition is unleashed. Be alert to notice the spark of recognition of an underlying profound truth beneath a simple tale.

Not all children see life alike. Yet the sensitivity of perceptions will often reveal a child's gifts. A good piece of literature is not one-way communication. It is a catalyst to facilitate the reader's own source of unfolding thought. Reading is only incidentally visual or aural; the print has no power in itself. It is the power of the gifted reader's deep personal intuition, knowledge, and understanding that activates the message.

Our gifted children do not need more and more words bombarding them from all sides. They need deeper, more beautiful, more heart-stretching and mind-stretching ideas to confront. They need to be offered books with a variety of levels of meaning to free their minds for the gymnastics of which they are capable.

Books such as Lois Lowry's *The Giver* can reinforce an awareness of the indomitable human spirit; hope, loyalty, and courage surmount the many obstacles that war and its consequences create in Theodore Taylor's *The Cay. Tuck Everlasting,* by Natalie Babbitt, leaves one pondering the meaning of temporal life. Would physical immortality be a blessing? Walter Dean Myers's *Amistad: A Long Road to Freedom* can impel a reader to contemplate the meaning of freedom, recognize courage and resourcefulness, and feel the subtle power of a timeless saga.

There are innumerable books to pump the bloodstreams of our talented children with feeling. And how many fine biographies inspire the reader to set his or her goals high? More than can be tallied here. By the largeness of one's dreams does one truly live! Books initiate and enhance those dreams. They tell us that nothing is impossible, that love heals, that different is not bad.

TRAITS AND NEEDS OF GIFTED CHILDREN

Gifted children may have both positive and negative traits. Many become bored with the standard curriculum and refuse to conform. These children can come from varied backgrounds and have social and emotional needs that may not be related to their superior intellects. Gifted children often have passions that they pursue to the exclusion of other subjects and many times study only those things in which they have a consuming interest. Not all gifted students are easy to identify, some may also have learning difficulties and may be highly gifted in one subject but not others. Gifted children who are also highly creative may have difficulty in adjusting to the structures of school.

An excellent example of the nonconforming gifted child is found in *Shy Charles,* by Rosemary Wells. Charles would never say hello, good-bye, please, or thank you, much to the dismay of his parents. They tried football and ballet but nothing worked ... until the baby sitter fell and Charles had to interrupt his spaceship building to take action.

Arthur Koestler has said that, "True creativity often starts where language ends."[6] Nonverbal Charles demonstrates his creativity by building a spaceship out of items found in his bedroom. Brian Aldiss, the science fiction writer, defines creativity as the solution to a problem.[7] Charles quickly solves the problem of the baby sitter's fall by calling for emergency assistance. And finally, from May Sarton comes a description of Charles's problem of giftedness that many children face: "The creative person who moves from an irrational source of power, has to face the fact that this power antagonizes."[8]

The basic premise of *Gifted Books, Gifted Readers* is that the creativity that is such a powerful part of the gifted child, no matter what the specific area of his or her giftedness, must be brought to the reading experience. The educator who guides these children must know literature and be able to help in extending their choices (and their minds) to ever-greater literature challenges. This book details two ways in which this can be done.

First, strategies and techniques are suggested to build excitement and anticipation for the reading experience. The literature guides, the areas of concentration, and the specific titles recommended were chosen to help children become sensitive to the personal and social as well as the technological problems of humanity; to realize that many problems require creative solutions and that creative thinkers may be the hope of humanity. The questions that are included for many suggested titles are not test questions or even comprehension questions. They are provided as a guide for the teacher or librarian in stimulating creative thinking; in helping children to analyze that which they read and to use the insights gained in creating new solutions for problems. The questions are best used for small group discussion, with each group having a secretary to record the main ideas. The secretary then reports on the group's discussion to the class or others who have read the book. Questions are open ended and might begin with "How many ways," "What if," "If you were," "Suppose that," or "How is _____ like ___?" The child whose reading horizons are expanded through the enthusiastic suggestions and support of a teacher or librarian who really cares will have an ever-widening area of experience for problem solving, decision making, and bringing his or her creativity not only to the reading experience but to life.

Second, *Gifted Books, Gifted Children* attempts to assist educators in providing those conditions in which the child can act upon what he or she has read. Suggestions are given for creative production, elaboration, rearrangement, and transformation of text. Both the pre- and post-reading activities are designed to help the child connect his or her own experiences with the experiences of literary characters. An activity such as "Find someone who ..." lists events that happen in the story and asks students to find someone in their class who has had the same experience. Vocabulary activities allow children to use their language storehouses combined with vocabulary from the literature to play charades, create super-long sentences, or group words in a variety of ways.

Post-reading activities are those that allow children to respond in an environment of psychological safety. Many research reporting patterns are provided for students to use in sharing information. The patterns can be used to report on either real or literary characters and events and require that the student show understanding of the information. Research data cannot be copied because the child must show understanding by organizing the information in new ways. Enough guidance is given so that the child feels comfortable exploring new ways of responding with original products in which he or she can take pride.

The titles chosen for inclusion in this text are not intended to be an inclusive reading list for gifted students. Rather, the titles are meant to be representative of the kinds of books that have appeal to the gifted reader at a variety of ages and stages.

This book is intended as a beginning. In any program of gifted education, there must first be an identified need for going beyond the standard curriculum. However, as the curriculum changes to meet this need, the effects of the change should be felt by every child in the school. For example, as bright underachievers begin to see the genuine excitement of others in exploring books, they, too, may want to peel the words off the page to get to the ideas underneath.

And that is what this book is all about.

NOTES

1. Grace Farrell, *Isaac Bashevis Singer: Conversations* (University Press of Mississippi, 1992).

2. Kornei Chukovsky, *From Two to Five* (University of California Press, 1963).

3. Ibid.

4. Helen Duke and Banesh Hoffmann, eds., *Albert Einstein: The Human Side: New Glimpses from His Archives* (Princeton University Press, 1981).

5. Madeleine L'Engle, *A Circle of Quiet* (HarperCollins, 1986).

6. Arthur Koestler, *The Act of Creation* (Arkana Publishers, 1990).

7. Brian Aldiss, *The Twinkling of an Eye* (St. Martin's Press, 1999).

8. May Sarton, *Crucial Conversations* (W. W. Norton, 1994).

Picture Books for Gifted Programs

Fine picture books can help to satisfy the intellectual, social, and emotional needs of elementary gifted children. Among these needs are:

The need to belong

The need to achieve and feel self-esteem

The need for beauty, order, and harmony

The need to cope with stress

The need for laughter, nonsense, and expanded vocabulary

The need to know and extend developing concepts

The titles chosen for this chapter are among the many excellent picture books that speak to these needs. The suggested activities for each book are designed to develop specific thinking skills in young gifted children: (memory skills, sequencing, perceptual skills, classification, reversible thinking, seriation, associative thinking, and audio and tactile perception) and higher level thinking in upper elementary students (fluency, flexibility, originality, elaboration, planning, forecasting, decision making, and problem solving).

THE NEED TO BELONG

The Memory Coat, by Elvira Woodruff. Scholastic, 1998.

Long ago, in faraway Russia, a young girl named Rachel and her cousin, Grisha, lived in a *shetel* with their family. Grisha had recently lost his parents in an epidemic. To help comfort him as he grieved, the two played a storytelling game that drew them close together.

But these bittersweet times came to a sudden end when the Tsar's soldiers invaded the Jewish community with their swords drawn. The family quickly made plans to flee to America, where they would be safe. But they faced one serious obstacle: the inspection station at Ellis Island. For any wrong move could cause one or all of them to be turned away and sent back to Russia.

Hoping to make a good impression at Ellis Island, the family pleaded with Grisha to let them replace his old tattered coat with a new one. But Grisha refused. The coat, which was made by his mother in her last year, still held the powerful memory of her love. This is the moving story of a close-knit family and of a coat that holds their loving stories.

Activities

A.   If you had to flee with your family to another land and could take only what you could carry, what five things you would take? List them in order of importance, with 1 being the most important and 5 being the least important.

1. _____

2. _____

3. _____

4. _____

5. _____

B.   A memory song: After reading *The Memory Coat*, fill in the missing words below. Sing the song to the tune of "My Bonnie Lies Over the Ocean."

This story in faraway (1) R _____

Of Rachel and (2) G _____ so young,

Their games cheered up (3) G _____ the sad boy

Who lost both his parents so young.

Chorus

Rachel, Grisha

When Tsar's soldiers came

They made plans to (4) f _____

To a new land

With freedom that they hoped to see.

Now Grisha would not wear a new (5) c _____

His (6) m _____ had made it with love

(7) I _____ might think he was shabby,

But he knew she smiled from above.

Answer key: 1. Russia 2. Grisha 3. Grisha 4. flee 5. coat 6. mother 7. Inspectors

Too Close Friends, by Shen Roddie. Dial, 1998.

Hippo and Pig are good friends until Hippo cuts the hedge between their houses. Then Hippo sees what a messy eater Pig is and Pig watches Hippo chew his toenails. They decide they don't want to visit each other any more, until time passes and they realize how valuable a good friend can be.

Activities

A.   Questions to think about:

1.   Why do you think Pig and Hippo were such good friends at the beginning of the story?

2.   What was the reason they stopped being friends?

3.   How did the hedge growing back help their friendship?

B.   List things the two do in the story:

drink tea

take mud baths

cut hedges

knit scarves

exercise

lick ladles

chew toenails

watch each other

Choose two and use them in a "London Bridge" song. Example:

> *Pig and Hippo watch each other,*
> *Watch each other, watch each other,*
> *Pig and hippo watch each other ...*
> *and drink tea.*

C.   Phonics: Make hippopotamus jokes by listing words that end in "ip" (slip, drip, etc.). Apply each word to a question about a hippo. Example:

What do you call a hippopotamus that falls down? Answer: A slippotamus.

What do you call a hippopotamus with a runny nose? Answer: A drippotamus!

Lily's Purple Plastic Purse, by Kevin Henkes. Greenwillow, 1996.

School was a wonderful place to be until the day Lilly took her new glittery glasses and purple plastic purse to school. She was so anxious to share her new things that she ignored her teacher's warning to wait and interrupted the class. When her teacher took the things to keep for her until the end of the day, Lilly was furious. She drew a terrible picture of Mr. Slinger and put it into his book bag. Can you guess what happened next?

Activities

A.   Sentence starters:

   1.   A really good day at school would be …

   2.   It would be nice to have a new …

   3.   The best school lunch would be …

   4.   When someone is not having a good day …

B.   Write a Lilly song by listing things Lilly did in the story.

Drew pictures
Taught her brother
Showed her purse
Became furious

Use two of the things in a "London Bridge" song about Lilly. Example:

Little Lilly drew pictures
Drew pictures
Drew pictures
Little Lilly drew pictures
And taught her brother.

C.   The Lightbulb Lab: Pretend you are in The Lightbulb Lab, where questions can have many right answers. What can you name that is:

   1.   As tall as a mountain?

   2.   As fast as a racing car?

   3.   Smaller than an ant?

   4.   Louder than a fire alarm?

   5.   Heavier than an elephant?

   6.   Sweeter than candy?

   7.   Longer than a river?

   8.   Happier than Lilly at school?

D.   A spelling game: Read the directions for making each word. Fill in the blank spaces with the words you make. Use only these letters to make the words: A R H C T E E.

   1.   Use three letters to name one of Lilly's favorite classes in school. ____ ____ ____

   2.   From the word you just made, take away one letter and add one letter to tell what Lilly does at lunchtime. ____ ____ ____

   3.   From the word you made in no. 2, take away one letter and add two letters to make a word that tells what a stomach does when you eat too much. ____ ____ ____ ____

4. Add one letter to the word you made in no. 3 and move letters around to tell what Lilly must do to get something from a high shelf. ____ ____ ____ ____ ____

5. Add two letters to the word you made in no. 4 and move letters around to tell what a person is called who doesn't follow the rules in a game. ____ ____ ____ ____ ____ ____ ____

6. Move the letters around in the word you made for no. 5 to tell what Lily wants to be when she grows up. ____ ____ ____ ____ ____ ____ ____

E. A writing pattern: Lilly thought of many things she wanted to be when she grew up: a dancer, a surgeon, an ambulance driver, a diva, a pilot, and a scuba diver. Choose one of Lilly's ideas and write about it using this pattern:

> *I wish I were a diva (tell what)*
> *Standing on an opera stage (tell where)*
> *Singing a beautiful song (doing what)*
> *Hitting high notes with the orchestra (tell how)*

THE NEED TO ACHIEVE AND FEEL SELF-ESTEEM

King of the Woods, by David Day. Illustrated by Ken Brown. Four Winds, 1993.

A battle is brewing deep in the forest … and one of these bragging creatures will become King of the Woods! Will it be little Wren or screeching Crow? Will it be regal Eagle, master Wolf, or terrible Bear? Or is the big bellowing Bull Moose the most clever and kingly creature of them all? The challenge is on!

Activities

A. To introduce the book, pull from students' experiences.

1. Organize children into groups of four. Give each group a blank sheet of paper. (For children who are not yet reading, use a box of animal pictures. The team chooses four to eight woodland animals. Continue with steps 4 and 5.)

2. Ask the question: What animals would you expect to find in the woods?

3. One team member writes an animal name (or chooses an animal picture) and passes the paper to the next team member. The paper is passed eight times so that eight animals are named.

4. One person from each team reads the team's list aloud. After team 1 has responded, team 2 reads aloud only animals on its list that have not yet been named. The reading of lists continues until all teams have responded. To promote careful listening, an animal name can be read only once.

5. Now challenge each team to select four of the animals team members agree will be in the story.

6. Read the story so that students can see if their guesses were correct.

B.   Animal poems: Complete each verse by adding the missing word.

> *I had a wren*
> *And her name was Twirp*
> *I don't know why*
> *But she loved to _____*

> *I had a wolf*
> *And his name was Carl*
> *I don't know why*
> *But he loved to _____*

> *I had a bear*
> *And his name was Glore*
> *I don't know why*
> *But he loved to _____*

> *I had a moose*
> *And his coat was yellow*
> *I don't know why*
> *But he loved to _____*

C.   A singing game: Sing the song and play the game.

1.   Place the children in a circle (standing).

2.   Give six children a picture of the animal each is to be (wren, crow, eagle, wolf, bear, moose). The wren stands in the center of the circle.

3.   When an animal is named in the song, the child holding that animal card chases wren (or whatever animal is in the center of the circle) around the circle one time. Wren (or the appropriate animal) takes the chaser's place in the circle and the next verse is sung.

4.   The game continues until all verses are sung. Sing to "The Farmer in the Dell."

> *The wren was on the stump*
> *The wren was on the stump,*
> *Sing a song about the woods*
> *The wren was on the stump.*

The _____ chased the wren

The _____ chased the wren

Sing a song about the woods

The _____ chased the wren.

The _____ chased the crow

The _____ chased the crow

Sing a song about the woods

The _____ chased the crow.

The _____ chased the eagle

The _____ chased the eagle

Sing a song about the woods

The _____ chased the eagle.

The _____ chased the wolf

The _____ chased the wolf

Sing a song about the woods

The _____ chased the wolf.

The _____ chased the bear

The _____ chased the bear

Sing a song about the woods

The _____ chased the bear.

The _____ was King of the Woods

The _____ was King of the Woods

Sing a song about the woods

The _____ was King of the Woods.

The Bears on Hemlock Mountain, by Alice Dalgliesh. Scribner, 1990.

Jonathan lived in a stone farmhouse at the foot of Hemlock Mountain. Grown-ups did not think there were bears on the mountain, but Jonathan did. Besides, Uncle James said he had once seen a bear.

When Jonathan's mother sends him over the mountain to borrow a large cooking pot from his aunt, the boy is late in returning and a search party goes out looking for him. What they find is a brave boy who is able to take care of himself.

Activities

A.   About black bears: Answer these questions about black bears. Guess if you do not know.

1.   Black bears weigh ___ pounds when born.

2.   A newborn black bear is ___ inches long.

3.   Black bears live about ___ years.

4.   The largest known black bear weighed ____ pounds.

B.   Introducing vocabulary: Put the following words on separate small cards. Use as many of the words as you can to make two or three sentences about bears. Other words can be added.

Jonathan	munched	bears	hungry
Hemlock Mountain	farmhouse	footprints	tracks
puzzle	creatures	cousins	arched
company	breath	cottontail	raccoon
politeness	relatives	brave	nonsense

C. Chapter projects: *Before* reading each chapter, or group of chapters, choose one of these open-ended sentence starters to complete. Then write two more sentences about it. Be ready to read what you have written to a small group of your classmates.

Chapter One

1. Wild animals get food in winter by …

2. A really good supper would be …

Chapter Two

3. Having lots of relatives would be …

4. Animals you might see in a walk through the woods are …

5. Having 20 people for dinner …

B. Write a food song: This is a verse about food Jonathan's mother cooked.

> *She cooked:*
> | *Brown* | *chicken* | *sizzling* | *in the skillet* |
> | *Yellow* | *corn* | *steaming* | *in the pot* |
> | *Apple* | *pie* | *baking* | *in the oven* |
> *Eat, all you people, eat!*

Sing the song to the tune of "Skip to My Lou."

Write another verse using *your* favorite foods:

I like:

_____	_____	_____	_____
_____	_____	_____	_____
_____	_____	_____	_____

C. Research project:

James taught Jonathan to look closely when he went into the woods. They saw a cottontail rabbit, a song sparrow, and a raccoon.

Choose an animal that lives in the woods. Find facts about the animal. List six facts and number them 1–6. One fact must be a "give away" fact. Ask a classmate to give you a number between one and six. Read the fact for that number. If the student passes, call on another classmate to give you a different number. The game continues until the mystery animal is guessed, or all clues are read. Example:

1. I am sometimes called a clown.
2. I can climb trees.
3. I have black fur.
4. I have four legs.
5. My name rhymes with pear.
6. I sleep in the wintertime.

In the Woods: Who's Been There?, by Lindsay Batt George. Greenwillow, 1995.
    Two children take a walk through the woods and see clues that tell them what animal has been there before them.

Activities

A. Questions and answers:

They see shells of nuts.
Who's been there? Answer: A squirrel.
Draw a picture of something an animal might have left in the woods.
Ask your reader: Who's been there?
On the next page of your book, draw a picture of the animal.

B. Writing patterns: Jonathan would see different things on the mountain at different times of the year. For example, he might see a tadpole in a mountain stream in the spring. By summer the tadpole would be a frog. What other living things change from one form to another? Can you add two more to the following list?

1. A tadpole becomes a frog.
2. An acorn becomes a tree.
3. _____
4. _____

Choose one of the items you added and write a poem about it, using the pattern below.

> *Look at the frog that grew from a tadpole*
> *Slowly, slowly from a tadpole.*
> *In the pond it grew and grew.*
> *Look at the frog, it's brand new!*

Look at the _____ that grew from a _____

Slowly, slowly from a _____

In the _____ it grew and grew.

Look at the _____ it's brand new _____

C. Predict:

Jonathan heads down the mountain when he sees two dark shapes. He hides under the cooking pot as the shapes come closer. Write what you think the shapes are and what will happen next.

Jonathan hid under the cooking pot. As the two shapes came closer and closer he peeked out

and saw _____. The _____ (did what?)

_____ and Jonathan (did what?) _____

_____. The (tell what happened)

_____.

D. Write about spring:

Jonathan continues his journey and sings a song about no bears on Hemlock Mountain. He hears a drip, drip of melting snow. If there were bears, is this a sign of spring? Are they waking up? Write a chant about spring. Follow this pattern for the winter chant.

Winter Things
Cold winds
Warm fires
Icicles
Fur coats
Warm mittens
Ear muffs
These are just a few
Snow boots
Sleeping bears
Bare trees
White snow
Road cleaners
Dark mornings
Fast sleds, too
From near and far
Here they are
WINTER THINGS!

Spring Things

_____

_____

_____

_____

_____

These are just a few

——————————————

——————————————

——————————————

——————————————

——————————————

—————————————— , too

From near and far

Here they are

SPRING THINGS!

About Black Bears

Black bears are sometimes called the clowns of the woods because they like to play, standing on their heads, dancing and falling over and over. Some black bears have brown fur instead of black. They are the smallest of all North American bears. They can climb trees and run fast. Bears spend much of the winter sleeping in caves or hollow trees. They eat fruits, berries, acorns, leaves, and roots of plants. A newborn black bear weighs one-half pound and is about seven inches long. The largest black bear known weighed 900 pounds. Black bears live about 25 years.

THE NEED FOR BEAUTY, ORDER, AND HARMONY

The Bird House, by Cynthia Rylant. Blue Sky/Scholastic, 1998.

A young girl, alone without home or family, sees birds fill the sky above a blue house by the river. A great owl roosts by the front door. The girl returns each day to watch the beautiful birds. And then one day, without warning, the birds take flight and find a way to change the girl's life forever. A modern day fairy tale about loss, beauty, discovery, and the healing power of the natural world.

A.   What do we know about owls? Answer yes or no. Guess if you do not know.

1.   Owls are social and live in groups.

2.   Owls hunt only at night.

3.   Owls eat rodents like mice.

4.   There are 525 different kinds of owls.

5.   The largest owl is the great gray owl.

6.   The smallest owl is the elf owl.

Support or disprove your guesses by reading the owl poem.

B. Questions to think about:

    1. Why was the girl alone?

    2. Where had the girl been before she found the blue house?

    3. Why did she hide from the woman and the birds?

C. Write about the setting of the story: In the woods, what did the girl:

See	Hear	Smell	Taste	Feel

Use the information in the boxes in the following pattern.

The forest is the color of _____

It looks like _____

It sounds like _____

It smells like _____

It tastes like _____

It made the girl feel like _____

Owl Poem
The kinds of owls now alive
Number five hundred and twenty-five
They live alone and hunt at night
Give rats and mice a fearful fright.
The Great Gray Owl is largest of all
The Elf Owl gets the prize for small.

Something Beautiful, by Sharon Dennis Wyeth. Illustrated by Chris K. Soenpiet. Doubleday, 1998.

A little girl longs to see beyond the scary sights on the sidewalk and the angry scribblings in the walls inside her building. When her teacher writes the word *beautiful* on the blackboard, the girl decides to look for something beautiful in her neighborhood.

Her neighbors tell her about their own beautiful things. Miss Delphine serves her a "beautiful" fried fish sandwich at her diner. Her friend Gerogina's "something beautiful" is the music that makes them both dance.

Beautiful means "something that when you have it, your heart is happy," the girl thinks. Her search for "something beautiful" has left her feeling much happier. She has experienced the beauty of friendship and the power of hope.

Activities

A.   Pre-reading activity: Before reading or hearing the story, name one beautiful thing for each letter in the word B E A U T I F U L.

B.   Post-reading activity:

1.   Add more words after each letter. Use some of the things the little girl found: (fried fish sandwiches, jump rope, beads, shoes, apples, moves, sounds, stone, baby).

2.   Use these patterns to write about a beautiful animal and/or a beautiful thing.

• Compare/contrast pattern:

If I had the beautiful coat of a _____ (name a beautiful animal)

I would _____ (tell something it does)

And I'd _____ (tell something else it does)

But I wouldn't _____ (compare with another beautiful animal)

Because _____ (do/does) that.

• Descriptive pattern:

Hey kids! I have a _____ (name something beautiful) for sale. It's

the most beautiful thing you will ever want to own since it _____ (tell three

things that make it beautiful)

and _____

and _____

and the greatest thing about it is _____

• "If I were" pattern:

Name the thing you want to be.
Where is it found?
One thing it would do for someone else.
A second thing it would do.
Repeat the first line.

If I were a blanket
All snug in your bed
I would curl all around you
And keep you warm from toe to head
If I were a blanket.

THE NEED TO COPE WITH STRESS

The Wolf Is Coming, by Elizabeth MacDonald. Illustrated by Ken Brown. Dutton, 1998.

The wary rabbit family is first to notice a crafty intruder on their quiet hillside, and they hurry to warn others: "The wolf is coming! The wolf is coming!"

The chase begins, and the comedy grows as an ever-expanding band of noisy animals flees before the hungry wolf. In a last attempt to escape from him, the enormous crowd of farmyard friends—quite by accident—finds the perfect way to terrify the wolf into leaving the farm forever.

Activities

A.   Writing patterns: List the animals on the board or chart paper:

wolf   rabbit   hen   pig   cow   donkey

Find two that are alike in some way and one that is different. Examples:

A rabbit has four legs
A wolf has four legs
A hen does not have four legs

A cow can make a loud noise
A donkey can make a loud noise
A rabbit cannot make a loud noise

B.   Make a wolf data bank. Use the information in the simple research reporting patterns that follow.

Eats	**Lives**	**Has**
gophers	U.S.	soft fur
rats	woods	bushy tail
rabbits	Alaska	erect ears
What It Does	**What It Looks Like**	
runs fast	large dog	
howls	yellowish gray	
talks	with ears	

A London Bridge Song

Crafty wolves have _____ and _____

_____ and _____

_____ and _____

Crafty wolves eat _____ and _____

And they like to _____

You should never, ever try to ride on a wolf's back because

_____

and _____

and _____

but you can listen when a wolf talks because it talks with its ears.

The Little Old Lady Who Was Not Afraid of Anything, by Linda Williams. HarperCollins, 1986.

Once upon a time there was a little old lady who was not afraid of anything, until one windy autumn night, while walking in the woods, she hears CLOMP CLOMP. "I'm not afraid of you," says the little old lady. But the noises keep growing—CLOMP CLOMP, WIGGLE WIGGLE, SHAKE SHAKE, CLAP CLAP—and the little old lady who was not afraid of anything has the scare of her life! But by using her head and coming up with a great idea, the little old lady finds that everything turns out just right in the end.

Activities

A. Introducing vocabulary: Find two words among the following that go together and tell why.

lady	glove	herbs
basket	silver	shoes
moon	chair	cottage
afternoon	shirt	basket
scarecrow	dark	home

B. Pre-reading sentence starters: Choose one sentence starter to complete. Add ___ more sentences on the topic.

1. Walking alone in a forest …

2. Things some people fear are …

3. People gather herbs because …

4. Reasons to walk fast are …

C. Higher order questions:

1. Suppose the old lady met only the shoes on the path. How would the story change?

2. The little old lady kept saying she was not afraid. Was this true? Why or why not?

D. Sequencing: Create the following story strips, then cut them apart and put them in order to tell the story. Add capital letters and punctuation marks where they belong.

1.   she met a shirt two gloves and a hat

2.   went for a walk in the forest.

3.   she ran home and sat in her chair

4.   the next morning she found a scarecrow

5.   she met two big shoes and a pair of pants

6.   one afternoon a little old lady

7.   on her way home

8.   she met a huge scary pumpkinhead

E.   Play the phonics game: Find two words that are alike and one that is different. Explain your choices. Example:

Which word does not belong?

shining   spices   windy

Windy does not belong because it has a short "i."

lady	woman	forest
cottage	clomp	wiggle
shake	herbs	clap
afraid	nod	spice
middle	silver	shining
windy	collect	pumpkin

F.   Sing the story to the tune "Are You Sleeping?":

Little old lady (name)
Little old lady (name)
In the forest (where)
In her cottage (where)
Gathering and walking (what)
Running and whispering (what)
Read this book. Read this book.

G.   Writing activities: What could you do with a scarecrow?

You could _____

And you could _____

It would be fun to _____

And _____

This is what you could do with a scarecrow.

Look at the scarecrow
That grew from some clothes
Slowly, slowly from some clothes
In the garden it grew and grew
Look at the scarecrow
It's brand new.

Use the same pattern to write about something else that changes.

H.   Research activity: Finding out about pumpkins. Find the answer to these questions.

1.   Where are pumpkins found?

2.   How big does a pumpkin grow?

3.   How long does it take a pumpkin to grow from a seed?

4.   What are pumpkins used for?

Use the answers in this pattern:

Some pumpkins have their own _____

Where they take _____ to grow.

Sometimes they grow as big as _____

And sometimes people _____

But to this very day, some pumpkins have their own _____

THE NEED FOR LAUGHTER, NONSENSE, AND EXPANDED VOCABULARY

Horton Hatches the Egg, by Dr. Seuss. Random House, 1940.

In this tale of faithfulness and responsibility, Mayzie, the lazy bird, takes off for a vacation, leaving Horton, the elephant, to sit on her nest. Horton sits through the fall and through the ice and snow of winter because "an elephant's faithful one hundred per cent." When spring comes, hunters capture Horton and sell him to a circus, tree, nest and all. While he is on display Mayzie happens to fly by. She stops to chat just as the egg begins to break apart. Now Mayzie wants to claim the offspring even though she did none of the work in hatching it. How Dr. Seuss solves the problem of custody makes for a satisfying ending.

Activities

A.   Topic talking. To develop oral language facility, have students talk to partners about their own experience with a topic. Over a period of time, increase the amount of time and the size of the group. Examples of three topics for introducing *Horton Hatches the Egg* are elephants, a circus, and being responsible.

B.   Before sharing the story, give students these open-ended sentences. Children can choose one to complete orally or in writing. Upper primary students can be asked to finish the sentence and write two more sentences on the topic.

1.   Going to a circus would be …

2.   Keeping a promise is important because …

3.   When winter comes the animals in the woods …

4.   To be lazy means …

C.   After reading, have a debate, with half the class giving reasons why Mayzie should get the egg and the other half giving reasons why Horton should get the egg.

D.   Skills should arise naturally from the literature and give the learner an opportunity to creatively use them. Example: For phonics, make elephant jokes:

1.   List words that end with "ell": Sell, Tell.

2.   Create a joke: What would you call an elephant who sells things? Answer: A sellephant!

E.   Pick a project to respond to *Horton Hatches the Egg*.

Pick a Verb	Pick a Topic	Pick a Product
Summarize	The plot of the story	Song
Compare	The characters of Horton and Mayzie	Compare/contrast
Describe	Life in the circus	Five senses poem
Create	Different kinds of eggs	List report

Sample statement: I will summarize the plot of the story in a song.

The Day Jimmy's Boa Ate the Wash, by Trina Hakes Noble. Dial, 1980.

Another boring day at school. Nothing exciting ever happens! Nothing unless you consider crying cows and pigs on a school bus exciting. Nothing exciting except maybe food fights with corn and eggs. Nothing exciting except spending the day with boa constrictors, pigs, sheep, chickens, and other assorted farm animals. I suppose it could be exciting, if you like that kind of stuff.

Activities

A. After reading the story, add the missing words below and sing the song to the tune of "London Bridge."

Jimmy's Boa ate the _____ (1)

Ate the _____ (1)

Ate the _____ (1)

Jimmy's Boa ate the _____ (1)

On our class trip

When the cow began to _____ (2)

Began to _____ (2)

Began to _____ (2)

When the cow began to _____ (2)

On our class trip

She cried because a _____ (3) fell

A _____ (3) fell

A _____ (3) fell

She cried because a _____ (3) fell

On our class trip

The _____ (4) ate the wash

Ate the wash

Ate the wash

The _____ (4) ate the wash

On our class trip

Now Jimmy has a fat pet _____ (5)

Fat pet _____ (5)

Fat pet _____ (5)

Now Jimmy has a fat pet _____ (5)

From our class trip.

Flossie and the Fox, by Patricia C. McKissack. Dial, 1986.

Flossie lives with Big Mama in the Piney Woods. One morning Big Mama asks Flossie to take a basket of eggs to Miss Viola at the farm on the other side of the woods. On the way Flossie meets the fox (who loves eggs), who has frightened Miss Viola's chickens so much that they won't lay eggs. To get through the woods safely and with all the eggs in her basket, Flossie fools the fox into believing that she doesn't know what kind of creature he is. Fox becomes more and more frustrated, trying to convince Flossie that he is, indeed, a fox. but to no avail, until the very last moment, when she reaches the farm.

Activities

A.   Sentence starters: Before reading the story, choose one sentence starter to finish. Share your completed sentence with the class.

    1.   Walking through a dark woods …

    2.   Living on a farm would be …

    3.   Meeting a fox in the woods …

    4.   A person carrying eggs has to …

    5.   Ways in which a fox and a squirrel are alike are …

    6.   When a fox scares all the chickens …

    7.   Things to see in the woods are …

    8.   It is okay to fool someone if …

    9.   Animals found on a farm are …

    10.   Being responsible means …

B.   Questions to think about:

    1.   Why do you think Flossie chose to walk through the _____ when she knew there might be a fox there?

    2.   Do you think Flossie really did not know what a fox looked like? Why or why not?

    3.   Suppose that the fox had taken Flossie's eggs. What do you think Flossie would do next? Why?

    4.   Do you think it was safe for Flossie to walk through the woods alone? Why or why not?

    5.   How is *Flossie and the Fox* like the story of *Little Red Riding Hood*?

C.   A spelling lesson: Write the following letters on small, separate pieces of paper: S H D U N O.

    1.   Take two letters and make a word that means the opposite of yes. ___ ___

    2.   From the word you made for no. 1, add one letter to tell what your head might do if you get sleepy. ___ ___ ___

    3.   Take away two letters and add two letters to the word in no. 2 tell what was shining when Flossie went for her walk. ___ ___ ___

4.   Add two more letters to the word in no. 3 to put the missing word in this sentence. When the chickens heard the _____ of the fox they were afraid. _____ _____ _____

5.   Add one more letter to the word in no. 4 and move letters around to make a word that describes the farm dogs. _____ _____ _____ _____ _____ _____

Answers: 1. no 2. nod 3. sun 4. sound 5. hounds

D.   Sentence strips: Create the following strips of words. Then cut them apart and put them in order to tell the story. Add capital letters and periods where needed.

1.   flossie meets the fox in the woods

2.   flossie sets out with the basket of eggs

3.   fox runs away

4.   she pretends it is not a fox

5.   the fox gets upset

6.   flossie arrives with the eggs at the farm

E.   An egg chant:

> *WE LIKE EGGS*
> *BIG EGGS*
> *SMALL EGGS*
> *OVAL EGGS*
> *WHITE EGGS*
> *BROWN EGGS*
> *SCRAMBLED EGGS*
> *THESE ARE JUST A FEW*
>
> *IN A BASKET*
> *ON THE GROUND*
> *IN A NEST*
> *ON A PLATE*
> *IN A PAN*
> *IN THE GRASS*
> *ON A SHELF, TOO*
>
> *STAND AND SHOUT*
> *BRING THEM OUT*
> *WE LIKE EGGS!!!*

Use the same pattern to write about foxes. In the first verse use words to describe foxes. In the second verse tell where you might find a fox.

WE LIKE FOXES

_____ FOXES

_____ FOXES

_____ FOXES

_____ FOXES

_____ FOXES

_____ FOXES

THESE ARE JUST A FEW.

IN _____

ON _____

UNDER _____

BETWEEN _____

OVER _____

ON TOP OF _____

_____, TOO

STAND AND SHOUT

BRING THEM OUT

WE LIKE FOXES!

THE NEED TO KNOW AND EXTEND DEVELOPING CONCEPTS

Let's look at protecting wildlife with:

Turtle Bay, by Saviour Pirotta. Illustrated by Nilesh Mistry. Farrar, 1997.

People think the old man is strange. He sits on the beach for hours, listening to the wind, sweeping the sand with a broom, and waiting, always waiting. But young Taro is fascinated with the old man, whom he considers wise and full of wonderful secrets. And when the old man reveals that some special friends—Japanese sea turtles, ready to lay their eggs—are about to visit the beach, Taro joins the old man to help with the preparations.

Activities

A.   Pre-reading question: Why would a person sweep a large, sandy beach with a broom?

B.   Introducing vocabulary: Use as many of these words as you can in one sentence to describe the cover of the book. Use other words as needed in your sentence OR make as many sentences as you can with the words to tell what you think this story will be about. Add other words as needed.

secrets	listening	seagulls	broom
rubbish	swept	cleaner	pointing
dolphins	waves	boat	whale
tomorrow	sand	turtle	eggs
digging	flippers	beach	patient
friends	message	sea	weird
seaweed	sweeping	beach	crabs

C.   Create a sea turtle data bank:

Eats	**Lives**	**Has**	**Does**
sea grass	warm climate	bone armor	born on dry land
crabs	in the sea	hard shell	breathe air
shrimps	Pacific Ocean	flippers	lay eggs on sandy beaches
			glide with ease through the water
			live 50 years

D.   Writing activities: Use the information from the data bank to complete the writing patterns that follow.

The "If I Were" Pattern

Name a sea creature: If I were a _____

Tell where found _____

Name two things it could do for someone

I'd _____

And I'd _____

If I were a _____ .

Sea Turtle Story Pattern

Some sea turtles have their own _____

Where they _____

Sometimes they go around _____

Or sometimes they just _____

But to this very day, some sea turtles have their

own _____ .

K-1 Pattern

London Bridge

Big sea turtles eat _____ and _____

_____ and _____

_____ and _____

Big sea turtles eat _____ and _____

And (name something they do) _____

I saw a _____ and the _____ saw me

It was _____ along (in/by) the deep blue sea.

_____ goes _____ , _____ , _____ .

E.   Additional reading: Share *The Stolen Egg,* by Tim Vyner and Sue Vyner (Viking, 1992).

THE NEED TO KNOW AND EXTEND DEVELOPING CONCEPTS: ANIMAL FAMILIES

Stellaluna, by Janell Cannon. Scholastic, 1993.

A young bat lands in a bird's nest and is adopted by the birds. She has trouble accepting the birds' habits and finally meets a family of bats.

Activities

A.   Recall the story using the song: "Are You Sleeping?":

_____ bat

_____ bat

With her _____

With the _____

_____ and

_____

_____ and

_____

Stellaluna, Stellaluna

B.   Questions to think about:

1.   How are birds and bats alike and different?

2.   Would you rather be a bird or a bat? Why?

3.   Was Mother Bird a good mother?

C.   Create another song, also using "London Bridge." Recall from the story:

Little bats have _____ and

_____

_____ and

_____

_____ and

_____

Little bats eat _____ and

_____

And _____

D.   List as many forest creatures as you can. Use the following pattern:

Stellaluna, Stellaluna, what do you see?

I see a _____ looking at me

_____ , _____ what do you see?

I see a _____ looking at me.

Blueberries for Sal, by Robert McCloskey. Viking, 1978.

Two mothers and their children go berry picking and find each other's children behind them: One mother happens to be a bear!

Activities

A. Sing the story to "My Bonnie Lies over the Ocean" (children supply the missing words):

Oh, Sal and her M _____ went walking

All over the Blueberry _____

They wanted to pick sweet, ripe _____

And each had a tin pail to fill.

Mother picked and she

Filled up her _____ to the very top

Sal dropped B _____

The sound that they made was ker-plop.

B. Questions to think about:

1. Why did Mother Bear want Little Bear to eat lots of berries?

2. How many things can you name that are made of berries?

C. Sentence starters (journal writing for grades 1–3):

1. Getting lost from your mother…

2. Picking berries is fun when …

3. Walking in the woods …

D. Sentence word banks: List describing words about bears, such as large, furry, etc.

List name words: cub, bear
List action words: runs, sleeps
List "where" words: in a cave, etc.
Put together to make sentences.

E. Create a bear chant:

We like bears!
(List six words to describe bears)
These are just a few
(List seven more describing words)
Stand and shout, bring them out
We like bears.

Make Way for Ducklings, by Robert McCloskey. Viking, 1941.

The Mallard family searches for a safe place for their ducklings and finally finds one with the help of Michael, a policeman.

Activities

A. Recall the story in song to the tune of "The Itsy Bitsy Spider":

A pair of D _____ was flying here and there.

_____ for a home to _____ their eggs with care

When cars on the _____

Wouldn't let them cross

A _____ named Michael

Showed them who was b _____.

B. Rewrite a Mother Goose rhyme:

> *Once I saw a little bird*
> *Come hop, hop, hop*
> *And I cried, Little Bird*
> *Will you stop, stop, stop.*

Once I saw a little duck

Come q_____ , q_____ , q_____

And I cried, Little Duck

Come b_____ , b_____ , b_____

Add verses about other animals.

C. Think of things the Mallard family saw on their way to the park. Create a big city ABC using the following pattern:

H IS FOR POLICE-OFFICER

WHY?

BECAUSE POLICE

OFFICERS

HELP PEOPLE

THE NEED TO KNOW AND EXTEND DEVELOPING CONCEPTS: COMMUNITY HELPERS

Let's look at construction workers in:

Mike Mulligan and His Steam Shovel, by Virginia Lee Burton. Houghton, 1967.

No one wants Mike and his steam shovel, Mary Anne, anymore. But Mike does not want to cast Mary Anne aside like the other old steam shovels. How can he convince the townspeople that Mary Anne can still be used?

Activities

A. Pre-reading activity. List from A to Z things in your town built by construction crews and machines.

B. Use the following pattern to answer: What can you do with a steam shovel?

You can climb on it, and _____

You might _____ and _____

That's what you can do with a steam shovel.

What can't you do with a steam shovel?

You can't take it to school for Show and Tell or _____

You can't _____

or _____

Because you can't do that with a steam shovel.

C. Mike treats Mary Anne as if she were a living creature. How is she like the following living things: a tree, a giraffe, an eagle, a dinosaur?

Let's look at doctors and nurses with:

Madeline, by Ludwig Bemelmens. Viking, 1960.

Madeline wasn't afraid of anything, even tigers! She loved winter and when she had to go to the hospital for an operation, a big surprise was waiting on her stomach!

Activities

A. A pre-reading activity: Predict how many in your class will answer yes to these questions. Then check your predictions.

1. Have you ever been in a hospital?
2. Have you ever had an operation?
3. Are you afraid of tigers?
4. Do you like winter?
5. Do you have any scars?

B. Write the missing words to the "Muffin Man" tune (write about nurses and doctors):

Nurses are _____ and _____

_____ and _____ _____ and _____

Nurses are _____ and _____ and _____

(Change nurses to doctors for verse two.)

C.   Draw your idea of what a present day Madeline would look like.

Let's look at news reporters with:

The True Story of the Three Little Pigs, by Jon Scieszka. Scholastic, 1989.

The wolf claims to have been framed for the murder of the three pigs and blames news reporters for not telling the real story. Rank order these excuses from (1), the one he is most likely to use, to (5), the least likely excuse.

___ I needed to borrow some aspirin for my headache.
___ I needed to borrow a cup of sugar.
___ I was selling magazine subscriptions.
___ I wanted to invite the pigs to dinner.
___ The pigs invited me to visit.

Now listen to the story to see what excuse the wolf really gave!

Activities

A.   Write your own news story about another fairy tale character. Perhaps you will choose to write about Red Riding Hood's meeting with the wolf, or the Little Red Hen who could not find anyone to help her, or Sleeping Beauty, who woke up after 100 years. Be sure to tell:

WHO the story is about.
WHAT happened.
WHERE it happened.
WHEN it happened.

Let's look at teachers with:

Miss Nelson Is Missing, by Harry Allard. Houghton-Mifflin, 1977.

Miss Nelson has the worst-behaved class in school until a substitute teacher, Miss Viola Swamp, arrives. When days pass and Miss Nelson does not return, the children know it is time to take action!

Activities

A.   Complete the bio-poem about Miss Nelson:

Name _____

Two traits _____

Who teaches _____

Who likes _____

Who dislikes _____

Who loves _____

Who gives _____

Who expects _____

Occupation _____

B.   Complete the following pattern to give Miss Nelson advice on how to improve the behavior of her students:

Dear Miss Nelson,

If I were you, I would _____ or _____

but I wouldn't _____

because _____

C.   Create an ABC guide for next year's students listing things you have learned this year. Example:

A is for adding numbers together
B is for behaving nicely

Let's look at tailors with:

Something for Nothing, by Phoebe Gilman. Scholastic, 1993.

A small boy sees his worn blanket made into a jacket by his grandfather. When the jacket gets too small, grandfather makes a vest. Over time the vest becomes a tie, the tie becomes a handkerchief, and the handkerchief becomes a button cover. When the boy loses the button, even grandfather can't make something from nothing. But maybe the little boy can!

Activities

A.   A guessing game: Match the object with the rhyming description: jacket, blanket, vest, tie.

   a.   It's frazzled, worn, unsightly, torn

   b.   It's shrunken, small, doesn't fit at all

   c.   It's spotted with glue, paint on it, too

   d.   It has a big stain of soup that makes the ends droop.

B.   Spelling: Use the letters T B L N A K E:

   1.   Choose 3 letters to make a color. __ __ __

   2.   Take away one letter and add two letters to name a vegetable. __ __ __ __

   3.   Take away one letter and add one letter to make a word the opposite of messy __ __ __ __

4.   Take away two letters, add three letters to describe a page with nothing on it ___ ___ ___ ___ ___

5.   Add two letters to tell what Joseph's Grandfather made for him. ___ ___ ___ ___ ___ ___ ___

Answers: 1. tan 2. bean 3. neat 4. blank 5. blanket

C.   Write a clothes chant:

Joseph likes clothes

All kinds of clothes

_____ jacket

_____ vest

_____ tie

_____ button

_____ pants

_____ shirt

_____ shoes

_____ hat

Add a describing word before each piece of clothing

Everyone knows
Joseph likes clothes!

D.   Read some books on recycling:

Gibbons, Gail. *Recycle*. HarperCollins, 1992.
Leedy, Loreen. *The Great Tree Bash*. Holiday House, 1991.

THE NEED TO KNOW AND EXTEND DEVELOPING CONCEPTS: AFRICA

Introducing the Unit

1.   Ask students:

   • Is Africa a country or a continent?

      (Answer: Africa is a continent with more than 50 countries.)

   • Does it snow in Africa?

      (Answer: It snows in the mountains.)

- What is the most common African animal?

     (Answer: Next to the little monkey, the camel is the most common animal.)

- Is Africa mostly jungle?

     (Answer: Africa is 80 percent desert.)

2.   Share *Who Is Coming?,* by Patricia McKissack. (Children's Press, 1989). Use the following pattern to recall what the animals did in the story:

If I were (animal)

I would _____ and _____

But I wouldn't _____

Because (another animal) does that.

3.   Show pictures of African animals. Use this pattern for writing: Find three animals alike in some way and one that is different. Have the children write four sentences. Example:

A lion has four legs.
A leopard has four legs.
An elephant has four legs.
A snake does not have four legs.

4.   Share Graeme Base's *Animalia* (Abrams, 1986). Create alliterative sentences about African animals.

Geography

On a map, show the different regions of Africa: the grasslands, the deserts, the mountains, and the jungle. Let children guess what animals might live in each region. Then share *We Hide, You Seek,* by Jose Aruego (Greenwillow, 1979).

Problem Solving

1.   Share *Who's in Rabbit's House,* by Verna Aardema (Dial, 1976). Set up a problem-solving grid for children to work to help Rabbit get the Long One out of his house. Then finish the story to see what happens.

Problem: How can Rabbit get the Long One out of his house?

Ideas	Fast	Safe	Effective
_____	____	____	_____
_____	____	____	_____
_____	____	____	_____
_____	____	____	_____

Score 1=no 2=maybe 3=yes

2.   Create an African giant. Complete this paragraph:

They used to tell stories about a giant called _____. They said he was as _____ as a _____

and that he could _____. He had _____ fingernails and _____ teeth. His feet were

_____ and his hair was _____ because he didn't comb it. But the most awful thing about

him was _____.

Share *Abiyoyo,* by Pete Seeger (Macmillan, 1988). Compare this giant with the one the class
created. Note that this tale is from South Africa and call attention to the wide variety of people
in the illustrations.

Additional Activities

A.   Make a dictionary of African animals following the pattern in Mary Elting's *Q Is for
Duck* (Houghton, 1980). Example: T is for elephant. Why?

B.   Choose a favorite African animal. Use the pattern from Seymour Simon's *Animal Fact,
Animal Fable* (Crown, 1979) to create a book about the animal. Make a statement about
the animal on one page. Ask the reader if the statement is fact or fable. Give the answer
and tell why on the next page.

C.   Share *I Hunter,* by Pat Hutchins (Mulberry, 1986). Which animal does not belong in
the story? Answer: Tiger, because there are no tigers in Africa.

D.   Africa has several areas where quicksand is found. Learn about quicksand in Tomie de-
Paola's *The Quicksand Book* (Holiday, 1977). List three things you saw in the story.
Complete this pattern and sing it to "Skip to My Lou":

We see …

Tall trees rising to the sky

Brown branches hanging from the trees

Scary quicksand bubbling in the ground

Look, little children, look

_____ _____ _____ _____

Adjective Noun ing word prepositional phrase

_____ _____ _____ _____

_____ _____ _____ _____

Look, little children, look.

E.   Share other titles by Verna Aardema. Note the country of origin of each.

Bimwili and the Zimwi (Dial, 1985)
Bringing the Rain to Kapiti Plain (Dial, 1981)
Oh, Kojo, How Could You? (Dial, 1984)
Princess Gorilla and a New Kind of Water (Dial, 1988)
Rabbit Makes a Monkey Out of Lion (Dial, 1989)
The Vingananee and the Tree Toad (Viking, 1983)
What's So Funny, Ketu? (Dial, 1982)
Why Mosquitoes Buzz in People's Ears (Dial, 1985)

Anansi Goes Fishing, by Eric Kimmel. Holiday, 1992.

Anansi, a lazy spider, is fooled by turtle into doing all the work. Turtle convinces Anansi that resting is very tiring indeed!

Activities

A.   Sing the following song to "A Hunting We Will Go":

> *To Kenya we will go*
> *We'll catch a fish and*
> *Put it in a _____*
> *To Kenya we will go.*
> *Echo read: My aunt came back*
> *I made a wish*
> *From Kenya she brought*
> *A great big _____.*

B.   Kenya is a country of grassy plains and jungles where most of the wild animals live. The people make their living from hunting and farming and understand the importance of nature and its influence on their daily lives. Animals found in Kenya include the monkey, elephant, lion, hippo, giraffe, and boa constrictor.

Compare two animals using this pattern:

If I were a _____

I would _____

And I'd _____

But I wouldn't _____

Because _____ do that.

THE NEED TO KNOW AND EXTEND DEVELOPING CONCEPTS: ROCKS

Sylvester and the Magic Pebble, by William Steig. Simon & Schuster, 1969.

Sylvester, the donkey, loves to collect beautiful pebbles. One day he comes upon a magic pebble that will grant him anything he wishes. On his way home to share his discovery, a lion frightens him. Without thinking, Sylvester wishes to become a rock. The only problem now is that he cannot hold the pebble to wish himself back. What will become of poor Sylvester?

Activities

A. Pre-reading sentence starters: Choose one of these sentence starters. On the lines below, finish the sentence and write two more sentences on the topic.

   1. Going on a picnic can be _____

   2. Many people have hobbies because _____

   3. Families help each other when _____

   4. Being alone all the time would be _____

B. Topic talking: Introduce topics related to the book: families, rocks, wealth. Have partners talk about the topics for increasing amounts of time.

C. Introducing vocabulary:

   1. How many ways can you group these words? A group must have at least three words.

inquire	pathway	green
police	vacation	donkey
quickly	disappeared	neighborhood
pigs	frightened	lion
pebble	bright	chickens
beautiful	colorful	houses.

   2. Use as many words as you can to describe one picture from the book. Add other words as needed.

D. Story strips: Create the following story strips. Cut the strips apart and put them in order to tell the story. Add capital letters and punctuation marks where needed.

   1. wishes he met a lion and wished

   2. stuck as a rock until spring

   3. on a rainy day sylvester

   4. pebble and turned him back

   5. he was a rock he was

6.   found a magic pebble that gave him

7.   while on a picnic his mother found a

8.   into her son again

E.   Problem solving: What could Sylvester have done to be safe from the lion other than turning himself into a rock? List your ideas on the lines below. Rank each idea 1 = no, 2 = maybe, 3 = yes

Ideas:	Fast	Safe	Can Do	Total
_____	____	____	_____	____
_____	____	____	_____	____
_____	____	____	_____	____

F.   Respond to these statements about rocks with "true" or "false." Guess if you do not know. Support or disprove your guesses by singing the song on pages 43-44.

1.   The softest rock is called talc.

2.   Granite is the hardest rock.

3.   A diamond is a rock.

4.   Igneous rocks are made by heat.

5.   Lava from a volcano is melted rock.

6.   Sandstone is a sedimentary rock.

7.   Metamorphic means change.

8.   Limestone is a metamorphic rock that turns into marble.

G.   Brainstorm: How many uses can you think of for rocks?

Rocks in My Pockets, by Marc Harshman and Bonnie Collins. Dutton, 1991.

The Woods family lived on a farm on top of the top of the highest mountain, where the wind was a neighbor all year round. Their farm was on old rocky soil, and they made their living as best they could. They raised knee-high corn and walnut-sized potatoes, but you'd hear no complaints from them. Their house was drafty, their animals skinny, their clothes patched.

But one thing they had was pockets, and in their pockets they carried rocks, yes, rocks. They were very important. They carried rocks to keep from being blown away; they played games with them; and they wrapped them in heavy socks after heating them by the fire, to keep warm at night. And they polished them 'til they were as smooth and shiny as glass.

But one early summer day, the rocks proved to be more important than all these things and changed life forever for the Woods family.

Activities

A. Predict how the rocks will change their lives.

B. Fluency:

1. List as many things as you can that you would find if you dug a hole to the center of the Earth.

2. Put a letter on each line that tells you where you would find the things listed. For example: If magma would be found 6 to 50 feet down, put the letter D on that line. Work with a partner. If you do not know, *guess!*

    1–6 feet _____   A. ball of solid iron
    6–50 feet ____   B. topsoil
    10–20 miles ____   C. diamonds, coal
    20–150 miles ___   D. magma
    3,000–3,860 miles __ E. basalt

3. To support or disprove your guesses, read *How to Dig a Hole to the Other Side of the World,* by Faith McNulty (Illustrated by Marc Simont. Harper, 1979).

C. Pick a project: Choose a verb, a topic, and a product and write a research statement. Example: I will describe volcanoes in a fact/fiction book.

Verb	Topic	Product
Label	Geysers	Poem
List	Volcanoes	Chart
Describe	Kinds of rocks	Story
Locate	Fossils	Model
Report	Diamonds	Mystery Report
Show	Oil	Model
Group	Your idea	Diorama
Discover		Bio-poem
Compare		
Create		

D. Write a singing report, and sing it to "Tiny Bubbles":

> *Rock collecting can be fun*
> *You can do it rain or sun*
> *Look for rocks of different hues,*

Pink, black, white, gray, rocks are
found beneath your shoes.
(Chorus)
Some are plain and some are rare
R O C K rocks are everywhere

Ancient Romans built rock roads
Pyramids took loads and loads
Scale your rocks for hardness then
Talc is one and diamonds
Score a mighty ten.

Igneous rock means made by heat
Found beneath most every street
Lava is a rock that flows
Melted in a volcano that
Tends to explode

Under igneous rocks on charts
We see granite, basalt and quartz
In rock operas are other players
Sedimentary rocks are made
by forming layers.

Metamorphic rocks are strange
Rocks like this go through a change
Shale with pressure becomes slate
Limestone turns into marble,
what a pleasant fate.

So collect many rocks
for a hobby that is great.

E.   Use the Internet: See the Smithsonian Gem and Mineral Collection at: http://galaxy. einet.net/images/gems/gems-icons.html.

THE NEED TO KNOW AND EXTEND DEVELOPING CONCEPTS: ROBOTS

The Sorcerer's Apprentice, by Ted Dewan. Doubleday, 1998.

The Sorcerer is a brilliant inventor whose work keeps him so busy that he never has time to clean. If only the amazing machines he creates could pick up after themselves! Soon a clever idea is put into action, and the Sorcerer invents a robot Apprentice, the perfect solution to his clutter problem. But the Apprentice, left alone in the workshop to vacuum up, has other ideas. What if he were to make his own little helper? And what if, in turn, each helper created HIS own helper? This is exactly what happens and soon there are dozens of robots frantically rooting around for parts to make more copies until all the tubes and wires and gears are used up. Then they turn their nozzles on the Apprentice. HELP! he howls. The Sorcerer leaps out of bed and runs to the workshop; he knows he has to do something to save the Apprentice. What will he do? Write down your ideas and rate them using the scale of 1 to 3.

Ideas:	Fast	Safe	Low Cost	Effective	Total
_____	____	____	_____	_____	____
_____	____	____	_____	_____	____

Score: 1 = no 2 = maybe 3 = yes

Activities

A. Pre-reading vocabulary activity: Work in teams of three. Looking at one illustration from the book, generate as many words as you can related to the illustration. Take turns naming nouns, verbs, adjectives, and adverbs. Each word should be written on small, separate pieces of paper. After 10 minutes of generating words, use as many of the words as you can in ONE sentence to describe the picture. You may add the noun determiners (articles and conjunctions) *a, an, and, the,* and any needed prepositions, but you may not add additional nouns, verbs, adjectives, or adverbs. The team using the most words in a sentence after 10 minutes is the winning team.

B. Pre-reading sentence starters: Choose one sentence starter to complete. Continue writing for five minutes on the topic. In a small group, share orally what you have written.

1. Having too many chores to do can be …

2. An inventor is one who …

3. Playing around with machines without understanding how they work …

4. When things get out of control …

5. If a machine were smarter than a person …

C. Compare tales: In two minutes list all the ways that this tale and Tomie dePaola's *Strega Nona* (Simon & Schuster, 1975) are alike.

D. Respond to the following statements about robots using "true" or "false." Guess if you do not know.

1. The first robots were in use in the Middle Ages.

2. The first robot arm to perform specific tasks was invented in 1925.

3. Robot arms can slide like a telescope or bend like an elephant's trunk.

4. Robots replace humans today for dangerous, unpleasant or repetitive tasks.

5.   Goods can be produced more cheaply because robots replace human workers on assembly lines.

6.   In the future small robots can travel inside human arteries to deliver medicine.

7.   In the future, surgeons will direct robots in operating on patients who may be great distances away from the surgeon.

Support or disprove your answers by singing the "History of Robots in Song."

E.   The origin of the story: In 1797 the famous German poet and scientist, Goethe, wrote his ballad "Der Zuberiehrling," about a sorcerer's apprentice done in by his own magical spell. A century later the French composer Paul Dukas won recognition for his *The Sorcerer's Apprentice*, an orchestral scherzo written in 1897. In the piece different instruments represented different characters.

Retell the story using the robot song pattern in item F. Example:

A man made a big machine
To sweep up and keep things clean
Handy robot, without a doubt
And he made other robots just to help him out.

Robots tangled in a fight

Hit each other, what a _____

_____

_____

F.   Write a singing report. Sing it to the tune of "Tiny Bubbles":

A History of Robots in Song
Clockwork robots moved in stages
Told time in the Middle Ages
Robot arm came in fifty-four
It could slide like a telescope or bend like a trunk to the floor.

(Chorus)
Ten feet tall
Or very small
Handy, dandy R O B O T

Does tough jobs that bring men pain
Measures a volcano or a hurricane.
Assembly line jobs done without mistake
Robots work very quickly and consider them a piece of cake.

Tiny robot, electric eye
Opens doors as folks walk by
Other robots that come to mind
Wash your clothes, cook your food, add up numbers, what a find!

(Repeat chorus)

Tiny robots enter veins
To relieve your aches and pains
Need to see a doctor today?
She can operate upon you even if she's far away.

In the future robots think,
Solve a problem, quick as a wink
If it breaks it can repair itself
Handy Robots on every 21st century shelf

HANDY ROBOTS ON EVERY TWENTY-FIRST CENTURY SHELF!

THE NEED TO KNOW AND EXTEND DEVELOPING CONCEPTS: EARTHWATCH

Sister Yessa's Story, by K. Greenfield. HarperCollins, 1992. For grades 1 through 4.

As storm clouds gather, Sister Yessa takes the animals to her brother's place, telling the tale of Great Turtle, who traveled the world dropping animals off his back. A delightful introduction to regions of the Earth and animal habitats.

Taking care of the Earth, which is home to us all, is an important area of study for young gifted children. The books create an awareness of the priceless resources we all share and of the many problems to be solved to preserve those resources for the future.

Activities

A.   Pre-reading activity: Match the animal with its setting:

| a. grasslands | b. arctic | c. desert |
| d. mountain | e. Australia | f. islands |

__ elephants	__ herons
__ dingoes	__ cobras
__ camels	__ lions
__ crabs	__ yaks

B.   The "mystery report": List 10 animal clues. Each student gives a number from 1 to 10. Read the clue for that number. Each student can guess or pass. The game continues until the animal is guessed or all clues are read. One clue must be a "give away" clue.

C.   Deserts: Name something in the desert that would:

   a.   bounce
   b.   dart
   c.   creep
   d.   sing
   e.   glide
   f.   sting

   Read *Mojave,* by Diane Siebert (For grades 3 through 6. Crowell, 1988). The Mojave is a mysterious place teeming with life that bounces, darts, creeps, sings, glides, and stings. Savor this poetic description.

   After sharing *Mojave,* write a five senses poem about the desert, using this pattern:

The desert is _____ (color)

It looks like _____ It sounds like _____

It tastes like _____ It smells like _____

It makes me feel like _____

D.   Rivers:

   If a river dried up in Texas, name four other places water could be found.

   Read *Alamo Across Texas,* by Jill Stover (For grades 1 through 4. Lothrop, 1993).

   Create a song using the following pattern. Sing it to "Yellow Rose of Texas" after sharing the book.

On the great (1) L_____ River

Alligator (2) A _____

Enjoyed the tasty (3) f _____

And watched the river (4) f _____

But a (5) d _____ dried up the river Alamo with much remorse

Went traveling throughout (6) T _____

To find a water source.

He walked and (7) w _____ a distance

At a ranch he saw some cattle,

The ocean was too (8) s _____

In the pool he had to (9) b _____

The fountain was too (10) n _____

The water was not deep

So at the end of a long, long trail

He curled up and went to (11) s _____ .

Answers: 1. Lavaca 2. Alamo 3. fishes 4. flow 5. drought 6. Texas 7. walked 8. salty 9. battle 10. noisy 11. sleep

E.   A research project for primary grades: Research river creatures. Use the pattern that follows to create a song. Sing it to "The Bear Went Over the Mountain":

We saw a ___ in the river. We saw a ___ by the river. We saw a __ on the river, for the river is its home.

F.   The forest: A readers' theater booktalk:

N1:	*Long ago Raven*
Raven:	*dreamed that the forests were gone*
N1:	*and he asked for*
Raven:	*a song of power*
N1:	*to change his dream*
N2:	*The world's spirit answered:*
Spirit:	*"Every song must have a singer and each singer must find someone who understands his song."*
N:	*Raven sings the song*
Raven:	*about the death of the forest*
N1:	*but he is known as a trickster*
N2:	*and the people don't heed his warning. Finally a little girl*
Girl:	*understands the song*
N2:	*and convinces her logger father*
Girl:	*to spread the word*
N2:	*in this Song for the Ancient Forest, by Nancy Luenn (Atheneum, 1993).*

G.   Write a song using this pattern. Sing it to "Skip to My Lou"

In the forest we see:

Green fir trees standing in the shade

_____   _____   _____   _____

_____   _____   _____

Look, little children, look!

H.   Compare *Song for the Ancient Forest* with *The World That Jack Built,* by Ruth Brown (Dutton, 1991).

A lush green forest is compared to a dying forest polluted by factory waste. How would the pattern differ using information from this book?

Writing about the forest: (can be a research OR creative writing pattern). List one word for each item: Use in a story.

1. A size
2. A color
3. An animal
4. Place to sleep
5. Human
6. Way to travel
7. Same as #5
8. something to read
9. Same as #3
10. Animal noise
11. Animal (not 3)
12. Animal
13. Animal
14. Same as #5
15. Same as #6

Use the words you chose in place of the numbers in this story:

> In the dark, grassy forest there was a (1) (2) (3) who was sound asleep on a (4). A (5) approached on a (6). The (7) was reading a (8) and stumbled over the (9) who awakened and gave a loud (10) that frightened the other forest animals including the (11) (12) and (13). The (14) left quickly on (15) vowing never to disturb the forest animals again.

Rain Forest, by Helen Cowcher. Farrar, 1988.

Many animals live in the forest, which is invaded by man and machines. A flood results, driving the animals to high ground, where they watch the man and machine be swept away by flood waters.

One-Eyed Tree Frog, by Joy Cowley. Scholastic, 1998.

This provides an exciting new way to see the natural world. Join the adventure as one plucky red-eyed tree frog searches for something to eat and avoids the many dangers of the rain forest. There are tempting but poisonous caterpillars and hungry boa snakes ready to swallow little tree frogs!

Activities

A. Put an N in front of something you would not want to see in a rain forest:

__ tapirs	__ trees
__ man	__ sloth
__ machines	__ macaw
__ jaguar	__ flood

B.   Choose one rain forest creature to research and write about using the following pattern: (Choose appropriate prepositions.)

In the tropical rain forest: Over ___ Under ___ Above ___ Between ___ Lives a (describe and name).

Heartland, by Diane Siebert. Illustrated by Wendall Minor. HarperCollins, 1989. For grades 3 through 6.
This story is a tribute to Midwestern farmers.

Activity

Look at the cover. On separate pieces of paper write nouns, verbs, adjectives, and adverbs related to the cover. After five minutes, arrange the words in a descriptive sentence.

Rushmore, by Lynn Curlee. Scholastic, 1999.
This book describes how the son of immigrants overcame many obstacles to create the world's most immense stone carving.

Activity

Read about a national park and use the pattern below to write about it.

Name: Yellowstone
Two features: Geysers, mountain trails
Three activities: Hike, camp, fish
Four sights: Huge trees, Old Faithful, brown bears, wild moose
Describe: Guardian of wildlife

Backyard Bear, by Jim Murphy. Illustrated by Jeffrey Greene. Scholastic, 1993. For grades 1 through 4.
A young bear enters a town to find food.

Arctic Spring, by Sue Vyner. Illustrated by Tim Vyner. Viking, 1993. For grades K through 4.
A mother bear will not leave an ice pack that is floating out to sea.

Komodo, by Peter Sis. Greenwillow, 1993.
Peter and his parents go to the island of Bali to see the only dragon left in the world today, the Komodo, but because of all the people, the dragon is hard to see.

Activities

A.   Write about endangered animals using the following pattern:

Name: Polar Bear
How it moves: Lumbering, plodding
Where: On the polar ice pack
Where: By her winter cave
Describe: White Giant!

B.   Create an ABC book of endangered animals.

C.   Ecosystems: Respond to the following statements with "true" or "false."

1.   Milk is a nutritious food.

2.   Cows eat sweet red clover.

3.   Mice eat honeycombs.

The Little Old Ladies Who Liked Cats, by Carol Greene. Harper, 1991.

On a small island, the old ladies' cats ate mice, but when the mayor ordered that cats be kept in at night, the mice ate the honeycombs, the bees could not pollinate the clover, and the cows had no sweet clover to eat and could not give milk to keep the sailors strong.

Activities

A.   Predict what will happen when pirates invade the island. How will letting the cats out at night help?

B.   Write about the Earth using the pattern in *Say Something,* by Mary Stolz (HarperCollins, 1993). "A mountain lasts forever. It covers its slopes with trees and snow, and inside it has a secret."

C.   Research riddle: going places.

Let us go to brand new places

And see the world's various faces.

We will find: (*list 6 specific details in phrases*)

But that's not all: (*list 6 more details in phrases*)

Do you know where we are?

(*In* _____ , *of course.*)

D.   For great ideas for keeping the planet clean, read:

Going Green, by John Elkington (Viking, 1991). Use the model in *Going Green* to write your own ABC book of caring for our planet!

Take Action, by Ann Love (Beech Tree, 1993).

FAVORITE PICTURE AND POETRY BOOKS OF THE 1990S

Agee, John. *So Many Dynamos and Other Palindromes.* Farrar, 1994. Grades 4–8. How many palindromes can you name?

Bang, Molly. *Goose.* Blue Sky Press, 1996. All ages. A small goose finds its wings with a little help.

Brown, Ruth. *Toad.* Dutton, 1997. All ages. List words to describe a toad. Then share this deliciously yucky treat!

Carson, Jo. *The Great Shaking.* Orchard, 1994. Grades 2–4. A bear is awakened from its winter sleep by the New Madrid earthquake. Write about a special day at school. Give copies to your local historical society.

Cribben, June. *Into the Castle.* Candlewick, 1996. A good model for creating a circle story. Grades Pre-K–2.

Cushman, Doug. *ABC Mystery.* Harper, 1993. Grades K–3. List words from A–Z connected with a mystery story.

Cyrus, Kurt. *Slow Train to Oxmox.* Farrar, 1998. Grades K–3. Edwin Blink is in a rush but by mistake boards the slow train to Oxmox. As the train meets more and more obstacles, Edwin pulls with the other passengers to help so that the destination is reached.

Day, David. *King of the Woods.* Four Winds, 1993. Grades Pre-K–2. A small wren captures an apple from a large moose. Try this pattern for different animals: "I had a wren, her name was Twirp, I don't know why but she loved to _____."

Dobrin, Arthur. *Love Your Neighbor: Stories of Values and Virtues.* Scholastic, 1998 Grades 2–4. Original animal fables with themes of tolerance, prejudice, love, and freedom, each ending with a question for the reader to ponder.

Dunrea, Oliver. *The Trow Wife's Treasure.* Farrar, 1998. Grades K–3. A kind farmer helps a trow-wife find her lost baby. In return she gives him a treasure. Can you guess what it will be? *Activity:* In small groups, have children rank order the following treasures as to the one the group would most want and least want. They should bee ready to explain their rankings: $100.00, A Nintendo Game, Fresh fruit every day, A good friend.

Edwards, Pamela. *Some Smug Slug.* HarperCollins, 1996. Grades 2–4. A slug takes an alliterative journey into the mouth of a toad. Try alliterative animal names: terrible tiger, etc.

Flor Ada, Alma. *Gathering the Sun.* Lothrop, 1997. All ages. An Hispanic alphabet book that celebrates the land and the culture. Create an ABC book about your community.

Garland, Sherry. *My Father's Boat*. Scholastic, 1998. Grades 2–4. A tale of three generations of fishermen separated by time and sea. *Activity:* Complete the pattern using information from the book. "If I went to sea in a small boat I would see _____ and _____ and _____ but I wouldn't see _____ for I would see that on land."

Gerrard, Roy. *The Roman Twins*. Farrar, 1998. Grades 2–4. Twins who seem doomed to be slaves begin a quest for freedom that involves a dramatic escape, a chariot race, and a threatened invasion of Rome.

Ginsburg, Mira. *Clay Boy*. Greenwillow, 1997. Grades Pre-K–2. Clay Boy eats everything in sight, including his Grandma and Grandpa. Compare with Nancy Polette's *The Little Old Woman and the Hungry Cat* (Greenwillow, 1989).

Hall, Zoe. *The Surprise Garden*. Blue Sky/Scholastic, 1998. Grades Pre-K–1. We're planting seeds and giving them lots of water. Soon the sun will help them grow and grow until SURPRISE!: vegetables and flowers appear. *Activity:* Complete this pattern: "Look at the _____ that grew from a seed. Slowly, slowly from a seed. In the _____ it grew and grew. Look at the _____. It's brand new." (Sing to "I'm a Little Teapot.")

Hindley, Judy. *The Best Thing About a Puppy*. Candlewick, 1998. Grades K–2. A good pattern book. The good thing about a puppy is …; the bad thing is … .

Hodges, Margaret. *Up the Chimney*. Holiday House, 1998. Grades 2–4. A young girl becomes a helper to a witch and is told she must never look up the chimney?

Hopkins, Lee Bennett. *Hand in Hand*. Simon & Schuster, 1994. U.S. History in Poetry series. Grades 3–6. Many poems suitable for choral reading for all eras of U.S. history.

Hutchins, Pat. *Shrinking Mouse*. Greenwillow, 1997. Grades K–2. As owl flies off, his friends watch him getting smaller. Will he disappear altogether? Examine a variety of illustrations. Where are the smaller things on the page? The larger things?

Kvasnosky, Laura. *Zelda and Ivy*. Candlewick, 1998. Zelda, the older sister, thinks she must always be the one in charge, and she usually is until Ivy makes a wish. Three charming tales of sibling rivalry. *Activity:* Complete the sentence: "Having an older brother or sister (is) (would be) __."

Lester, Alison. *Yikes*. Houghton Mifflin, 1995. Grades 3–6. Introduce geographic regions with wild adventures in which the reader takes part.

Levitin, Sonia. *Boom Town*. Orchard, 1998. Grades 2–4. During the Gold Rush days Amanda and her family settle in a California boom town, where even a pie pan is hard to find. But in spite of there being no pie pans, Amanda goes into the pie baking business in a big way. *Activity:* Rank order the things you feel are most needed in a new town: a bank, sidewalks, paved streets, a hotel, a library. Explain your rankings.

Lund, Julian. *Way out West Lives a Coyote Named Frank*. Dutton, 1993. Grades 1–4. An excellent pattern for reporting on an animal.

Maestro, Guilio. *Riddle City U.S.A*. Harper, 1995. Grades 3–6. What state do cars visit? Answer: Rhode Island.

Martin, Jr., Bill. *A Beautiful Feast for a Big King Cat*. Harper, 1994. Gades Pre-K–2. A small mouse learns it isn't wise to tease a big cat. Good repeating patterns.

Martin, Rafe. *The Brave Little Parrot*. Putnam's, 1998. Grades K–3. A brave parrot has a way to save a forest from a raging fire, but will the other animals listen to her? *Activity:* It takes 75,000 trees to produce one Sunday issue of the *New York Times*. Brainstorm ways to save paper.

McBratney, Sam. *The Dark at the Top of the Stairs*. Candlewick, 1996. Grades Pre-K–2. "Seeing a shadow at the top of the stairs is scary but _____ is REALLY scary!"

Munsch, Robert. *Ribbon Rescue*. Scholastic, 1998. Grades K–3. "I'm late, I'm lost! I'm late. I'm lost!" cry a groom, a bride, the ring bearer, and the wedding guests. Jillian saves the day by sharing ribbons from her new dress.

Novak, Matt. *Mouse TV*. Orchard, 1994. Grades 1–3. Each page can be a starter for a writing project as a mouse family tries to live without TV.

Polette, Nancy. *The Hole by the Apple Tree*. Greenwillow, 1992. An ABC Adventure. Grades K–3. Write an "Are You Sleeping" song about the cat. "__ cat, __ cat In the ___, on the ___ (4 -ing words) read this book."

Roth, Susan. *My Love for You*. Dial, 1997. "Is bigger than one bear, taller than two _____ ."

Sciszka, Jon, and Lane Smith. *Squids Will Be Squids*. Viking, 1998. Grades 2–6. A fresh twist on fables, with unusual morals.

Shannon, George. *Tomorrow's Alphabet*. Greenwillow, 1996. Grades K–3. Q is for scraps, tomorrow's quilt. Create a tomorrow alphabet book about your school. *Example:* D is for chalk, tomorrow's dust.

————. *True Lies*. Greenwillow, 1997. Students are asked to guess the solution to 18 tricky tales.

Shles, Larry. *Nose Drops*. Squib Publications, 1996 (1264 Moncoeur, St. Louis, MO. 63146). Grades 4–8. A small nose wants to achieve greatness like Julius Sneezer. A book filled with puns.

Smith, Lane. *The Happy Hockey Family*. Viking, 1993. Grades 4–6. A parody of the Dick and Jane readers.

Speed, Toby. *Water Voices*. Putnam's, 1998. Grades Pre-K–2. "What kind of water waits for sunrise? Morningmist." Seven water riddles told in verse. *Activity:* Let children guess what kind of water is described in each riddle.

Stanley, Diane. *Rumplestiltskin's Daughter*. Morrow, 1997. Grades 1–4. The greedy king learns a lesson from this young miss! *Brainstorm:* What other NEW characters could arise from familiar tales?

Walton, Rick. *What to Do When a Bug Climbs in Your Mouth*. Lothrop, 1996. Grades 2–4. Gross poems about insects that kids will love.

Wegman, William. *William Wegman's Mother Goose*. Hyperion, 1996. Grades K–4. Mother Goose characters portrayed by dogs.

Wisneiwski, David. *The Secret Knowledge of Grown-ups*. Lothrop, 1998. Here are the real reasons for rules imposed by grown-ups. Rule #1, "Eat all your vegetables," isn't because they are good for you but because if the vegetable population is not checked, vegetables will grow to enormous sizes and eat people. Other silly explanations for familiar rules follow. *Activity:* Creative writing: Students choose a rule (like brush your teeth, drink milk, wash your hands, etc.) and write a REAL reason for the rule.

Woodruff, Elvira. *The Memory Coat*. Scholastic, 1998. Grades 2–5. Grisha refuses to replace his tattered coat to pass through Ellis Island because it was made by his mother and holds the memory of her love.

Exercising
the Imagination
Fairy Tales and Fantasy

Fairy tales and fantasy can create a startling new environment for the mind. Once a child has ventured beyond earthly restrictions, he or she can never crawl back into old mental modes of thought. Fairy tales and fantasy can throw new light on the outer world through the upheavals it generates in the inner world.

Let us not be afraid of affording our children who are gifted with supple and energetic minds the opportunity to use them. Children need to develop the inner resources to cope with the complex world around them. Gifted young thinkers will not use a fairy tale or fantasy as a drowsy voyage into never-never-land, but will feel an awakening, and leap to challenge the suggested answers that come not from the tale but from one's own deep and intuitive wells of thought.

The intellectually quick need to wrestle with good and evil as well as with calculus, to contemplate the humanity and inhumanity of man as well as historical facts, to plunge into the deeper meaning of life and death instead of memorizing batting averages. The world needs gifted thinkers to raise the values that appear to govern society. Fairy tales and fantasy do relate specifically to the conditions of contemporary society. Consider the Washington, D.C., scandals in relation to Anderson's immortal "The Emperor's New Clothes." Ask your bright children if they recognize a Hitler or an Adi Amin in *Watership Down.* And surely Anderson's "The Nightingale" is a powerful comment on what technology could be doing to our values as it outraces conservation of nature.

If our gifted children are at home in the land of fairy tales and fantasy, perhaps they can help to make our world home a bit more secure. If they have reached a higher resource beyond pure knowledge or reason, if they have caught a vision from a myth, if they have been touched by the inspiration of a fairy tale, their lives will attest to this new-found awareness.

The books and suggested activities in this chapter are designed as a starting point to help gifted children make that mental leap that ties everything together, to catch the subtle inferences and symbolic innuendoes beneath the tales and link them to life's challenges.

READING THE WORLD WITH FOLKTALES: CHINA

Fa Mulan, by Robert D. San Souci. Hyperion, 1998.

When news breaks that one man from each family must join the Kahn's army to fight the Tartars, Fa Mulan is distraught. Her father is too old and frail. Her brother is too young. She realizes that it is up to her to save the family from disgrace.

Disguised as a man, Mulan joins the Kahn's troops and with her skill and intelligence rises swiftly through the ranks. But as she fulfills her dream of being a great warrior, Mulan realizes she must choose between this gallant role led in secret or the noble life she left behind: that of a future wife, bride, and mother.

Activities

A.   Introducing vocabulary:

   1.   Find four words that go together & tell why.

   2.   Use as many words as possible in ONE sentence to describe the cover of the book.

Add other words as needed.

Mulan	fatal	swordsman
bamboo	Tartars	companions
strength	anxious	disorganized
scrolls	honor	battlefield
enemies	valor	protested
stallion	position	sorrowful

B.   Pre-reading sentence starters: Choose one to complete. Continue writing for ten minutes. Share what you have written with a small group.

   1.   Most nations have an army because…

   2.   When two people disagree they should…

   3.   Long ago there were no women in the army because…

   4.   Family honor means…

   5.   Parents are proud of their children when…

   6.   Things a visitor might see in China are…

   7.   When a person is very brave he or she…

   8.   Sometimes it is hard to choose because…

   9.   A woman leading men into battle is…

   10.   Rather than going to war it would be better for two countries to…

C. Questions to think about:

1. List as many ways as you can that Fa Mulan's everyday life in ancient China was different from your life today.

2. List as many ways as you can that Fa Mulan's everyday life with her family is like your daily life with your family.

3. Was it fair for the Khan to demand a man from each family to be in his army? Why or why not?

4. Why do you suppose that the other soldiers did not guess that Fa Mulan was a girl?

5. Did Fa Mulan like leading the army as a general? Why or why not?

6. Why do you think Fa Mulan's parents agreed to let her join the Khan's army?

7. Why did Fa Mulan keep apart from the soldiers in her squad?

8. Fa Mulan dreamed of becoming a bride, a wife, and a mother. Why then did she remain in the army?

9. List all the words you can to describe Fa Mulan. From your list choose the two words that best describe her and tell why.

D. Understanding Mulan—proverbs: Complete each proverb as Mulan might have done.

1. Curiosity killed...

2. Don't cry over...

3. Every cloud has a...

4. Two wrongs don't make...

5. Look before you...

E. Creative writing: Mulan led the army over the plains and through the valley to the Black Mountain. Follow this pattern to write about the Black Mountain:

> *Valley*
> *Sinking, Sloping*
> *Delves, dips, dives*
> *Earth's expression of time*
> *Wrinkle*

The Pattern:
Line 1	One word for the title
Line 2	Two words that describe the title
Line 3	Three words that show action
Line 4	Four words that show feeling

MORE TALES FROM CHINA

The Journey of Meng, by Doreen Rappaport. Dial, 1991.

Meng's scholar husband is sent to work on the building of the Great Wall. The workers are treated badly by the cruel emperor and many die, including Meng's husband. She is determined to take his bones back to their home but must seek the emperor's permission.

Activities

A.   Pre-reading activity: The Great Wall of China

The battles between the Chinese and the Tartar invaders from the North went on for many years. Finally, just after the time Mulan led the army against the Tartars, the emperor decided to build a great wall to keep the enemy out. Today astronauts can see all of the Great Wall from space.

Working with a small group, list what you know and what you think you know about the Great Wall of China. Let your teacher or group leader read these questions for the group to answer. Don't be afraid to guess if you don't know. After all questions have been answered (without the use of reference books) the leader can read aloud the short article on the Wall that follows so that your group can support or disprove its guesses.

1.   The Great Wall is located in what part of China? _____

2.   How old is the wall (in years)?_____

3.   How tall (in feet) is the wall? _____

4.   How long is the wall (in miles)? _____

5.   How wide (in feet) is the wall? _____

6.   Can you name some famous visitors to the Great Wall of China? _____

B.   Information about the Great Wall of China:

The Great Wall of China is the longest fortified line ever built. It stretches 1,500 miles, winding through northern China from Lin-yu on the eastern coast to Kanso province in north-central China. The wall stands about 25 feet high. Towers from 35 to 40 feet high were built into the wall every 200 to 300 yards. The wall tapers from a width of 25 feet at the base to about 15 feet at the top. Its sides are made of earth, brick, and stone. The Great Wall was built entirely by hand and traces of the wall indicate that it is over 2,000 years old. It was built as a main defense against attacks by nomads. Famous visitors to the wall include the magician, David Copperfield, President Richard Nixon, and Big Bird.

Use the information about the wall in the reporting patterns that follow.

Compare/Contrast Pattern Action Pattern

If I had the _____ of a _____ If I were in charge of

I would _____ There would be

line And I'd _____ You wouldn't have

But I wouldn't _____ I'd cancel

And _____ But the most important thing I would do is

Because _____ (do/does) that.

READING THE WORLD WITH FOLKTALES: SOUTH AFRICA

Abiyoyo, by Pete Seeger. Illustrated by Michael Hayes. Macmillan, 1988.

A boy and his father are banished from the village because they play too many tricks on people. Then the giant, Abiyoyo, appears and the villagers run for their lives. The boy and his father do not run, however, and by tricking the giant they become the heroes of the village.

Activities

A. Pre-reading activity: Complete the description of an African giant by filling in the blanks. After reading, compare your description with the giant in the story.

They used to tell stories about a giant named ___ . They said he was as ____ as a ____ and that he could ____ . He had ____ fingernails and ___ teeth. His feet were ___ and his hair was ___ because he didn't comb it. But the most awful thing about him was _____.

B. Pre-reading activity: Write an acrostic poem about an African animal.

> *L   ions live in Africa*
> *I   n tall grasses*
> *O   ne lion can move very quietly*
> *N   anny goat is a favorite meal.*

C. Pre-reading activity: Write about an animal using this pattern:

If I had the feet of a rhino
I'd have an odd number of toes on each foot
And I'd have poor eyes but good ears
But I wouldn't be very active at night
Because armadillos do that.

D. Pre-reading activity: OR use the "Important Pattern" from *The Important Book,* by Margaret W. Brown (Harper & Row, 1969).

The important thing about a lion is _____ (add three or four details).

But the important thing about a lion is _____.

E. Write a bio-poem about Abiyoyo:

First name	Who needs
Four traits	Who gives
Related to	Who fears
Cares deeply about	Who would like to see
Who feels	Resident of

READING THE WORLD WITH FOLKTALES: GREAT BRITAIN AND SWITZERLAND

Tattercoats, by Joseph Jacobs. Putnam, 1989. [Great Britain]

A child rejected by her grandfather is cared for by the kitchen staff. She has only scraps to eat and clothes from the ragbag. Only the gooseherd boy can bring a smile to her face. One day a stranger appears and falls in love with her. She refuses to go to the ball with him because of her ragged clothes. But the magic of the gooseherd's pipes saves the day.

Activities

A. Retell the story using the "Fortunately, Unfortunately" pattern. Example:

Fortunately Tattercoats had a friend who was a gooseboy.
Unfortunately she had to wear rags and eat only scraps from the table.

Continue the story using the "Fortunately/Unfortunately" pattern.

B. Take a poll. Which sight would be the one most of your classmates would like to see in London: the changing of the guard at Buckingham Palace, the Tower of London where two young princes were murdered, the royal jewels, or the statue of Peter Pan?

The Singing Fir Tree, by Marti Stone. Putnam, 1992. [Switzerland]

The villagers love the singing that comes from the ancient fir tree on the mountain. Pierre, the woodcarver, wants to cut it down to carve from it an ornate tower for the town clock. The people object but Pierre knows no other tree will do. How can Pierre create his masterpiece and keep the villagers happy?

Activity

Debate: Should Pierre be allowed to cut the tree down?

Reasons to Cut	Reasons Not to Cut

READING THE WORLD WITH FOLKTALES: MEXICO

Borreguita and the Coyote, by Verna Aardema. Knopf, 1991.

Coyote would like nothing better than to make a tasty meal out of Borreguita, the little ewe lamb. But the little lamb tempts him with even tastier food like the big round cheese her master eats with his tacos. That night when coyote arrives at the pond to get the cheese he finds it is floating on the pond. He jumps in the water but finds nothing. Can you guess why?

The Sleeping Bread, by Stefan Czernecki and Timothy Rhodes. Hyperion, 1992.

Beto, the baker, always had bread to give to the beggar, Zafiro. To prepare for a big celebration, the townspeople ban all beggars from the town. As Zafiro bids Beto a sad good-bye, a tear falls into the water jar used to make the bread dough. The next morning the bread won't rise. Has the village lost more than a beggar?

Activities

A.   Use this pattern to write a song about Beto's village:

As I was walking in Beto's village.
I saw _____ and _____
I saw _____ and _____
A village for everyone to see.

Sing to the tune of "This Land Is My Land."

B.   A research project: Find the capital, a large city, three products, and three crops of Mexico. Use the information in this song pattern. Sing to "She'll Be Coming Round the Mountain."

She'll be coming from (capital)_____
When she comes.
She'll be coming from (large city) _____
When she comes.
She'll bring (three products) _____ and _____ and _____

She'll bring (three crops)_____ and _____ and _____
She'll be coming from Mexico when she comes.

READING THE WORLD WITH FOLKTALES: PERU

Chancay and the Secret of Fire, by Donald Charles. Putnam, 1992.

By sparing the life of the water spirit Tambo, Chancay proved himself worthy. But to win the secret of fire he must prove himself to be strong and brave. In three days' time Chancay faces lightning bolts, poisonous spiders, angry panthers, a molten volcano, a terrible condor, and the wrath of the moon and the sun. As Chancay reaches the golden temple where the sun and moon live he must have a clever plan to take the secret of fire home, for if he fails the sun will turn him into a shower of sparks. What do you think Chancay will do?

About Peru

Peru is located on the Pacific coast of South America. The Andes Mountains run the entire length of the country. Most people are farmers. The mountain people raise cattle, llamas, or sheep. The people use the llama for transportation and carrying goods. Its hair is used to make clothing and the hide is used for sandals. The Indians of Peru eat llama meat.

Activity

A "mystery animal report": Several animals are mentioned in the story: spiders, panthers, and condors. Also in Peru one might see deer, monkeys, anteaters, and boa constrictors as well as llamas. Find ten facts about an animal native to Peru. List the facts in any order. One must be a give-away clue. Ask classmates to give a number from 1 to 10. Read the clue for that number. The student can guess or pass. The game continues until the animal is guessed or all clues are read. Examples:

1. I grow four to five feet tall.
2. I do not have a hump.
3. I have thick, long, coarse hair.
4. I can be brown, buff, gray, white, or black.
5. I am useful as a pack animal.
6. I can carry about 100 pounds.
7. I can be very stubborn.
8. I spit when angry.
9. My name begins with two lls.
10. I can live for weeks without water.

Mystery animal: llama.

READING THE WORLD WITH FOLKTALES: RUSSIA

Salt, by Alexander Afanasiev. Retold by Jane Langton. Hyperion Press, 1992.

A merchant father sends his three sons in cargo-laden ships to make their fortunes. The two older sons lose their cargoes but the youngest son, Ivan, finds an island with a mountain of salt and trades the salt to the Tsar for gold, silver, jewels, and the Tsar's daughter.

On the return journey Ivan sees his brothers' battered ships and takes them aboard. The jealous brothers toss Ivan overboard and make their way home with the Tsar's daughter. With the help of a giant, Ivan arrives home just in time to put things straight and to marry the Tsar's daughter, proving that he is not so much of a fool as everyone thought.

About Russia

Today Russia is an independent nation but many years ago the land was ruled by a Tsar. Most royal families lived in St. Petersburg, which is today called Leningrad. The largest city in Russia is Moscow. There are few private homes. Most children go to school for ten years. In the time of the Tsars, Russia was a part of the Russian Empire, which was so large that when people in Moscow were going to bed those in Vladivostok were having breakfast.

Activities

A. Make a true/false book about Russia. Make a statement about Russia on one page. Example: "For hundreds of years Russia was called the sleeping bear of the world." Ask your reader if this statement is fact or fiction. On the next page, tell the reader the answer and explain why. Example: Fact: Long after other countries had modern factories, the people of Russia were farming using the same hand tools their ancestors used to till the land.

B. Share the story in song. Sing to "My Bonnie Lies Over the Ocean":

Young (1) I ____ sailed over the ocean.

Most people thought he was a (2) f_____

But while at sea (3) I_____ would learn more

Than if he were going to (4) s_____.

Chorus:

Ivan questioned

The shape of the (5) E_____ Was it flat or (6) r_____?

(7)F_____ answered

"It's flat, son, just look at the (8) g_____.

The boy traded (9) s_____ for some treasures

His brothers threw him (10) o_____

Then counted the (11) g_____ and the (12) s_____

A truly magnificent hoard.

Answers: 1. Ivan; 2. fool; 3. Ivan; 4. school; 5. Earth; 6. round; 7. Father; 8. ground; 9. salt; 10. overboard; 11. gold; 12. silver.

READING THE WORLD WITH FOLKTALES: AUSTRALIA

Koala Lou, by Mem Fox. Illustrated by Pamela Lofts. Harcourt, 1988.

There was once a baby koala so soft and round that all who saw her loved her. Her name was Koala Lou. The emu and the platypus loved her, but it was her mother who loved her most of all. A hundred times a day she would shake her head and say, "Koala Lou, I DO love you."

The years passed and brothers and sisters were born. Soon her mother was so busy she didn't have time to tell Koala Lou she loved her. Every night as she curled up under the stars, Koala Lou longed for the times when her mother said, "Koala Lou, I DO love you," and she longed for her to say it again. How could she get this to happen?

Criteria for Choosing the Best Idea

Your Ideas	Fast	Safe	Low cost	Effective	Total

Score each idea: 3 = yes, 2 = maybe, 1 = no. Total the scores for each idea.

Activities

A.   Find someone who (a name can be used only once):

1.   Has a younger brother or sister. _____

2.   Can name a movie or a book that takes place in Australia. _____

3.   Knows what a koala is. _____

4.   Can tell you what time of year it is in Australia right now. _____

5.   Can name one city in Australia. _____

6.   Has entered a contest. _____

7.   Has won a race. _____

B.   Find information about Australian animals and report the information as a chant or in a song. Prepare a data bank about the animal you choose.

```
┌─────────────────────────────────────────────────────────────────────┐
│                        Data Bank—Wombat                              │
│                                                                       │
│  Lives               Eats                  What It Does               │
│  Australia           roots                 carries its young in a pouch│
│  in a burrow         vegetables            makes an affectionate pet  │
│  Tasmania             leaves               digs large earth burrows   │
│                                            comes out only at night    │
│                                                                       │
│  What It Has         What It Looks Like                               │
│  a pouch             2–3 feet long                                    │
│  tough hide          yellow/black color                               │
│  long fur            furry possum                                     │
│  sharp claws                                                          │
│  small ears                                                           │
│  whiskers                                                             │
└─────────────────────────────────────────────────────────────────────┘
```

Wombat Chant

Facts about wombats
Has a pouch
Tough hide
Long fur
Sharp claws
Small ears
Whiskers
These are just a few.
Vegetable eater
Carries young
Good pet
Digs burrows
Yellow-black
Night creature
Eats leaves, too.
From near and far,
Here they are,
Facts about wombats!

FOLKTALES IN U.S. STUDIES

Let's visit colonial New England with:

The Red Heels, by Robert San Souci. Dial, 1997.

Deep in the woods a traveling cobbler, Jonathan, finds a cottage and in exchange for food and shelter he offers his services as a shoemaker to the young woman, Rebecca, who lives there. When she pulls out a pair of worn red heels, Jonathan is frightened because it is rumored that red heels are a sign of a witch. That night when Rebecca puts on the red shoes, something magical happens and Jonathan has an amazing adventure dancing in the clouds with her.

"Dancing ever faster, Rebecca with the cobbler in tow, mounted into the sky. Above the pond and the woods they whirled, beneath the silver fires of the moon and the stars. From the shadows below will-o'-the-wisps flashed up and capered beside them. Jonathan's fear left him. He felt carefree and feather-light."

Activities

A. Vocabulary: How many ways can you group these words from the story?:

colonial	shoemaker	workbench
spellbound	awl	Plymouth
journey-cake	affixed	porridge
hasty pudding	daydreamed	calfskin
chimney	hearth	tarry
farmwife	cobbler	Goodwife

B. Debate: Did Rebecca and Jonathan really fly up the chimney and dance in the clouds or did this happen only in their minds?

Let's visit the Hudson River Valley with:

"Rip Van Winkle," in *American Fairy Tales,* compiled by Neil Philip. Hyperion, 1996.

The story is set in the Kaatskill Mountains just before the Revolutionary War. Rip is a well-liked but lazy fellow with a shrewish wife who goes to sleep and awakens 20 years later to find his wife and friends deceased, his home in ruins, and that he is a citizen of a new country rather than a subject of King George.

Activities

A. Suppose you went to sleep in 1978 and awoke in 1998. Brainstorm with a group the changes you would experience. From your list choose the five changes you feel would be most startling to you.

B. What does Washington Irving mean when he says:

"The great error in Rip's composition was an insuperable aversion to all kinds of profitable labor."

"He inherited but little of the martial character of his ancestors."

"Men most apt to be conciliating abroad are those who are under the discipline of shrews at home."

"Her tongue was incessantly going to produce a torrent of household eloquence."

C. Why do you think our language is simpler today than in Washington Irving's day? (1783–1859).

Let's visit the Algonquin Indians at the shores of Lake Erie with:

The Rough-Face Girl, by Rafe Martin. Putnam, 1992.

Her two cruel sisters forced the Rough-Face Girl to feed the fire while they dressed in their finest garb to go to the wigwam of The Invisible Being to seek to become his wife. They were turned away because they could not say what he looked like. But the Rough Face Girl knew and her sweet nature won the heart of The Invisible Being.

Activities

A.   Using the Venn Diagram, compare Cinderella and the Rough-Face Girl:

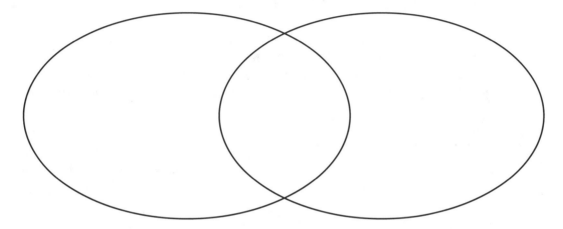

B.   Describe the village in a riddle poem using this model:

Let's go to long ago places and see the Earth's changing faces. We will see (list 4-6 sights). But that's not all. (List 4-6 additional sights.) Where am I? In an Algonquin Indian village.

C.   Cause and effect. List at least one for each statement:

The girl's face was marked by scars.
The sisters lied about seeing the Invisible Being.
The girl made a dress from birch bark.
The girl bathed in the water.

Let's visit the Appalachian Mountains with:

Ashpet, an Appalachian Tale, by Joanne Compton. Holiday House, 1994.

Ashpet was a serving girl to the widow Hooper and her two greedy and ugly daughters. She did all the work around the cabin and when visitors came she was hidden away. When it was time for the annual church social, Ashpet was left at home with more work to do than she could accomplish "in a month of Sundays." The Old Granny shows up and Ashpet's life changes for the better. At the social she meets the Doctor's son and the two hit it off so well that she nearly forgets Granny's warming to "be home by midnight."

Activities

A.   Before reading this Cinderella variant, answer these questions:

Where would she live?
What jobs will she do?
Who would all the girls want to marry?
What would be the big event all want to attend?
Who will help Ashpet?
What will her new dress look like?

B.   Try creating your own Cinderella tale set in a time in American history. Consider a colonial Cinderella, a Cinderella during the Industrial Revolution (see *The Bobbin Girl,* by Emily McCully), a Civil War Cinderella, a Depression era Cinderella, a World War II Cinderella, or a space age Cinderella. Research the facts carefully for your story setting.

FANTASY

Bunnicula: A Rabbit Tale of Mystery, by Deborah Howe and James Howe. Atheneum, 1979.

This book is written by Harold. His full-time occupation is dog. He lives with Mr. and Mrs. X (here called Monroe) and their sons Toby and Pete. Also sharing the home are a cat named Chester and a rabbit named Bunnicula. It is because of Bunnicula that Harold turned to writing. Someone had to tell the full story of what happened in the Monroe household after the rabbit arrived.

It all began when the Monroes went to see the movie Dracula. At the theater Toby found something on his seat: a baby rabbit that he took home and named Bunnicula. It proved to be an apt name, at least as far as Chester was concerned. A well-read and observant cat, he soon decided that there was something odd about the newcomer. For one thing he seemed to have fangs. And the odd markings on his back looked a little like a cape. Furthermore, Bunnicula slept from sunup to sundown. He was awake only at night.

When the family started finding white vegetables, drained dry, with two fang marks on them, Chester was sure Bunnicula was a vampire. But what to do about it? None of the family seemed to grasp the trouble, and Chester's hilarious hints were totally misunderstood.

Was Bunnicula really a vampire? Only Bunnicula knows for sure. But the story of Chester's suspicions and their consequences makes uproarious reading.

Activities

A.   Introducing vocabulary: Cut apart the words that follow. Work with a partner to group them in as many ways as possible. How many groups can you make?

Use as many words as you can to create a sentence describing the cover of the book. Add other words as needed.

Harold	Chester	Bunnicula
admonition	reverie	tranquil
circumstances	friends	independence
decipher	hysteria	preference
traumatized	sustenance	curiosity
energetic	indulgent	exhausted
criticize	imagination	significant
vampire	fascinating	aghast
inexplicable	vegetables	immobile
determination	pathetic	behavior
exemplary	devious	distressed
commotion	imminent	petrified
bewildered	starvation	fraught

B. Sentence starters:

Chapter One: The Arrival

1. A small bundle with tiny, glistening eyes might be ...

2. Treating others with respect means ...

3. When two people want a single object ...

Chapter Two: Music in the Night

4. A story that has a storm, cold chills, and haunting music will be ...

5. One way gypsies travel is ...

6. A person with a vivid imagination might ...

C. Questions to ponder:

1. List all the reasons you know that this novel is a fantasy rather than realistic fiction.

2. Why did Chester believe that Bunnicula was a vampire rabbit? Why was Harold not sure this was true?

3. What did Chester do to convince the Monroe family that Bunnicula was a danger to them? Why did they not understand Chester's message?

4. The vet said that Chester was jealous of Bunnicula and that was why Chester was behaving so badly? Do you think this was the real reason for Chester's behavior? Why or why not?

D. Chapter projects:

Chapters One and Two

Harold, the dog, and Chester, the cat, are alone in the Monroe house as a storm rages outside. The Monroe family returns from a Dracula movie with a small rabbit they found on a seat. They name the rabbit Bunnicula.

Activity: The first two chapters of Bunnicula tell you quite a bit about the Monroe household. You learn who lives there, what pets they have, what the house looks like, and many things that are in the house. Use the pattern below to write about the Monroe house. The free verse pattern can be framed in the shape of the "house."

This is the house where _____ lives.

This is where

_____

_____

This is where

_____

_____

And you can hear

_____

_____

And you can see

_____

_____

And you can feel

_____

_____

And _____ cares.

Chapters Three and Four

Chester sees Bunnicula go into the kitchen at night. The next day the Monroes find in their refrigerator a dry, white tomato. Toby reads *Treasure Island* late on a Friday night and shares snacks with Harold. Chester tries to convince Harold that Bunnicula is a vampire rabbit.

Activity: Using the patterns below, describe Harold, Chester, and Bunnicula.

If I were Chester

I would _____

And sometimes I would feel _____

And something I would do often is _____

And the thing I am most concerned about is _____

_____

But I wouldn't _____

Because Harold does that.

If I were Harold

I would _____

And sometimes I would feel _____

And something I would do often is _____

And the thing I am most concerned about is _____

_____

But I wouldn't _____

Because Bunnicula does that.

If I were Bunnicula

I would _____

And sometimes I would feel _____

And something I would do often is _____

And the thing I am most concerned about is _____

_____

But I wouldn't _____

Because Chester does that.

Chapters Five and Six

The Monroe family is puzzled to find more white vegetables in the kitchen. Chester pretends to be a vampire but the family does not get the message. Chester takes a steak off the table, puts it on Bunnicula and hits it. He then throws water, missing the rabbit but soaking Harold. Harold gets to eat the steak and Chester is put outside.

Activity: Chester read that to kill a vampire one needs a stake (a piece of wood). Chester did not know about homophones and he got a steak (meat) instead. Following are homophones Chester can learn:

ant, aunt
arc, ark
ate, eight
ball, bawl
bare, bear
beat, beet
cell, sell
fair, fare
hair, hare
knot, not
lead, led
made, maid

meet, meat

peak, peek

role, roll

sail, sale

tail, tale

Write three sentences about Harold, Chester, or Bunnicula using two homophones in each sentence. Example: Chester should have used a stake instead of a steak to do away with a vampire.

Chapters Seven through Nine

Chester's behavior seems to improve but Bunnicula is getting weak and listless. Harold discovers that Chester is keeping the rabbit from eating at night. Harold carries Bunnicula to the diningroom table to eat from the salad bowl. Chester chases the rabbit, causing a disaster at the table.

The vet discovers that Bunnicula suffers from hunger and puts the rabbit on a liquid diet. The vegetables stop turning white and the household settles down.

Activity: Using alliteration. Use of alliteration is one key to writing about animals. You will find using a dictionary and thesaurus helpful. Use the following pattern to write about an animal that lives with the Monroes and what it might do to make it a better place to live. (Choose Harold, Chester, or Bunnicula.)

This is a _____

 (Name of the pet)

_____

_____

(On these lines use at least four words beginning with the first letter of the pet's name to tell where he lives.)

_____

_____

(Using the same letter, tell his favorite things to eat)

_____

_____

(Tell what the pet liked to do).

This _____

_____ me.

(Tell about something the pet does that makes the house a better place to live.)

The Whipping Boy, by Sid Fleischman. Greenwillow, 1986.

A spoiled prince runs away taking his whipping boy with him and is changed by a series of harrowing adventures.

Activities

A. Pre-reading activity: journal writing: Choose one and write for ten minutes before reading the book. Share your writing with others.

   1. Playing a prank on your parents' dinner guests can lead to …

   2. Being lost in the woods on a dark and foggy night …

   3. Starving people sometimes eat …

   4. Going home after a dangerous journey can be …

B. Post-reading activity: discussion questions:

   1. Why did Prince Brat run away?

   2. If you were Jemmy would you prefer palace life or life in the sewers? Why?

   3. What caused the change in behavior in Prince Brat? Do you think it will last?

C. Chapter projects:

Chapters One and Two

Prince Brat causes constant trouble in the palace but is never punished because Jemmy, the whipping boy, gets the blows the prince deserves. The schoolmaster gives up on the prince, who always has an excuse for not having his homework.

Creative writing: Choose three of the following items and use them in an excuse about why the Prince does not have his homework.

apple core	a string	a rattlesnake
a dead rat	a tin soldier	a kite
a rusty key	six firecrackers	road tar
a one-eyed cat	a doorknob	crazed deer
bad shadows	a broken window	a mousetrap

Chapters Three and Four

The prince decides to run away and orders Jemmy to go with him. They get lost in a fog-filled forest and are captured by thieves. Research the causes of fog. Write about the causes in a chant. Describe fog in a five-senses poem.

A Fog Chant
Clear nights, gentle winds
Chill layers of warm air
Above the earth, mixing it
With cold air, at the surface
Fog forms, drains down
Lowest point, Of the ground.

The Fog: A Five Senses Poem
Fog is the color of a gossamer spider's web
It looks like a shroud covering the trees
It sounds like the soft hiss of a tea kettle
It tastes like fizzy water
It smells like a steam bath
It makes me feel like Sherlock Holmes

Chapters Five and Six

The outlaws, who are highwaymen, discover the prince's crown and decide to hold the boys for ransom. A highwayman was made famous in the poem by that name by Alfred Noyes. Find and read a copy of the poem. Summarize it using an acrostic.

T	he landlord's daughter and the
H	ighwayman
E	njoyed each other's company.
H	e told her to look for him
I	n the moonlight when he would
G	o to the inn door
H	is words were overheard
A	nd the king's men tied Bess
Y	onder to the bedpost, she
M	anaged to shoot the gun
A	nd warn her lover who
N	ever saw her again.

Chapters Seven and Eight

The outlaws decide Jemmy is the real prince because he can read and write, and they force him to write a ransom note to the king.

Use these words from chapters seven and eight in a sentence to describe the cover of the book. Add more words as needed:

rummaged	chest	stolen	scribblement
message	villains	oblige	calculating
scheme	ignorant	arrogant	flummox
genuine	haughty	ransom	scoundrels
reward	quill	rogues	trifle

Chapters Nine through Twelve

The thieves want to send Prince Brat to deliver the ransom note. He refuses to go and foils Jemmy's plan for escape. Jemmy tries to frighten the thieves by describing the king's punishments ... like boiling oil.

Using exaggeration, complete these sentences:

Getting a beating you don't deserve is scary but _____ is terrifying.

Walking in a dark woods at night is scary but _____ is terrifying.

Meeting a bear is scary but _____ is terrifying.

Add seven more, related to the novel.

Chapters Thirteen through Sixteen

The boys escape and meet a girl and her dancing bear and get a ride in a coach with a hot-potato man.

Creative thinking: A Potato Contest! Assign teams: How many ways can your team list to fix potatoes (3 minutes)?

OR

How many uses can your team list for a potato other than as a food? (3 minutes)

Chapter Seventeen

The boys reach the city and see acrobats, a stilt walker, a magician, a fiddler, and a ballad seller, among others. The ballad seller is singing about the thieves.

Using the tune "Yankee Doodle," write a ballad about the Prince and Jemmy.

> *Prince Brat ran away one night*
> *Caused his parents grief,*
> *Jemmy tried to stop him but*
> *Was captured by a thief.*
> *Both the boys tried to escape*
> *Helped by girl and bear,*
> *In his travels the young prince*
> *Began to trust and care.*

Chapter Eighteen

Jemmy hears a news seller telling about the Prince's disappearance and charging him with the crime. Jemmy is wanted dead or alive!

Write a news article giving the real facts of the prince's disappearance from the palace. Include WHO, WHAT, WHEN, WHERE, WHY, and HOW. Be sure your first line is a "grabber" to get the reader's attention.

Chapter Nineteen

Jemmy heads for the safety of the sewers, where he and the prince are pursued by the robbers. In the darkness they try to avoid the hundreds of rats. The rats attack the thieves, who run for their lives.

Make a data bank about rats. Add more items under each heading.

	Classifying—Rats	
Eats	**Lives**	**What It Looks Like**
grain	in sewers	a giant mouse
ruits	on ships	8"long
eggs	all parts of world	9 inch tail
		black or gray
What It Does	**What It Has**	
gnaws through wood	long tail	
produces 22 young	whiskers	
smells danger	sharp teeth	
carries disease		

Chapter Twenty

The boys return to the palace ,where all is forgiven and the king is pleased with the prince's changed behavior.

Write a poem about the changes the prince underwent from the beginning to the end of the novel using this pattern:

Reporting with Free Verse
Your are changing, changing.
You feel: describe the atmosphere
You are: two adjectives
You: two verbs or verb phrases
You are: color
The color of: name an object the same color
You are: give size and shape
And are: use participle and prepositional phrase
You do not walk upright anymore as you: three verb phrases
It is: adjective to move like this
So: one adjective and one simile
You are: name

James and the Giant Peach, Roald Dahl. Knopf, 1996.

James Henry Trotter had a happy life until he was about four years old. That was when his parents were eaten up by an enormous rhinoceros in broad daylight! His house by the sea had to be sold and James had to go and live with his horribly hideous aunts with the strange names of Aunt Sponge and Aunt Spiker. They lived in a ramshackle house on a hill surrounded by a garden that was desolate, with the exception of a clump of old laurel bushes. James would often gaze wistfully toward the sea. Then a strange thing happened. James found a giant peach that grew and grew until it was the size of a small house. He found a secret path into the heart of the peach, where he met a shorthorned grasshopper, a spider, a ladybug, an earthworm, a centipede, a glowworm, and a silkworm. Together they leave the hillside and begin a great adventure, which ends 1,250 feet up in the air on the top of the Empire State Building in New York City. Share the adventures of James and his friends and the new home they learn to love and enjoy in *James and the Giant Peach.*

Activities

A. Questions to think about:

1. What fairy tale is similar to *James and the Giant Peach?*

2. How many ways can you list that *James and the Giant Peach* and the tale of Cinderella are alike?

3. Why do you think Roald Dahl made Miss Spider a character rather than any other animal or insect?

4. Each character plays a special part in the story; list the things that each character did to help James and his friends arrive in New York.

B.   Chapter projects:

Chapters One through Four

James Henry Trotter's parents were killed in a freak accident in London while shopping. So James was sent to live with his Aunt Spiker and Aunt Sponge. They didn't seem to like little children at all.

One day James met an old man. He held in his hands a bag, a bag full of glowing stones. The old man told James that the magic inside the bag would free him from his life with his horrible aunts. He warned James not to drop the bag because the magic would go to someone or something else.

Activity: Write a report by using a bio-poem about one of the four characters you have met so far in the book. An example is provided for you below.

> *First Name: James Henry Trotter*
> *Four Traits: Sweet, sensitive, hard-working, lonely*
> *Related to: Aunt Spiker and Sponge*
> *Cares deeply about: his life and his mom and dad*
> *Who feels: sad*
> *Who needs: love and nurturing*
> *Who gives: 100 percent of himself*
> *Who fears: his aunts*
> *Who would like to see: his mom and dad again*
> *Resident of: England*

Chapters Five through Nine

James dropped the bag of glowing stones while running back toward the house. They sank into the ground surrounding the old peach tree. One peach at the top of the tree started to grow and grow. It grew until it was as big as a house. Aunt Spiker and Sponge sold tickets to see it. One night James went outside and was standing near the peach when he noticed what looked like a door on the side of the peach.

Activity: Creative writing peach contest. In groups of four, choose which question to tackle. The questions are: How many ways can your team think of to prepare peaches? OR How many uses can your team think of for a peach other than for food?

Chapters Ten through Sixteen

James went inside and found an entire room of insects the size of human beings. He met an Old-Green-Grasshopper, Spider, Ladybug, Centipede, Earthworm, and last, a Glow-Worm. They soon fell asleep in beds made by the Spider. The peach fell from the tree and it started to roll down the hill. Inside everyone was jostled from one side of the peach to the other. Aunt Spiker and Sponge were in for a shock when they went outside to let those who bought tickets see the peach. It was heading straight for them. It rolled right over them. It rolled all the way to the ocean.

Activity: A sample research report. Name different kinds of spiders and tell where each is found in a chant.

Spider Chant

Where can you find a spider?
Trapdoor Spider
In a burrow
Wolf Spider
Underground
Balloon Spider
On a fence
In the air, too.
Crab Spider
On a flower
Water Spider
Under water
Black Widow
In a corner
These are just a few.
Now you know,
There you go,
Off to see a spider.
These are just a few.
Now you know,
There you go,
Off to see a _____.

Use the same pattern to write a chant about other insects found in *James and the Giant Peach.*

Where can you find a:

_____

_____

_____

_____

_____

_____, too

_____

_____

_____

These are just a few,

Now you know,

There you go,

Off to see a _____.

Chapters Seventeen through Twenty

Inside the peach was a disaster. They had no idea where they were. James believed they were near an ocean. When the spider had finished spinning a rope they all climbed out. They were floating on the ocean. Panic began to run throughout the group. They were starving and were stuck out at sea without food. James wasn't worried, the peach would work just fine. Then James had a plan to get the peach out of the water. His plan was to tie a knot in the string the Silkworm had woven and toss it up and around a seagull's neck; if enough seagulls could be hooked they would pull them out.

Activity: Choose a character in the story and write an acrostic poem. Include as much information as you can.

Chapters Twenty-One through Twenty-Four

The plan had worked; they were in the air floating. As they were traveling in the air they spotted a ship below. The ship thought the peach was a secret weapon, until the Captain took a closer look and saw a small boy in trousers standing next to a ladybug and a grasshopper.

Activity: As James and the Giant Peach are floating through the air it is uncertain where they will land. You are a travel agent and you are to plan their destination, but you can't tell us what it is. We have to figure it out from the clues you give. Research some cities, towns, states, or countries. The world is open to you. Describe it in a research riddle below. A format has been provided.

Destination Unknown
Let us go to brand new places
And see the world's many faces.
We will find: (list six specific details in phrases)
But that's not all: (list six more details in phrases)
Do you know where we are?

Chapters Twenty-Five through Twenty-Nine

As the novel progresses, James finds that each of the insects has an important contribution to make to the world. The traveling peach is spotted by the Cloud Men, who make hailstones to throw on the people of the world. When the Cloud Men throw hailstones at the peach it is damaged and its inhabitants run for cover. When the storm ends and James and his friends come out of hiding they see the Cloud Men lowering a rainbow from the sky. Unfortunately the string they are using becomes tangled in the string the silkworm had spun and the peach and the rainbow crash into each other.

Activity: Mystery report. List six things about a mystery character from the book. Mix up the clues. One must be a giveaway clue. Ask a friend to give a number from 1 to 6. Read the clue for that number. The person can guess or pass. You may get more people to join in until all the clues are read or the character is guessed. A collection of mystery reports will be kept throughout the year and combined into a book. An example is provided for you.

1. Was very snippy throughout the story.

2. Was saved by James.

3. He became a Vice-President-In-Charge-Of-Sales.

4. Was essential in getting away from the Cloud Men.

5. Said he had 100 boots while everyone knew he had only 41.

6. Always took the longest to get ready.

WHO AM I???

Chapters Thirty through Thirty-Four

Just when James thinks they are out of trouble the sky opens up and they have to hold on for dear life. They then have to battle the snow and blizzard the Cloud Men sent them. Once morning comes the peach is over land once again and James knows how to get the peach down. If they cut a few of the strings at a time, that would gradually set the peach down. The peach is spotted from the ground and speculations spread fast on what it could be. The strings are being cut and it gets down to the last few; the peach begins to plummet to earth. Everything seems to be ending for the peach's inhabitants.

Activity: News report. The news is spreading fast about the peach falling to earth and you are a reporter for the *London Gazette.* Your editor has sent you to interview anyone who survives the fall. You must plan your questions wisely because others are covering your beat as well. Make sure your questions are thorough and leave out nothing the other reporters could get.

Chapters Thirty-Five through Thirty-Nine

They continue to plummet until they hit the Empire State Building. Once the people on the ground realize that this couldn't possibly be a flying saucer they come out of hiding to see exactly what it is. The Head of the Fire Department can't understand what is going on when he sees all of the insects on the peach. Then James comes out and introduces them to his friends the insects. They are given a parade to celebrate and the children climb all over the peach, taking bites out of it. Once the parade is over everyone who was on the peach ride becomes very important, especially James. In the park he lives in the peach stone and lets children by the thousands into his home, telling them of his adventure in the peach.

Activity: Analyze a character. Use the pattern below to write about any character in the book.

YOU ARE: Changing, changing,
YOU FEEL: Describe the atmosphere
YOU ARE: Two adjectives
YOU: Two verbs or verb phrases
YOU DO NOT: What is different?
AS YOU: Three participle phrases
YOU ARE: Name

The Boggart, by Susan Cooper. Margaret McElderry Books, 1993.

In a tumbledown castle in the Western Highlands of Scotland lives the Boggart. He is invisible, an ancient mischievous spirit, solitary and sly, born of a magic as old as the rocks and the waves. He has lived in Castle Keep for centuries, playing tricks on the owners. But the last Scottish owner has died and left the castle to his great-nephew, Robert Volnik of Toronto, Canada. The Volnik family, including Emily and her nine-year-old computer-genius brother Jessup, visit Castle Keep, and when they return to Toronto they unwittingly take the Boggart with them.

The astonishments, delights, and horrors that invade their lives with the arrival of the Boggart fill this swiftly moving story. The collision of modern technology and the Old Magic brings perils nobody could have imagined and, in the end, an amazing and touching solution to the problem of the Boggart who has found himself on the wrong side of the ocean.

Activities

A. Introducing vocabulary: Use as many of the following words as possible in ONE sentence to tell what you think a Boggart might do.

Emily	Jessup	Boggart
invisible	mischievous	solitary
Toronto	technology	peril
loch	dinghy Castle	keep
provocative	hysterical	outrageous
revenge	affectionate	incredulous
ululation	maladjusted	distracted
treacherous	ominous	immigration
imperiously	bereft	capacious
astrolabe	frustrating	indistinctly
disdain	investigate	aggravate
heartrending	endowment	preoccupied

B. Open-ended sentence starters:

Chapter One:

　　1. Apples that fly through the air ...

　　2. An example of outrageous behavior is ...

Chapter Two:

　　3. Being nice to paying customers is not easy when ...

　　4. To discover you have inherited a castle ...

Chapter Three:

　　5. Driving in a rain storm ...

　　6. Exploring an old castle ...

C. Questions to ponder:

　　1. The Boggart assumed that he would become a treasured member of his new family. What was wrong with this assumption?

　　2. Why do you think the family did not immediately realize they had a boggart in the house?

　　3. Boggarts are not supposed to cause harm to people. How do you explain Emily's injury?

　　4. What reasons can you give for Dr. Stigmore's interest in Emily? Which was the most compelling reason?

D. Chapter projects:

Chapters One through Three

　　The last owner of Castle Keep of Scotland dies and the Boggart, a mischievous spirit who inhabits the castle, feels the misery of loneliness. The Volnik family of Canada inherits the castle and decides to fly from Toronto to Scotland to inspect it. On their way to the castle the family stops in London to see the sights. Arriving in Scotland, they purchase supplies and take the boat to the castle for a five-day stay.

About the British Isles: The island of Great Britain, just off the coast of continental Europe, includes England, Scotland, Wales, and Northern Ireland. The British have a deep love for their land and the sea. The land ranges from the hills and mountains of Wales, to the Highlands of Scotland, to the green and rolling plains of England. The Queen of England is Elizabeth II, who reigns but does not rule. Members of Parliament actually rule the country. If you visited London, the capital city, you would see ships from every land sail to and from the Port of London. You could take a tour of the Tower of London and see the royal jewels. You might also watch the changing of the guard at Buckingham Palace. You could go horseback riding on Rotten Row and see the statue of Peter Pan at Kensington Gardens.

TAKE A POLL! What would members of your class most like to do in London?

> Port of London
> Tower of London
> Changing of the guard
> Rotten Row
> Peter Pan statue

Chapter Four

On the first night in the castle the Boggart tries to aggravate the family, to no avail. Jessup and Emily explore the shoreline and see seals. They have trouble communicating with Tommy, a local boy, because of differences in word meanings. The Boggart investigates the children's room at night and ends up trapped in a desk to be shipped to Toronto.

Activity: Find out more about Toronto and report the information using the Diamante pattern.

Diamante

_____

noun

_____ _____

two adjectives that describe it

_____ _____ _____

Three verbs that tell what the noun does

_____ _____ _____ _____

Two nouns relating to first line Two nouns relating to last line

_____ _____ _____

Three verbs that tell what the noun does

_____ _____

Two adjectives to describe it

_____

Noun

Chapters Five and Six

The family returns to Toronto. The desk is delivered and opened and the Boggart is once again free to do his tricks. The cat discovers the Boggart first and is frightened of it. The tricks accelerate. The Boggart goes to school in Jessup's lunchbox and becomes visible during a hockey game but is mistaken for a puck. It fouls another player and Jessup is blamed.

Activity: *Proverbs—Wise Sayings!* A proverb is a wise saying that can often be applied to many situations. Choose three of the proverbs below. Tell how each is advice a character from this novel might need.

Birds of a feather flock together.

Curiosity killed the cat.

Don't cry over spilt milk.

Every cloud has a silver lining.

Still waters run deep.

Two wrongs don't make a right.

Haste makes waste.

Look before you leap.

Chapters Seven and Eight

Emily tells Dai, the costume man at her father's theater, about the mishaps at home. Willie, an actor, immediately identifies the cause as a boggart. On Halloween the Boggart throws furniture out the window, barely missing Maggie. The children realize they have a boggart in the house. In a shop the creature makes dolls dance and furniture fly as the children, their mother, and a psychologist watch.

Activity: About characters. Choose a shape that, in your opinion, best represents a character from the story. Give specific reasons why/how the shape you have chosen or drawn represents the character you have chosen. Use the back of this paper. Shapes to consider: rectangle, square, circle, triangle, hexagon, pentagon, or any other of your choice.

Chapters Nine and Ten

The Boggart goes to the theater with the children and takes over the lightboard, creating extraordinary lighting. When an actor's sad words touch the Boggart, his grief is so overwhelming that everyone in the theater feels it. On the way home the children stop for ice cream. When the Boggart plays with the streetcar wires and traffic signs and signals, Emily tries to stop him but is injured by a car. Dr. Stigmore, a psychologist, upsets Emily when he labels the strange events a result of her "repressed anger." Jessup calls Tommy to find out more about the Boggart.

Activity: The Boggart experiences many different feelings in the story. Choose three of the feelings listed below. Write a sentence for each, explaining when and why the Boggart experienced that feeling in the story. Follow this pattern:

The Boggart felt _____ when _____

wicked	optimistic	ecstatic	dismal	fearful
cautious	foolish	impatient	upset	helpless
unhappy	confused	thoughtful	pensive	apprehensive

Chapters Eleven and Twelve

Winter snows cover Toronto and the Boggart awakens to a deep homesickness. He is shocked by the cold Canadian winter. Dr. Stigmore visits the family and the Boggart throws things at him. Dr. Stigmore wants Emily in the hospital for observation.

Willie translates a message left on Jessup's computer by the Boggart. "I want to go home." In the computer, the Boggart disappears down a black hole in a game Jessup has invented.

Activity: Help the Boggart return to Scotland.

1.   State the problem _____

_____

2.   List problems that contribute to the major problem.

_____

_____

3.   In the box below, list as many possible solutions and probable consequences as you can.

Consequences	Possible Solutions

4.   Decide on the best solution. Tell why you chose that solution.

_____

_____

_____

The Phantom Tollbooth, by Norton Juster. Random House, 1961.

This is a tale about a little boy named Milo, "who didn't know what to do with himself." Through the Phantom Tollbooth lies a strange land and a series of even stranger adventures in which Milo meets King Azaz the Unabridged, the unhappy ruler of Dictionopolis; the Mathemagician; Faintly Macabre, the not so wicked Which; Alec Bings, who sees through things; and the watchdog, Tock, who ticks, among a collection of the most logically illogical characters ever met on this side of that side of reality. In his quest for Rhyme and Reason, Milo helps settle the war between words and numbers, visits the Island of Conclusions (which can only be reached by jumping), and ventures into the forbidden Mountains of Ignorance, whose all-too-familiar demons menace his every step.

Activities

A.   Introducing vocabulary: Work with a partner. Cut the following words apart. Use as many words as you can to develop a sentence that either describes the cover of the book or predicts what the book will be about. Add other words as needed.

Milo	Tock	Humbug
King Azaz	dejectedly	punctuated
enormous	dimension	precautionary
cartographer	expectations	destination
accelerator	monotonous	doldrums
lethargy	procrastinate	ferocious
inscribed	inconvenient	disrepute
Dictionopolis	advantageous	medallion
quagmire	flabbergasted	fraud
competition	macabre	ominous
consensus	disconsolate	exasperated
dissonance	mirage	illusions
exaggeration	promontory	chaotic

B.   Open-ended sentence starters:

Chapter One: Milo

1.   Seeking knowledge is a good thing when ...

2.   An enormous package might contain ...

Chapter Two: Beyond Expectations

3.   If thinking were unlawful ...

4.   To get out of the doldrums one must ...

Chapter Three: Welcome to Dictionopolis

5.   Many words that mean "yes" are ...

6.   Time is very important when ...

C. Questions to ponder:

1. Which do you think are more important, words or numbers? Why?

2. Explain the Dodecahedron's words: "The more you want the less you get and the less you get, the more you have."

3. What is the difference between reality and illusion? Give specific examples.

4. List the things Milo learned from his journey. Which item on your list do you think is most important? Why?

5. Explain this statement: "Without rhyme or reason wisdom withers."

D. Chapter projects:

Chapters One and Two

Milo, a boy bored with life, receives a package with directions for constructing a tollbooth "for those who have never traveled in lands beyond." He begins the trip, making a stop in The Doldrums (where nothing ever happens).

Milo will visit many strange places in his travels, including:

The Foothills of Confusion The Sea of Knowledge
The Word Market   The Castle in the Air
Point of View   The Silent Valley
City of Illusion   The Island of Conclusions

Choose one of the above settings and describe it using the questions below. Compare your descriptions with the actual setting when Milo arrives there.

1. Name the place: _____

2. What objects could usually be seen in this place? _____

3. What is the usual temperature and what are the general weather conditions around this place?

_____

4. What unusual smells would be present? _____

_____

5. What sounds might one hear all of the time, or some of the time? _____

_____

6. What objects would one find here that would tell the time in history the story takes place?

_____

7. Is this a place people would like or fear to visit? Why? _____

_____

8. Is there anything especially strange or unusual about this place? What? _____

_____

Chapters Three and Four

Milo meets Tock, the watchdog, and the dog explains the importance of time. They travel together to Dictionopolis, where words are freely used. Milo and Tock visit the Market Place, where words are for sale. They meet the Spelling Bee and the Humbug.

Activity: Milo meets the first of many strange characters in Dictionopolis, as well as other strange characters. Some of these are:

Short Shrift	Faintly Macabre	Rhyme and Reason
The Humbug	Dr. Dischord	The Dodecahedron
The Mathemagician	Terrible Trivium	Gelatinous Giant

Choose one character to describe using the questions below. Compare your description with the author's when you meet the character in the novel.

1. What is the character's name? _____

2. How old is this character? _____

3. Is this character's height or weight unusual in any way? _____

4. Does this character have any special characteristics that would easily identify the character?

   _____

5. What would most people like about this character? _____

   _____

6. Does this character have any habits that might bother, irritate, or alarm other people?

   _____

7. What does this character do for a living? _____

8. What does this character most like to do for fun? _____

   _____

9. What can this character do that most others cannot do? _____

   _____

10. What kind of voice does this character have? _____

11. What would children do if they met this character on the road? _____

    _____

12. What is this character's favorite food? _____

13. Would this character represent good or evil forces in this story? Why? _____

    _____

14. Who would this character most likely have for friends? _____

    _____

Chapters Five through Eight

Short Shrift, the policeman, gives Milo a short sentence (I am), and jails Milo and Tock for causing confusion. Faintly Macabre tells the two about the early days of Dictionopolis, when words and numbers had equal value; the decline of the City of Wisdom; and the banishment of the two princesses, Rhyme and Reason. Milo and Tock enter the palace, which looks like an enormous book where citizens literally eat their words. The Royal Ministers speak in proverbs and the Humbug explains the difficulties in rescuing the badly needed princesses from Digitopolis. King Azaz decides that Milo, Tock, and Humbug should go to rescue the Princesses.

Activity: Using the book outline as a base, design the Royal Palace of Dictionopolis in a sketch. Add whatever details you wish.

Chapters Nine and Ten

The travelers meet a boy who grows down (not up), get lost in a forest, meet a giant and a midget, and see a concert in which the orchestra plays the sunset as well as morning, noon and night. Milo tries to conduct the orchestra but fails. They continue the journey and meet Doctor Dischord, who makes all kinds of noise with his assistant Dynne, who collects unpleasant noises.

Activity: Thinking about noise. Use these creative thinking skills to think about NOISE!

1. FLUENCY: The ability to make many responses.

Name as many very loud noises as you can.

_____   _____   _____

_____   _____   _____

_____   _____   _____

_____   _____   _____

_____   _____   _____

2. FLEXIBILITY: Finding new categories.

How many ways can you group the noises you named in item 1?

_____   _____   _____

_____   _____   _____

_____   _____   _____

_____   _____   _____

_____   _____   _____

3. ORIGINALITY: Giving many responses.

Describe a way to make a loud noise that you do not believe anyone else will think of.

_____

4. ELABORATION: Adding details.

Choose a musical instrument. What can you add to it to increase its sound? Draw a sketch below and describe what your addition(s) will do.

Chapters Eleven through Fourteen

Milo tries to rescue one small sound from the Soundkeeper to restore sound to the Valley of Silence. He is successful. The travelers then enter a country where it doesn't pay to jump to conclusions, numbers are valued, and jewels are thrown away.

Miss Hickory, by Carolyn Sherwin Bailey. Viking, 1946.

When Great-Granny Brown packed up and moved to the Women's City Club in Boston, Miss Hickory was faced with the problem of spending a severe New Hampshire winter alone. This might not have been so bad if Miss Hickory had not been a country woman whose body was an apple-wood twig and whose head was a hickory nut. Also, if her house had been built of stronger material than corncobs, however neatly notched and glued together.

This is the story of how she survived those trying months, in the company of neighbors like Crow, who was tough, wise and kindly; Bull Frog, who lost his winter clothes; Ground Hog, a surly character afraid of his own shadow; and a host of others. It is a fantasy full of the peculiar charm of the New Hampshire countryside, seen from an angle that most of us, city-bound in the winter, know little about.

Activities

A.   Introducing vocabulary: Group as many of the following words as you can. A group must have a minimum of three words.

Miss Hickory	New Hampshire	severe
country	twig	corncobs
notched	survive	company
neighbors	Crow T.	Willard Brown
Chipmunk	Barn-Heifer	difficulty
ruffles	doorsill	discarded
clodhoppers	pretensions	ancestry
gossip	hardheaded	essence
checkerberries	haunches	desperate
occupied	despair	bedraggled
orchard	scurry	rustling
conscience	appetite	excavated

B.   Open-ended sentence starters:

   1.   When forest animals prepare for winter …

   2.   Dangers a small creature would face in the woods …

   3.   Crows are only bothersome when …

   4.   Survival of the fittest means …

C.   Questions to ponder:

1.   Miss Hickory did not see what was in the manger on Christmas Eve. What do you think the animals saw?

2.   Explain how Miss Hickory arranged for spring to come earlier than expected.

3   Why do you suppose Miss Hickory did not try to get her house back when Chipmunk stole it?

4.   Robin accused Miss Hickory of being completely selfish. Do you agree or disagree with Robin? Why?

5.   Tell three ways the story might have ended if Squirrel had not eaten Miss Hickory's head.

D.   Chapter projects:

Chapters One and Two

Miss Hickory, a doll made from an apple twig with a hickory nut head, learns that the family has gone to Boston for the winter, leaving her behind. Both the crow and the cat bring the bad news.

This story takes place in New Hampshire. Find the information asked for below and write a New Hampshire song. Sing to the tune of "She'll Be Coming Around the Mountain."

She'll be coming from _____ when she comes,
(capital)

She'll be coming from _____ when she comes,
(large city)

She'll bring _____
(three products)

She'll bring _____
(three crops)

Chapters Three through Six

Chipmunk takes over Miss Hickory's home, leaving her shivering under the trellis. Crow finds her a new home in a robin's nest in an apple orchard. She makes winter clothes from moss and leaves. She discovers that Squirrel (who likes nuts) lives at the bottom of her tree. Miss Hickory shows Hen-Pheasant how to protect her winter feeding place from Cock by getting all the hens together to make a quilt. The cat looks for Cow to get her daily milk but Cow turns up with a stomachache.

Activity: Draw a story quilt! Include:

three objects that represent the time of the story

three objects that represent the place or setting of the story

three objects that are important to plot of the story

Chapters Seven through Ten

Fawn goes exploring and returns home to find his mother missing. Wild-Heifer offers Fawn her friendship. Miss Hickory sees the two feeding together in the barn. Squirrel invites Miss Hickory to a Christmas celebration in the barn. She sees a parade of animals from near and far but does not hurry and misses the wondrous sight in the manger. Ground Hog sees its shadow and darts back into its hole. Miss Hickory talks the hens into leaving food for Ground Hog on a cloudy day to make spring come faster.

Activity: There are many superstitions about animals and nature. Some may have basis in fact. Choose three of the superstitions listed below and find out if they are true or false. Report your findings to the class.

1. Deer shed their horns every year.
2. Foxes charm squirrels out of trees.
3. A skunk cannot discharge its odor without raising its tail.
4. It's bad luck for a rabbit to cross your path from left to right.
5. Buzzards winter in Ozark caves.
6. The whippoorwill and the night hawk are the same bird.
7. The raincrow lays its eggs in other birds' nests.
8. The bite of a wren is poisonous.
9. Young crows are white before they leave the nest.
10. Loud thunder kills young turkeys in the egg.
11. The eel is a male catfish.
12. Gars are deadly poison.
13. Stepping over a fishing pole means you will catch no more fish that day.
14. Hearing a screech owl means a coming sickness.
15. It's good luck to find a dead crow on the road.

Chapters Eleven through Fourteen

The crows return, attacking the hens and stealing their corn. Crow takes Miss Hickory on a flight to see signs of returning spring on the farm. Miss Hickory pulls Bull Frog out of the ice and he slips out of his skin, showing a fresh new suit. She is shocked when he eats his old "suit." Miss Hickory sets off to find new clothes. When she returns she discovers that Robin has reclaimed the nest. Miss Hickory is homeless. She ventures into Squirrel's home and Squirrel eats her hickory nut head. Headless, Miss Hickory climbs an apple tree and rests there.: Use the form below to tell how Miss Hickory felt when she lost her head.

Activity: Add words to the story below that describe Miss Hickory's feelings.

Miss Hickory was _____. She was so

_____ that she (action)

_____. Crow knew that Miss Hickory felt

_____. Crow knew because

_____. Bull Frog knew that Miss Hickory felt

_____. Bull Frog knew because

_____. The ways in which Miss Hickory
showed her feelings were

_____

_____ and

_____. Because she felt

_____, Miss Hickory decided to

_____. This made her feel

_____   _____.

Chapter Fifteen

Ann returns to find Miss Hickory gone. The children discover a new branch on an old apple tree that looks like Miss Hickory, up to the neck. Miss Hickory has found a permanent home at last!

Activity: Create a Miss Hickory ABC. There are many forms of wildlife mentioned in *Miss Hickory,* both plants and animals. Some lines are completed with creatures Miss Hickory met. Complete the other lines with names of more plants and animals from the story.

A _____   N _____

B _____   O _____

C crow _____   P _____

D _____   Q _____

E _____   R _____

F _____   S squirrel _____

G _____   T _____

H hen _____   U _____

I _____   V _____

J _____   W _____

K _____   X _____

L _____   Y _____

M _____   Z _____

The Forgotten Door, by Alexander Key. Westminster Press, 1965.

Little Jon is watching the shooting stars streaming across the sky when suddenly he falls through the Door: the one that leads to another place, the one that has been closed for so long.

On the first page of this enchanting book you meet Little Jon as he is gathering himself together, cold and sore and bruised, in a mossy cave. He can remember nothing, not even who he is. So he starts down the mountain in search of people to help him. It is a strange journey, full of mystery and magic. As he travels into our world we gradually realize that he is from another one.

Following a friendly deer, Little Jon eludes the first dangers and meets, in the valley, the Bean family, the kindly people who take him to their home. They think he cannot speak because of some shock, but as he quickly learns their English they realize he can also read their minds.

The local folk call Jon the wild boy and are afraid of his extraordinary powers. He is astonished to learn about their fear and hate, which he has never known, about the tangle people have made with their laws and their money and their fighting for power. There is suspense and adventure, magic and meaning, as Jon tries to find the Door back to his own peaceable kingdom.

Activities

A.   Introducing vocabulary: Use as many of the following words as you can in one sentence to describe the cover of the book. Add other words as needed.

Little Jon	enthralled	astonishing
cleft	pondered	lichens
cultivated	disbelief	incredulous
Cherokee	pursuer	varmint
vaguely	impersonal	furiously
liniment	unnatural	venison
mercenary	concoction	deceived
concussion	geology	bewilderment
heir	enclosure	misgivings
temporarily	filigree	profit
theory	dispute	civilization
intelligent	observant	ferret
reputation	investigate	guardian
recuperate	threshold	conspirator

B.   Open-ended sentence starters:

Chapter One: He Is Lost and Found

1.   Awakening in an unfamiliar place ...

2.   Communicating with a wild animal is ...

3.   The ability to sense the feelings of others ...

Chapter Two: He Gains a Home

4.   The kindness of strangers can be ...

5.   The ability to read minds ...

6.   A good meal for a vegetarian is ...

Chapter Three: He Learns a New Language

    7.   The exact truth is often a hard thing to manage ...

    8.   A deception is not wrong when ...

    9.   Learning a language in one day ...

C.   Questions to ponder:

    1.   What stereotypes of good and evil can you find in this novel?

    2.   How would your life be different if no animals were ever killed?

    3.   List the advantages and disadvantages of being able to read minds.

    4.   Jon's presence meant trouble for the Beans. Why do you suppose they didn't give him up to the authorities?

    5.   Explain the significance of the title.

D.   Chapter projects:

Chapters One and Two

A careless step plunges Little Jon through a dark hole on his planet and he awakens in a strange world, not knowing who he is. A confrontation with mean humans sends him back to the safety of the forest and the friendly animals he finds there. Jon senses the friendliness of a family in a passing truck. The Bean family take him home, dress his wounds, and care for him. Gilby Pitts, the hunter who first saw Jon and was cruel to him, stops by the Bean house. Thomas Bean does not reveal the boy's whereabouts.

Activity: Describe the forest in literary terms by completing the following form.

The author creates an ideal forest setting amid the mountains. Use the form below to describe this setting as Jon sees it.

I am a forest green and _____. My floor is a bed of

_____ where _____. Tucked within the pockets of rugged

cliffs I shelter _____. I

am old, older than _____. Yet I am young,

younger than _____. My trees in bloom are covered with

showers of _____ that

_____. Familiar sounds of a hidden spring and the clatter and fuss of

_____ blend with the cautious steps of _____

_____ who shelter in the home I provide for them. Under the rocky

ledges that jut from the mountainside are hidden _____

_____. I am the forest looking on as

man approaches _____. Feeling fear as man

_____. Yet harboring hope as others

_____.

Chapters Three and Four

Mrs. Bean realizes that Jon must be from another world when he shows his ability to read animals' thoughts and learns English in one day. After listing what they knew about Jon, the Beans conclude that he is from another world where ideas like war, lies, profit, and thievery are unknown. A neighbor drops by and sees Jon.

Activity: Using pictures from the newspaper or old magazines, make a collage to show Jon what one of these words means:

WAR	LIES	PROFIT	THIEVERY

Under your collage write a two-line couplet to explain the word.

Chapters Five and Six

Mr. Bean, who is a geologist, and Jon take rock hammers to the place where Jon awoke from his fall. Before they can leave, Deputy Bush arrives, looking for the thief whom he suspects is the "wild boy" others have reported seeing. Jon and Mr. Bean find the place Jon landed. Mr. Bean finds igneous rocks that shouldn't be there. Mr. Pitts recognizes Jon as the "wild boy" and accuses him of being a thief.

Activity: Be a geologist! Find out about rocks. Rocks can be placed in three main groups:

1. Igneous Rocks	2. Metamorphic Rocks	3. Sedimentary Rocks

Find a book about rocks or look in the encyclopedia. Put the following rocks in the group above where they belong.

Basalt	Flint	Pumice
Chalk	Coral	Syenite
Gneiss	Quartzite	Slate
Marble	Mica Schist	Soapstone
Clay	Lava	Sandstone
Coal	Obsidian	Shale

Find out more about one of these famous rock formations. Tell where it is and what it looks like. Draw a picture of it on the back of this page.

Garden of the Gods	Gibraltar	Mount Rushmore

Chapters Seven through Nine

The Deputy accuses Jon of stealing. They drive to the Macklin place, where the Macklin boys have hidden the stolen goods. Jon leads the Deputy to the place where the goods are hidden. The Deputy still thinks Jon is the thief. Rumors fly among the neighbors about Jon and a summons arrives ordering the Beans to bring him to Juvenile Court on Monday. Jon faces his accusers in the court and tells the truth. The Macklin boys confess to the theft but the welfare people want to take Jon away from the Beans.

Activity: Character sketch. By now you know quite a bit about Jon. Write a character sketch for Jon by answering the character sketch questions that follow. Then write the sketch in paragraph form.

1. What adjectives can be used to describe Jon's appearance?

_____

_____

2. What adjectives will you use to describe Jon's personality?

_____

_____

3. What would Jon think about or how would the character feel about everyday things like school, television, computers, pizza, etc.?

_____

_____

4. What would others say about Jon and/or how would others react to him?

_____

_____

5. How would Jon normally respond to a problem or a crisis?

_____

Chapters Ten through Twelve

Reporters descend on the Beans. Warning notes are thrown through their windows. The military is taking legal steps to take custody of Jon to use him for their own purposes. The house is surrounded by enemies preventing escape, when Jon hears a voice telling him that his people have come for him. Jon knows his family has come to rescue him, but if he leaves the Beans will be in trouble. They agree to come with him, and after a harrowing chase they all escape to Jon's planet.

Activity: Mr. Bean assures Jon that there are many good people on the planet Earth. Jon's love for animals and respect for their lives can be compared to that same love and respect for animals shown by Dr. Albert Schweitzer. His love of peace is similar to that of the great Indian leader, Gandhi. Mr. Bean compares Jon's ability to carve figures with that of the great sculptor, Rodin.

Find out more about Schweitzer, Gandhi, or Rodin. Report your findings in the bio-poem model that follows.

Bio-Poem

First Name _____

Four traits _____

Related to _____

Cares deeply about _____

Who feels _____

Who needs _____

Who gives _____

Who would like to see _____

Resident of _____

Sources of Information:

Title _____

Author: _____

Castle in the Attic, by Elizabeth Winthrop. Dutton, 1981.

Mrs. Phillips, who has taken care of William for a long time, is moving back to England. William has grown too old to need a nurse. But William is very fond of Mrs. Phillips and does not want her to leave. He is determined to find some way to make her stay. As a farewell present Mrs. Phillips gives him a wooden and stone model of a real medieval castle, complete with a Silver Knight. She tells William how the Silver Knight was thrown out of his kingdom by an evil enemy and one day will come back to life and return to reclaim his lands.

Later that night, after everyone has gone to bed, William creeps up to the attic and takes the Silver Knight from its box. To his surprise the Knight feels soft and squishy and even warm. And then it moves!

Activities

A. Chapter projects:

Chapters One and Two

William is the smallest kid in the class, without much confidence in himself. He is upset because his trusted nurse, Mrs. Phillips, is leaving. She takes him to the attic and gives him a gift of a castle with one soldier, Sir Simon.

A research project: Two castles are very important to the story: the castle in the attic and Alastor's castle. After reading this chapter see if you can tell the purpose of each of these rooms, places, or objects:

1. Great Hall _____
2. Allure _____
3. Buttery _____
4. Armory _____
5. Portcullis _____
6. Moat _____
7. Benfry _____
8. Drawbridge _____
9. Crossbow _____
10. Courtyard _____

Chapters Three through Six

The Silver Knight comes alive and tells William a tale of treachery. A wizard has stripped the knight of all of his powers except a small medallion, which is to be used to get the knight his lands back. William shows his friend, Jason, the castle but does not reveal the secret of the knight. He catches bugs and takes them to Sir Simon, who tries the power of his medallion on them successfully. Watching the bugs shrink gives William an idea.

Activity: Knighthood was a rank that had to be earned. It had to be learned. Only the sons of nobles and knights were allowed to train. This training began when the boys were about nine years old, and it prepared them to be fighters. They first became pages, then squires, and, finally, were made knights. While most of their training concentrated on fighting techniques, they also learned a code of conduct called chivalry. This conduct centered on many abstract concepts, such as loyalty, honor, bravery, generosity, courage, and gallantry.

Make a banner. Write on the banner a metaphor for the knight, using an abstract concept from above or another one you think describes a knight. In a few lines, explain why you chose the concept. Can you create more banners? Make them larger and hang them around the classroom.

Chapters Seven and Eight

William decides to shrink Mrs. Phillips without her consent. Sir Simon is pleased with the idea because every castle needs a lady in residence. When the deed is done, she refuses to speak to William until she is returned to her normal size, an impossibility unless the evil wizard who has the other medallion can be conquered.

Have a debate:

List reasons that it was a good idea to shrink Mrs. Phillips.

List reasons it was not a good idea.

What conclusions did you draw from looking at your lists?

Good Idea	Not a Good Idea

Chapters Nine and Ten

William allows the knight to make him smaller. Sir Simon acquaints William with the Rules of Knighthood and he and William set off to conquer Alastor the wizard and get the magic medallion back.

Activity: Rules for today's society would be very different from the Rules of Knighthood. Make a list of six rules that William might give the Knight if the Knight were to enter William's world. List the rules from the most to the least important for surviving in today's world.

_____

_____

_____

_____

_____

_____

Chapters Eleven and Twelve

William and Sir Simon travel through a dark and dangerous forest, where they are separated. William emerges from the evil forest and helps a stranger. He wonders how he will get past the dragon that guards the castle doors.

Activity:

List Ideas Here	List Consequences Here

Chapters Thirteen and Fourteen

William defeats the dragon and meets Alastor, the evil wizard, who has captured Sir Simon and turned him into lead once again. The only way William can save Sir Simon and Mrs. Phillips is to get the medallions that hang around Alastor's neck. How can he do this? Use the problem-solving model below to work out a solution. Then read the next two chapters to see if your solution and the author's solution are the same or different.

1. What important facts can you state about the situation?

_____

_____

_____

2. State the major problem.

_____

_____

3. List as many ways as you can to deal with the problem. These are your alternatives.

_____

_____

_____

_____

_____

4. Select the four best ideas and enter them on the decision grid below.

5. Two criteria for judging ideas are provided in the grid. Add a third of your own.

6. Evaluate each idea on a scale of 1 to 5. A poor rating is 1; a high rating is 5.

Ideas	Fast	Safe	Possible	Effective	Total

Chapters Fifteen through Seventeen

Because of his courage and good heart, William defeats the wizard, who is turned to lead. His touch brings Sir Simon to life and they return to the castle in the attic, where Mrs. Phillips is brought back to her true size. Their parting is easier now that William has learned to believe in himself.

Activity: Abstract thinking. In this story, William finds there are many doors to trust, courage, freedom, and love. These are abstract concepts and are sometimes hard to define or evaluate. Look at the questions below. Work alone, in pairs, or in groups, and try to find answers.

What are some examples of courage that you can think of?

_____

_____

What are some examples that seem to be a lack of courage?

_____

_____

When you are courageous, you can or will do what?

_____

_____

Is fear the opposite of courage or is it a part of courage?

_____

_____

Do you know anyone who is truly courageous? Who?

_____

_____

Are there different kinds of courage? What kinds?

_____

What is the most courageous thing you have ever done?

_____

Is there a difference between being courageous and being foolhardy? Give an example of each.

_____

_____

What kinds of courage are these?:

physical courage _____

mental courage _____

ethical courage _____

Can you now give a definition for courage?

The Classics
and Poetry

INTRODUCTION

The classic books written by great authors are a never-ending source of enjoyment to the young reader. In addition, they can serve as motivators for study units and as tools for integrating thinking skills into the curriculum. And, finally, they can be used as a theme, or a topic focus, such as "ocean voyages."

Diversity is a state with which gifted children must learn to be comfortable in this rapidly changing world of ours. Students can be led to a greater knowledge and appreciation of the many different perspectives, viewpoints, and concepts of the multifarious world in which we live.

The activities in this chapter emphasize creative and critical thinking about a variety of peoples, cultures, customs, beliefs and places—real and imagined. The classics are a wonderful source for emphasizing these concepts.

These are the stories, "tried and true," that have endured throughout the years and never cease to delight and excite young minds. Their familiarity could cause us to overlook the store of ideas that lend themselves to expansion and elaboration into many units of study. As adults, we can remember the fascinating travels on a river raft, to a treasure island in a steamy jungle, or leagues under the sea found in the classic tales. To share this fascination with young gifted students is to relive our youthful dreams and continue these enriching sagas for new generations to enjoy.

TO THE TEACHER

To be successful in our pluralistic society, we must be able to understand and to value the diversity of cultures that make up our own civilization and others throughout the world. We can pass on that knowledge and appreciation to our students through literature.

The classics in this chapter, and many others, are an excellent source for learning about the languages, customs, beliefs, traditions, and inventions affecting many different ways of life. To know and understand the many diverse cultures of the world is the first step toward valuing them. In valuing them, we can instill the desire to preserve, rather than destroy, ways of life other than our own.

ACTIVITIES TO IMPROVE SKILLS THROUGH CLASSIC LITERATURE

Creative Thinking

List the adversities the characters in the *Swiss Family Robinson* had to overcome to survive.
Create a new society on a desert island—a perfect world.
Elaborate on this new world to show what could be added to make others want to copy it.
Examine how different our own society could be if five critical laws were changed.

Critical Thinking

Associate by identifying characteristics common in people, places, and experiences. Use metaphor, simile, and analogy.
Analyze the attributes of characters found in the classics.
Clarify the moral lessons that can be found in these stories.
Predict how the main character will solve his or her problem in the story.

Vocabulary

Research the origin of complex words found in the classic stories.
Compare the words used to describe the good versus the evil characters.
Note how words and descriptions influence your judgment of people.

Problem Solving

Decide which problem was most critical for the Robinson family.
Gather evidence; write down all the facts you can about this problem.
Select the best solution based on judgments concerning safety and possibility.

Imaging

Who is the most interesting character in *20,000 Leagues Under the Sea?* (Describe.)
What makes him or her so interesting? (Describe.)
Where would he or she want to live for the rest of his or her life? (Describe.)

Observation

Look at the world around you right now.

Listen to all the sounds you hear.

Taste whatever is in the air or edible near you.

Touch the things that are near.

Feel … how would these things change if you fell asleep and woke up in 20 years?

ACTIVITIES FOR CLASSICS

Pre-Unit Activities

Brainstorming: Students can be led to an expansion on classics by realizing the many areas associated with the word *classic.*

Defining: Students learn to define words and concepts such as "classic" and "diversity" by attaching attributes and characteristics that belong to those words.

Listing: Students start a list on tagboard of all the many kinds of people, places, and adversities found in children's classics. Add to the list as classics are read.

Predicting: After arranging books and book jackets of classics around the room, students are allowed to predict what the story is about.

Mid-Unit Activities

Integrating: Expand on a unit of Canada with *Call of the Wild*; measure fathoms with *20,000 Leagues Under the Sea*; expand on a Middle Ages unit with *Robin Hood*; introduce alliteration with *Peter Pan.*

Metaphoric thinking: Compare famous people to characters in the classics. Create a book of classic character metaphors.

Abstract thinking: Define the qualities found in classic story characters through the use of attributes connected with the abstract.

Decision making: Students decide what ten things they would choose to have if they were marooned on an island.

Problem solving: Using the sequential steps of problem solving, discover new solutions for the many obstacles faced by the characters in the classic story.

Personification: What human characteristics were given to the mole, the toad, the water rat, and the badger in *The Wind in the Willows*?

Post-Unit Activities

Create a parody of *Peter Pan.* This time, make the hero a girl. Give her a different method to get to Never Never Land, and create a new ending for the story.

Deductive reasoning: Give students six generalizations that fit the concept of a children's classic. They can find data to support the generalizations. Give them a chance to add to the list.

Forecast: If Rip Van Winkle fell asleep 20 years ago and woke up today, what are all the things he would have missed? Ask students, "What would be the most important historical event(s) he missed?"

Research: Have a "Night of Classics" for parents. Students dress as their favorite classic characters and tell their stories.

Associate: Create associations by comparing the problem found in the classics to modern day problems. Students can find solutions through the problem-solving process.

Clarify: Stage a debate to determine values found in the classic stories. Students can learn the skills of persuasive argument.

Elaborate: Find new or different endings to classic stories; create some surprise or unhappy endings.

Analyze: Look at the classic story from a different viewpoint or perspective. Make the hero a villain and vice versa.

CHILDREN'S CLASSICS

Treasure Island, by Robert Louis Stevenson. Illustrated by Robert Ingpen. Viking Press, 1992. (Original, 1883).

This is a classic story of "gold and greed." While trapped in an apple barrel, Jim Hawkins overhears the plan of pirates and thieves, who want to take over the ship on which he is sailing. Long John Silver, the villain, tries to reach the lost map and the buried treasure before anyone else. Silver doesn't stop at murder or mutiny to reach his goal. He is cunning and merciless, but in the end his evil is no match for the loyalty and goodness of Jim Hawkins.

The action and adventure never stop in this story of the race for riches on a deserted island, with a hidden map as the key to success.

The island isn't as deserted as everyone thought! That's when old Ben Gunn is discovered. He seems more animal than man, after three years alone on the island. His help is invaluable to Jim as he plans his dangerous attack on Long John Silver and the pirates.

Classic Author: Robert Louis Stevenson

Robert Louis Stevenson was born in 1850 and lived only 44 years, but his stories may live forever. He spent most of his childhood in Scotland, in bed, because of sickness. He left the cold climate of Scotland after he contracted tuberculosis. He visited Europe, America, and the South Pacific. He finally settled in Samoa with his family and wrote many absorbing stories, as well as essays and poems. In addition to *Treasure Island,* he wrote *Kidnapped* and *The Strange Case of Dr. Jekyll and Mr. Hyde.*

Activities

A.   Pre-reading activity: Before we begin our journey into the many adventures of children's classics, let's make sure we understand what a classic is. Work with partners to answer as many of the following as you can:

1.   Name all the things you can that are connected with the word "classic":

a. Classic music   d. _____   g. _____

b. _____   e. Classic Coke   h. _____

c. _____   f. _____   i. Classic cars

2.   For each classic named in part 1, write approximately how long we've had that classic.

a. hundreds of years   d. _____   g. _____

b. _____   e. 75 years   h. _____

c. _____   f. _____   i. 60 years

Can you now define what classic means?

B.   Pre-reading activity: The word *classic* is connected to many different ideas or concepts. You might hear a song described as a real "classic." A woman could be called "classy." A deed can be performed "with class," or a hairstylist could give a "classic cut." What are the connections between a song, a person, a deed, and a haircut? Form groups to brainstorm as many adjectives as you can that you think are connected with "class," "classy," or "classic." A thesaurus will help. Don't add a word unless you know its meaning. A dictionary will help with meanings. Examples:

olden   tasteful   excellent

_____   _____   _____

_____   _____   _____

_____   _____   _____

_____   _____   _____

C.   Symbolic thinking: *Treasure Island* is filled with pirates and piracy. We can always recognize their ships by the symbol of the skull and crossbones on their flag. What other famous symbols can you match below?

1.	Star of David	A.	Barber
2.	Serpent and Staff	B.	America
3.	Cross	C.	Judaism
4.	Red-striped pole	D.	Poison
5.	Crown	E.	King
6.	Eagle	F.	Medical
7.	Compass rose	G.	Christianity
8.	Happy Face	H.	Good paper
9.	White flag	I.	Map direction
10.	Skull with an X	J.	Surrender

Answer key: 1. C 2. F 3. G 4. A 5. E 6. B 7. I 8. H 9. J 10. D

D. Associative thinking—vocabulary variety: *Treasure Island* is filled with the cunning and cruelty of Long John Silver and his fellow pirates. Piracy is robbery on the high seas. It started thousands of years ago. The Minoans, the early Greeks, and the ancient Romans all had their pirates and piracy. There are many words that are associated with pirates and piracy. How many can you find that start with the letter "B"? Think of different pirates, their ships, and how they lived. Start a list. See how many words you can add to it. Be prepared to explain the association.

buccaneer   Black Bart   brotherhood

_____   _____   _____

_____   _____   _____

_____   _____   _____

_____   _____   _____

_____   _____   _____

Can you think of other words to associate with pirates? Let's connect a pirate word with an animal. We can create a simile. Use the words "like" or "as" when comparing. Example:

1. Pirates are like vultures.

They can be as cunning as _____ .

2. Treasure coins are like fireflies.

They shine as bright as _____ .

3. Pirate ships are like _____

_____ .

4. Blackbeard was like a _____

_____ .

Do other similes (comparisons) for Mary Read, Black Bart, Jolly Roger, Captain Kidd, and Calico Jack. You may have to research the subject of piracy. There are many sources of information in your school library.

E. Describe in literary terms:

Alliteration: Repeating beginning sounds (Peter Piper picked).

Hyperbole: Absurd exaggeration; doing something to excess. (Davy Crockett killed a bear when he was only three.)

Imagery: Use of the senses in describing (taste, smell, touch, sight, hearing).

Metaphor: Comparing without the use of "like" or "as." (The sea was a cauldron.)

Personification: Giving life to nonliving objects. (Fingers of wind plucked the clothes.)

Repetition: Repeating phrases for emphasis. (His right foot, his enormous right foot, lifted up and out.)

Simile: Comparing using "like" or "as." (As neat as a pin.)

In the novel, *Treasure Island,* find:

A sentence that contains a simile.

_____

_____

A sentence that contains alliteration.

_____

_____

A sentence that contains hyperbole.

_____

_____

A sentence with good imagery.

_____

_____

A sentence that contains a metaphor.

_____

_____

A sentence that uses repetition for effect.

_____

_____

A sentence that shows personification.

_____

_____

20,000 Leagues Under the Sea, by Jules Verne. Waldman Publishing Corp., 1979.

This classic story is about "Nemo and the *Nautilus.*" It takes us to yet another place of adventure on this planet. And what a place—under the sea! The book is filled with all the wonders of the ocean depths.

When the president of the United States decides to rid the seas of a terrible monster, the excitement begins. Monsieur Pierre Aronnax, an expert on undersea life, is on board the ship that will destroy the monster, and he tells the story. What a story he has to tell!

Aronnax faces shipwreck; capture by a crazed genius, Captain Nemo; and an unbelievable journey on Nemo's ship, beneath the sea. The ship, the *Nautilus,* takes them to faraway lands and oceans. They live through cannibal attacks, experience funerals beneath the sea in coral kingdoms, and find treasure on the ocean floor.

Lost continents, mythical monsters, and gigantic icebergs are all part of the adventure. Will they ever be able to escape to tell their tale? Nemo vows that whoever enters the *Nautilus* never leaves it!

Classic Author: Jules Verne

Jules Verne was born and grew up in a town by the sea in France. He yearned for the excitement and adventure in the sea stories he listened to as a young boy. But his father had other ideas for him, so his travels took place only in his imagination.

Jules Verne was a great, creative thinker, as he confirmed by inventing things in his mind that the world would not see for decades. His many books and stories take readers to other planets, to the moon, under the sea, and to unexplored islands.

The diversity found in Jules Verne's stories is not only in his unusual locations but also in his characters and their modes of transportation. They traveled in hot-air balloons, submarines, rocket ships, and electric automobiles. And he wrote of these travels over a hundred years ago! This was the age when people were traveling by horse and carriage.

Jules Verne died in 1905. He lived to see many of his fantasy inventions become reality. His adventures will live forever in the stories he left for future generations.

Activities

A.   Creative writing (setting)—terrifying travelogue: All aboard the Nautilus! Your travel agency has created a vacation cruise for intrepid adventurers.

This vacation trip will include a diversity of locations, activities, and modes of travel. You will begin your trip in a hot-air balloon, carrying you to your first port of call. The setting (time and place in which the event occurs) for your first experience is high in the sky.

Try to imagine the setting for the rest of the trip as you board the *Nautilus* and plan the next 10 days' itinerary. As in the story, you may visit cannibal islands, find sunken ships, dive in undersea coral creations, or fight dangerous sea monsters.

Read the description below for the setting and activities planned for the seventh day of the vacation adventure. After reading Jules Verne's book, write your own itinerary, carefully describing the setting for each day's adventure. Display your travelogue in the classroom. Could you entice a classmate to take the trip?

Day seven: We are at the bottom of the world! This is the icy wasteland of Antarctica—the South Pole. You will see many whales, and today the captain will lead you on an attack of the cruel and destructive sperm whales. But take caution! These waters are filled with dangerous icebergs. The Nautilus is equipped to split these ice fields open, but if we become trapped, we will be forced to dive beneath the ice. After surfacing, we will travel by dinghy to one of the rocky islands for a party with the penguins. Bring a healthy appetite.

B.   Creative thinking—denizens of the deep:

There were many different obstacles and life-threatening situations facing Captain Nemo and the men of the *Nautilus* as they traveled under the sea. They witnessed great coral kingdoms, wrecked ships, and huge icebergs. They fought island cannibals, man-eating sharks, and sperm whales. But the most terrifying danger of all was the giant squid.

Sea and land monsters have fascinated us through the ages. Some are believed to have been real, while others are considered pure fantasy. The men on Christopher Columbus's ships were afraid of the demons below the sea, and even today scientists are still investigating the Loch Ness monster in Scotland.

One monster found in *20,000 Leagues Under the Sea* has turned out to be real. The living legend is the Viraken! The ancients described it as a creature that looked like an uprooted tree, with a beak-like mouth and eyes as large as dinner plates. It has eight tentacles and two additional rubber cable-like arms that can stretch out to great lengths to snare their victims. They were describing the giant squid. This squid is the very real and terrifying animal that lives in the depths of the sea. It can measure more than 50 feet long. Squid have been known to tear sailors from life rafts, destroy large tuna, and even attack sperm whales. They have terrible suckers on their tentacles; can change color; and can shoot out black, ink-like liquid to help them escape enemies. Scientists say there are millions of them. Aren't we fortunate that these sea monsters prefer the depths and are seldom seen by humans?

Fluency: The giant squid is well known for all the monstrous things it does, such as randomly killing fish and frightening seamen. How many good uses could you think of for the giant squid?

1.   Use in scientific study of nerves   3.   _____

2.   _____   4.   _____

Flexibility: If you could make a pet of the giant squid, what duties could it perform for you with its 10 arms, its beak-like mouth, its great strength, and its ability to rocket through water?

The Merry Adventures of Robin Hood, by Howard Pyle. Waldman Publishing Corp., 1979.

This is the classic story of the "merry adventures of Robin Hood." Robin Hood is the outlaw everybody loves! Sherwood Forest was his home, and the band of men who followed him were a diverse group, who united under the cause of justice.

In the olden times of merry England, when Prince John ruled the land, Robin and his men ruled the forest. They made the Sheriff of Nottingham's life a misery. The sheriff had forced Robin and the men who joined him into their outlaw life by his terrible injustices. They fought back with arrows, swords, and various acts of bravery. Sherwood Forest rang with the clash of their swords and the whir of their speeding arrows. It also echoed with the laughter of this happy band of men.

How long could they hide from the evil sheriff and Prince John's vengeance? Would Prince John's death and King Richard's return make a difference? Robin Hood is wanted … dead or alive!

Classic Author: Howard Pyle

Howard Pyle, born in 1853, enjoyed fantasy and imagination. He wrote and illustrated adventure stories about pirates, early America, and the legends of medieval times.

The story of Robin Hood came from songs and ballads that Pyle gathered together and wrote in his own way, taking us back to the times of knights and castles, a time of excitement and enchantment.

Activities

A.   Vocabulary: The words below are all labels for people found in Medieval times and in *Robin Hood.* Form groups of two or four and see if you can connect the word to the correct definition. You may need a dictionary for some of them.

1.	yeoman	A.	The first step in training to be a knight
2.	minstrel	B.	One who mends kettles and pans
3.	lord	C.	The superior or head of the monks in the monastery
4.	villain	D.	Nobleman of the church. They had land and knights under them.
5.	rogue	E.	The nobleman who ruled the castle and estate
6.	abbot	F.	A nobleman, similar to being a count
7.	monk	G.	A man who is a rascal, a scamp, and a cheat
8.	page	H.	A gentleman attendant to the lord
9.	earl	I.	They owned nothing, had no freedom, and worked for the lord
10.	tinker	J.	Musician who traveled and entertained
11.	bishop	K.	Man who lived in monastery to pray and work
12.	squire	L.	One in training for knighthood

Answer key: 1. H 2. J 3. E 4. I 5. G 6. C 7. K 8. A 9. F 10. B 11. D 12. L

B.   Creative writing (attribute listing):

Robin Hood needed many men to wage his fight against the Sheriff of Nottingham. His army would have to live and fight in a very different way than most fighting groups. Put yourself in Robin's place in Sherwood Forest in olden England. Think of all the attributes a man should have to live and fight like Robin's band did. Make a list of as many as you can of the abilities they would need to live in a forest and fight against great odds.

Create a "want ad" poster that Robin Hood might have put out to enlist men for his band.

WANTED

C. Vocabulary (creative thinking)—wise and wonderful witticisms: Proverbs are wise sayings that should teach us how to act and behave toward each other. You can find these proverbs in every language and country in the world. They have been repeated for centuries and found in the classic works of Homer, Tolstoy, Ben Franklin, and many others. They are as diverse as human culture, but all have the common element of wisdom. They make us think!

Do you know any proverbs? They are just short messages of good advice, such as "The early bird catches the worm," or, "Don't cry over spilt milk." What advice are these sayings giving us?

Look at the proverbs below. Work in groups and see if you can associate these proverbs and their advice to the story of Robin Hood. Can you think of other proverbs to associate with the story?

Proverb	Association
1. Two wrongs don't make a right.	The Sheriff of Nottingham stole from the people, while Robin Hood stole from the rich. Was either one right?
2. Birds of a feather flock together.	
3. Misery loves company.	
4. Nothing ventured, nothing gained.	

D. Letter writing:

The men who joined Robin Hood in the forest had to give up their homes and families. They were homesick at times, and wanted to get in touch with mother, father, wife, or child. Pretend you are one of Robin's men after a great adventure fighting the king's soldiers or the Sheriff of Nottingham. Write a letter to someone at home, telling about your life and your latest escapade. Make it so exciting they'll wish they could be with you. Don't forget to give yourself an appropriate name for the time period.

Sherwood Forest
Merry Old England
April 15, 1238
Dear _____ ,

The Swiss Family Robinson, by Johann Wyss. Waldman Publishing Corp., 1987.

This is a classic story of the "perils of paradise." Traveling from Switzerland to a remote island in the South Pacific and learning to survive there were the greatest challenges the Robinson family would ever have to face. They did not choose this challenge for themselves, but when your ship goes down in an unfamiliar sea, any land is a paradise!

The parents and their four sons share their new island home with penguins, flamingos, monkeys, monstrous porcupines, and wild buffalo. They learn to eat sea turtle and wild kangaroo and to drink coconut milk. Their shelter is a tree house, and the barn for their animals is fashioned from the large roots of an island tree.

Tropical storms, dangerous animals, and quicksand are some of the dangers the family faces, but the great salt mine they discover in the island interior gives them a safe and comfortable haven.

The island interior provides the family with many exciting new adventures and reveals the fact that the family is not alone on the island. Ten years passed. Would they continue to survive? And, if rescued, would they choose to stay, or go back to their other life?

Classic Author: Johann Wyss

Johann Wyss, like the Robinson family, came from Switzerland. He was born in 1781 and was educated in Germany. He became a professor and head librarian at a Swiss university.

He loved literature and wrote many stories about the tales his father told him as a child. These stories were combined and made into the book, *The Swiss Family Robinson*, which is famous worldwide. The book has been translated into many different languages and has been enjoyed by Europeans and Americans for generations.

Activities

A. Reptiles: There were many dangerous reptiles in *The Swiss Family Robinson*. Look at the statements below. Decide if they are true or false, and label them T or F.

1. When a snake eats an egg whole, the eggshell aids in digestion. _____
2. A chameleon can catch a bee with its tongue. _____
3. An alligator hisses with its mouth open. _____
4. A baby alligator stays close to the nest after hatching. _____
5. Turtles have sharp teeth to snip and cut. _____
6. An alligator roars with its mouth shut. _____
7. Reptiles have scales, lungs to breathe, and are cold-blooded. _____
8. A reptile swallows its food whole. _____

Answer key: 1. F 2. T 3. T 4. F 5. F 6. T 7. T 8.

B. Analysis (compare and contrast—connect):

The story of the shipwrecked Robinson family involved a South Pacific island. Think about islands and all you know about them. Then expand on your ideas by working in groups to answer the following questions.

1. How would you define "island"?

2. Would you ever find an island in a large city? Where?

3. Is the sun an island? Why, or why not?

4. What do you think is meant by the famous saying, "No man is an island"?

5. Could you turn the saying around to "Every man is an island"? How would you interpret that saying?

Do you understand the word "island" in a more expanded way now? Think of the things that could be called islands in certain situations. Make a list of them. Use them in creative writing examples: one great idea surrounded by mediocre ones—one boy in the dance class, surrounded by ballerinas. Can you think of others?

Connecting words and ideas:

1. What is an oasis?

2. Would you ever find an oasis in a large city? Where?

3. Could a park be an oasis? Why?

4. How could you connect Las Vegas and Salt Lake City to an oasis?

Could you now create an analogy between "island" and "oasis?"

The Adventures of Tom Sawyer, by Mark Twain. Children's Press, 1985.

This is the classic story of "bribes, betrayal, and beautiful Becky." If there was trouble, excitement, or adventure anywhere near, Tom Sawyer managed to find it. However, Tom was a schemer, and always managed to plot a way out of his predicaments with clever and cunning solutions.

Tom not only talked other boys into whitewashing a fence for him, he insisted on receiving bribes for the privilege of assisting in this chore. He had many inventive ways to escape going to school, and his becoming involved with the homeless Huck Finn did not alleviate Tom's problems! Tom and Huck, after witnessing grave-robbing and murder, sealed their silence in blood. They were bound in brotherhood and found many exciting adventures in midnight meetings, river rafting, and running away from home.

Tom was in love with beautiful Becky, with her long, blond hair and lovely smile; this was the magnet that drew Tom back home. He might have settled into a more peaceful way of life, but remember, he and Huck had witnessed murder—which was blamed on the wrong man—and only Tom and Huck knew the truth! Will their fear of the vicious Injun Joe keep them from telling the truth? Will Injun Joe's treasure be found in the haunted house? And what dark secrets do Tom and Becky find in the cave as they desperately seek a way out of the endless passageways? Read and find out!

Classic Author: Mark Twain

Samuel Clemens, better known by his pen name, Mark Twain, was born in Hannibal, Missouri, in the year of Halley's Comet, 1835, and died in the year of the next appearance of the comet in 1910. He predicted that since he came into the world with the comet, he would leave it the same way. This seems appropriate because his stories are like bright comets, spanning the years with their interest, excitement, and adventure. They appear and reappear, giving us a true picture of American life and spirit.

Activities

A. *Fluency:* Tom Sawyer and Huck Finn traveled down the river in a raft. How many other things can you name that will carry you down the river? Think of the rivers in other countries to get more ideas.

sampan   felluca   oceanliner   _____ _____ _____

_____ _____ _____ _____ _____ _____

Was "oceanliner" a mistake, or is there a river large enough to accommodate one? What was your most unusual idea of river transportation?

B.   River research (making connections): Mark Twain wrote extensively about the Mississippi River and the adventures his characters found on their river travels. There are many, many rivers in the world. They are diverse in their size, length, location, history, and notoriety. There are thousands of rivers that are little known, while others are famous because of their associations with famous people, places, or things. Listed below are some of these well-known people, places, or things. Can you connect them to the river associated with them and tell why they are associated? You may have to do some research to find out.

Famous Nouns   **River Associations**

1 Lewis and Clark _____

2 Hindu religion _____

3 Henry Hudson _____

4 Grand Canyon _____

5 William Shakespeare _____

6 South America _____

7 Victoria Falls _____

8 London _____

9 Johann Strauss _____

Can you think of other rivers that are connected with a particular person, place, or thing?

1 _____   Tiber _____

2 _____   Volga _____

3 _____   Rhine _____

4 _____   Congo _____

5 _____   Yangtze _____

6 _____   Mississippi _____

7 _____   St. Lawrence _____

Can you think of others?

Answer key: 1. Missouri 2. Ganges 3. Hudson 4. Colorado 5. Avon 6. Amazon 7. Nile 8. Thames 9. Danube 1. Rome 2. Russia 3. Germany 4. Africa 5. China 6. U.S.A. 7. Canada

C.   About rivers: There are many interesting and exciting things connected with rivers. Both people and animals use them in a great variety of ways. Rivers serve in transportation, as a source of fresh water, for hydroelectric power, for entertainment, for irrigation, and as a home or home base. Can you think of other uses for a river? We will protect our rivers if we learn more about their importance.

Form groups of two or four and follow the letter clues below to find out more about rivers.

1.   The place where a river begins is called its …

    The first letter is in PLEASE, but not in PLEA

    The second letter is in SOIL, but not in SILL

    The third letter is in OUR, but not in OR

    The fourth letter is in SPRING, but not in PINGS

    The fifth letter is in CALL, but not in ALL

    The sixth letter is in USE, but not in US

    ANSWER: ___ ___ ___ ___ ___ ___

2.   The place where a river flows into the sea is called its …

    The first letter is in LAMB, but not in LAB

    The second letter is in TONE, but not in TEN

    The third letter is in ABOUT, but not in BOAT

    The fourth letter is in THIS, but not in HIS

    The fifth letter is in WASH, but not in SAW

    ANSWER: ___ ___ ___ ___ ___

3.   The rich soil and sediment that builds up at the mouth of the river, before it flows into the sea is called a …

    The first letter is in DARK, but not in ARK

    The second letter is in FEAST, but not in FAST

    The third letter is in LATE, but not in ATE

    The fourth letter is in RATE, but not in ARE

    The fifth letter is in MATE, but not in MET

    ANSWER: ___ ___ ___ ___ ___

4.   The low land drained by a river is called its …

    The first letter is in BALL, but not in ALL

    The second letter is in TEACH, but not in TECH

    The third letter is in CATS, but not in CAT

    The fourth letter is in THEIR, but not in THERE

    The fifth letter is in LINE, but not in LIE

    ANSWER: ___ ___ ___ ___ ___

Now it's your turn to create letter clues for more river terms. Then let your class-mates discover the words. Some you might try are *estuary, tributary, meander, sediment, channel,* or *waterfall.* Use the dictionary if you're not sure of their meanings.

Answer key: 1. Source 2. Mouth 3. Delta 4. Basin

Call of the Wild, by Jack London. Macmillan, 1963.

This is the classic story of "Buck and betrayal." Buck had strength and size. He had health and heart. He had pride in himself and loyalty to his owner, Judge Miller. However, this magnificent dog had no defense against greed and betrayal! When the judge's caretaker decides to dognap Buck and sell him to the gold seekers in the Klondike, his ordeal begins. He finds himself in a frigid, alien land, in the company of other great, furry dogs destined for the Arctic regions.

Buck's life is changed forever as he learns the brutal lessons of the club, the whip, and the harness of the dog sleds. He learns about survival as he watches his friend Curley die and as he fights off the attacks of wild dogs. He learns the lesson of the wild: kill, or be killed! The great dog finally finds love and loyalty again when he meets John Thornton, but can even this great affection between the two stop what Buck hears louder every day—the call of the wild?

Classic Author: Jack London

Jack London looked for riches when he traveled to Alaska and the Yukon. He found his riches, not in the gold for which he searched, but in the stories and experiences he brought back from the north. He was born in San Francisco, California, in 1876. He had a hard early life, with no father in the home, and he quit school at an early age.

Jack London was a great reader and traveled to many parts of the world, such as London and Japan, gathering experiences. After the time he spent in the Gold Rush areas, he returned to school and began to write his many books, stories, and newspaper articles. His exciting tales have fascinated readers for almost a hundred years. Today, movies and television productions of stories like *Call of the Wild* and *White Fang* are being made.

Jack London became wealthy and famous, but his personal life was not a success. He suffered from alcoholism, had two failed marriages, and died at the age of 40. His life was short, but his stories may live forever!

Activities

A.   Creative writing: Jack London lived an exciting, dangerous life. Many other classic authors also lived "on the cutting edge." If you had to write an epitaph (brief writing on a tombstone) for London, what might it be? Could you put it in rhyme?

> *Here he lies*
> *He looked for gold*
> *He found adventure*
> *But didn't grow old*
> *Jack London*

B.   Problem solving—glitter and gold: Gold fever is a disease that is hard to cure or ignore. When gold was discovered in California in 1848, many prospectors rushed to the West Coast, hoping to strike it rich. Nine years later, gold was discovered in lower Canada, then in the Yukon Territory, and finally in Alaska. Thousands and thousands of men rushed to the gold regions to make their fortunes. Jack London was one of them.

Many men found gold, and some of them became very wealthy, but scores of others were not so lucky. The men who found themselves in desperately over-crowded cities with few provisions, few resources, and little chance to find gold had a BIG problem. Only the good problem solvers would survive.

Pretend that you are a prospector in the town of Dawson, Yukon Territory, in 1860—you, and 40,000 other prospectors. You have little chance of finding gold. What can you do to survive? Follow steps 1 to 6 to solve your problem.

1. What are the facts?

   A. You're far from home and family

   B. You came here to find gold and get rich

   C. _____

   D. _____

2. What is the problem?

   You can't find gold, and you may not survive

3. What choices do you have?

   A. Latch on to someone who has found gold

   B. Open a restaurant

   C. _____

   D. _____

4. What standards will you use to evaluate your choices?

   A. Is it dangerous?   C. _____

   B. Is it possible?   D. _____

5. Score your standards on a scale of 1 to 4, with "1" being the best idea.

6. Give your solution.

Can you think of situations other than a gold rush in which people try to "get rich, quick?" Are there problems involved with these opportunities? Take one of these situations, such as playing the lottery, and go through the steps of problem solving for a decision you might face.

"Get-Rich-Quick" Scheme:

_____

What are the facts?

_____

_____

_____

What is the problem?

_____

_____

What choices do you have to solve the problem?

_____

_____

_____

What standards will be used to evaluate your choices?

_____

_____

C.   Originality—metaphoric thinking:

Many of Jack London's stories focused on the relationship of man and dog. The bond between the two can grow to great strength under the unusual difficulties and dangers of the Yukon. The two depend on each other for love, loyalty, and, sometimes, life itself. London's stories are good examples of the old saying, "A dog is man's best friend."

If a dog is man's best friend, what can you attribute to other pets? Look at the list that follows and try to think of an original phrase for them that might become as well known as the one about the dog. Can you think of a metaphor for your pet? It could lead to an original saying.

Pet	Metaphor
Cat	
Horse	streak of black lightening
Rabbit	
Canary	
Cow	
Goat	eating machine
Donkey	
Gerbil	
Snake	ribbon of fear
Turtle	
Mouse	

Can you add to the list of pets and metaphors?

Now that you have a new concept for your animal, could you write an original phrase for it? Examples:

A cat is man's reminder to take life easy!

A canary is man's one-voice symphony!

A turtle is man's secret messenger from ancient times!

Rip Van Winkle, by Washington Irving. Illustrated by Arthur Rackham. Dial Books, 1992. (First published 1819–1820).

This classic story is an "amazing adventure." Rip Van Winkle found escape from his nagging wife in the Catskill Mountains, high above his little village. Rip lived in early American times, before the Revolutionary War. He was a simple farmer, a good neighbor, and a good storyteller to the many children who loved him. His one big fault was his laziness. He did *not* like to work, and his run-down farm showed it. His wife nagged and screamed at him, but Rip and his dog always found escape in the mountains.

It was on one of these escapes that Rip experienced his great adventure. Imagine meeting strange men in the mountains who give you a drink that puts you into a sound sleep—a sleep that lasts for *twenty years*!

Classic Author: Washington Irving

Washington Irving was America's first author to make a living as a writer. He also became famous in Europe for *Rip Van Winkle* and *The Legend of Sleepy Hollow.*

Washington Irving was born in New York City during the Revolutionary War, which freed us from England, and he died just before the Civil War, which made all Americans free. He was named after George Washington and even got to meet the great first president. Washington Irving was a real "All American Man"!

Activities

A. Research (setting): The setting for Irving's *Rip Van Winkle* is the Dutch province of New York, in colonial times. Look at the words below. Can you find a connection between them and the setting? Write a short explanation.

Connection

Dutch <u>the people who first settled in this area of America</u>

Henry Hudson _____

Catskills _____

Colonist _____

Peter Stuyvesant _____

Province _____

Appalachians <u>the mountains on the American east coast</u>

American Revolution _____

B. Compare-contrast:

Rip Van Winkle slept for 20 years and found the world greatly changed when he woke up. It has been said that if Rip Van Winkle could have slept for hundreds of years and awakened today, the only thing he would recognize would be a school classroom. What do you think that statement means?

_____

_____

Think about and research the schools and classrooms of early America. Look at the list below of things found in ordinary classrooms. Add to the list if you can. Write "yes" if you still find it in the modern classroom of today, or "no" if you do not find it. Write "yes" or "no" in the second column to answer the question about whether you would have found that item in an early American classroom.

Modern Classroom	Early American Classroom
Teacher	
Desks	
Students	
Paper	
Pencils	
Books	
Chalkboard	
Maps	
Computers	
Globes	
Coathooks	
Stove	
Dunce hat and stool	

Count your "yes" and "no" answers. Do you think there is much difference between the old and new classrooms? _____ Explain _____

The Jungle Book, by Rudyard Kipling. Classic Press, 1968.

This is the classic story of "Mowgli the Man-Cub." If you can imagine being lost in the jungles of India, rescued by a black panther, and raised by a pack of wolves, you'll understand the life of the man-cub Mowgli.

Mowgli learns quickly how to survive in his dangerous surroundings. Of course, he gets help and advice from his jungle friends. If not for this, Mowgli would never have survived the deadly coils of Kaa, the constrictor snake, or Shere Khan, the evil tiger, who is determined to eat the boy.

Mowgli's friends in the jungle decide to return him to civilization, but Mowgli is just as determined to stay in his jungle home. He almost dies in his attempt to stay, and Baloo, the bear, is ready to give his life to save Mowgli.

What could it be that finally changed Mowgli's mind about returning to live among humans again?

Classic Author: Rudyard Kipling

Rudyard Kipling was born in India in 1865. His family was British, but they lived in Bombay, India, where his father was a university professor.

Kipling loved India and was very unhappy when he and his sister were sent to England to live for six years. He called his home in England "the House of Desolation."

He finally returned to India at the age of 17, and laid the foundation for his writing fame through his work on a newspaper. His other works include many classic short stories, ballads, and books such as *Kim*, *Captains Courageous,* and *The Jungle Book*, which are read and enjoyed to this day.

Activities

A.   Vocabulary (descriptive words):

Mowgli was befriended by a wolf and a panther. He was threatened by a snake and a tiger. Use the letters in each animal name to describe them. A thesaurus will help to paint a picture with words.

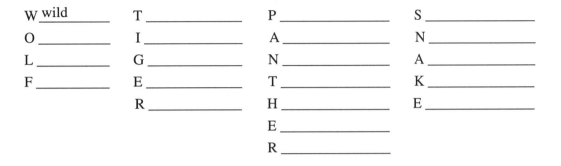

W wild	T	P	S
O	I	A	N
L	G	N	A
F	E	T	K
	R	H	E
		E	
		R	

B.   Elaboration:

Wild animals such as those found in *The Jungle Book* have different qualities or attributes to aid them in survival. Many perils are found in the deep, dark thicket of jungle, and life is precarious. These animals adapt to the dangers by using their diverse methods of defense. Look at the animals listed below. Think about what you consider their best physical quality of defense. Is it their teeth, claws, or perhaps their sound?

elephant _____   tapir _____

lion _____   zebra _____

monkey _____   cheetah _____

giraffe _____   cobra _____

anaconda _____   hyena _____

Draw a picture of Mowgli. He has no physical qualities to defend himself against the wild animals who want to kill him. Add all the physical things he would need to protect himself in the jungle. What would you add to his teeth, his body, and his feet? Can you think of something original?

Draw Mowgli here:

C.   Analysis (define by listing qualities):

In the previous activity we elaborated on Mowgli by adding physical attributes to allow him to defend himself in the wild jungle. Think of the dangerous animals and what their qualities are that make them fierce and dangerous. Could you list these qualities and write about them in a few sentences? It would be an interesting way to define an animal. Look at the example below. Can you figure out the animal from the list of attributes?

Jungle Animal: Dark as night, cold as a witch's heart, she is death waiting in a rough nest of twigs. She moves with quiet danger, standing high at times, when she must bite or spit the poison to protect her nest. She is poor in eyesight, and her world is soundless, but man and beast tremble at the sight of her. A violent hiss, spreading her hood and lying in coils, she is an endless tail. She is a _____ . (Answer: Cobra)

Can you create an animal definition by listing qualities and describing words to make a "picture paragraph" of your jungle animal? Use similes, metaphors, and adjectives to paint your picture of words.

Jungle Animal

_____

_____

_____

_____

It is a(n) _____

D.   Creative thinking (alliteration)—the "hissing hypnotizer":

   In the story of Mowgli, we find protagonists (the "good guys") and antagonists (the "bad guys"), as found in all stories. There must always be a struggle between good and evil, right and wrong, or strong and weak to make a good story.

   Kaa, the sly and slithering snake, was one of the antagonists in _The Jungle Book._ He did his best to trick Mowgli into his suffocating coils.

   Work in groups to create some interesting and original ideas about Kaa, the jungle snake.

Fluency: Practice fluency by listing all the many adjectives starting with the letter "S" to describe a snake.

Flexibility: The letter "S" looks something like a snake. How many ways and places can you picture it as a snake (e.g., in a desert, under a rock, in the water, on a tree)?

Originality: Create a picture showing your "S" snake in a particular setting, as in the suggestions above. Write an alliterative sentence about your picture.

Example: The slithering snake sailing the sea was a spectacular sight.

The Wind in the Willows, by Kenneth Grahame. Scribner, 1961.

   This is a classic story of a "Road Rebel." Toad was "the King of the Road"—a king with a desire for fast cars and a zeal for reckless driving. Toad was always in trouble! His conceit led him to snatch a motor car, imprisonment, unlawful escape, and pursuit by the authorities.

   Who knows what sad end poor Toad would have come to if not for the loyalty of his friends: Rat, the romantic poet; Mole, the staid bachelor; and Badger, the reclusive philosopher.

   Life for Toad reaches an all-time low when the stoats and the weasels take over his home, Toad Hall. Can his friends help him recover his mansion? If they succeed, will Toad ever learn to change his ways?

Classic Author: Kenneth Grahame

Kenneth Grahame was a British storyteller, who was born in 1859 (two years before the American Civil War) and died in 1932 (three years after the start of the Great Depression).

Grahame wrote *The Wind in the Willows* for his son, Alastair, who was ill at the time. The story is a fantasy filled with personification and shows his love for the rustic life of England.

Activities

A. Escape: In *The Wind and the Willows* and many other classics, the main character has a yearning for escape, and the escape is usually by waterways. Look at the classic stories listed below. How did the main character plan his escape in each story, and from what was he escaping?

Classic	Means of Escape	Why?
Kidnapped		
The Time Machine		
Huckleberry Finn		
The Count of Monte Cristo		
White Fang		
20,000 Leagues Under the Sea		
Black Beauty		
The Wizard of Oz		
Journey to the Center of the Earth		

If you were writing a story, how would your main character escape his or her problem? Try to think of an original idea. It may give you the beginning of a good story.

B. Personification: Personification is a literary technique in which human characteristics are given to an animal or an object. Kenneth Grahame used personification throughout *The Wind in the Willows*.

Poets, as well, use personification extensively to lend beauty and imagery to their writing.

Look at the words of imagery and personification below and decide what is being described.

1. They run over pages filling in blank spaces with dabs of color.

What are "they"? _____

2. Its sharp fingers scrub away ocean pollution.

What is "it"? _____

3. You put the sun to bed, holding a lighted match that flickers and then dies.

   What is "you"? _____

4. I dance to a beat with the shirt I hold together.

   What is "I"? _____

Can you describe a star, the ocean, or a camel using personification?

Answer key: 1. crayons 2. coral 3. twilight 4. safety pin

Try to create imagery and personification when you think of the things you know about. Give these things human characteristics and you will produce more original ideas, connections, and creative writing. Start with the words below. Add one human characteristic to each. Then try to elaborate to create a phrase or sentence.

Thing	Human Characteristic	Elaboration
wind	skipped	lightly among the leaves, creating little leaf dances
seagull		
storm		
hawk		
tree		
flower	embraced	the bee as it served a liquid lunch
clouds		
snow		
sun		
book	sighed	gently as the leaves were turned
toaster		
lawn mower		

How many can you add to the list?

Peter Pan, by James Barrie. Viking Press, 1991.

This is the classic story of "Darlings and daring deeds." Peter Pan did not want to grow up! In fact, Peter absolutely refused to leave his childhood.

This little elf-like person lures the children of the Darling family to his home in Never-Never Land, where they meet the terrible pirate Captain Hook and the little fairy Tinker Bell.

Peter and the pirates engage in many exciting encounters, and there are times when you wonder if the children will ever reach home again. John, Michael, and Wendy Darling also meet a fierce, unrelenting crocodile and an Indian princess. Their adventures are unusual and exciting, but do they, like Peter Pan, want to escape their responsibilities forever?

Classic Author: James Barrie

Sir James Matthew Barrie was born and grew up in Scotland. His life, which began in 1860 (a year before the American Civil War), was not an easy one. During his 77 years he knew tragedy and sorrow. He never recovered from his brother's death and the sorrow it brought to his mother. Like Peter Pan, Barrie did not want to grow up or face the adversities of life.

Activities

A.   Analyze-synthesize:

Pan was a very simple last name for Peter. How many more words can you make from it by adding letters? You may add letters before, after, or in between, to make new words.

1.   plan_____   6.   _____   11.   _____

2.   span_____   7.   _____   12.   _____

3.   pane_____   8.   _____   13.   _____

4.   Spain_____   9.   _____   14.   _____

5.   _____   10.   _____   15.   _____

B.   Story starters (alliteration—elaboration): Many titles, such as *Peter Pan, Wind in the Willows,* and *Black Beauty,* and characters, like Tiny Tim, King Kong, and Red Riding Hood, are examples of alliteration.

Alliteration is a way to generate ideas for a story. By expanding on a character with an adjective and finishing with many words that start with the same letter, you can create your own story starter with many ideas already in mind.

Look at the names on page 133. Put an alliterative adjective before each name and finish the sentence with as many words that start with the same letter as you can. (See examples.) You are creating story starters!

Adjective	Name	Finish the sentence with alliterative words
Mysterious	Maurice	met the messenger by the manor house.
	Joan	
	Ben	
	Kim	
	Tommy	
	Sam	
	Luke	
	Dan	

Look at the first example. Would the story be different if we substituted words such as:

Miserable Maurice's mistake meant misfortune for Michael.

If you tell why Maurice is miserable, what his mistake was, and what misfortune it lead to for Michael, you will have a complete story. Try some on your own!

Robinson Crusoe, by Daniel Defoe. Playmore Publishing, 1987.

This is a classic story of "sea, ships, and survival." Shipwreck!! What an exciting and thrilling word! Of course, you must survive the shipwreck to enjoy the breathtaking experiences that follow, and Robinson Crusoe was a survivor!

There are men who cannot deny the siren call of the sea. Neither his father's pleas to stay home nor being enslaved by Turkish pirates could deter Crusoe from sailing the seas. He yearned to see the world, and he saw a good part of it before he found himself alone and marooned on an island far from any civilization.

Robinson Crusoe felt desolation and loneliness. He felt fear and despair. But he also found joy and comfort in small accomplishments, and he discovered courage and hope in learning to survive by his own wits. Crusoe also realized a power and presence much stronger and higher than his own.

Earthquakes, fever, storms, and cannibals were great threats to life on the island. Could Crusoe survive them all, and, if so, would he spend the rest of his life alone on this tiny island?

Classic Author: Daniel Defoe

Daniel Defoe was an English writer who traveled the world and experienced exciting adventures. He was captured by Algerian pirates and lived to tell the tale! Defoe became a friend of the king of England, but he found himself in trouble many times for writing against the Church of England.

Daniel Defoe lived before America became a free nation. He is remembered for his classic book, *Robinson Crusoe*, but his writing didn't bring him much money, only popularity. He died in 1731, at the age of 70, but his tale about Robinson Crusoe may live forever.

Activities

A.   List the advantages and disadvantages of living alone on an island.

Advantages	Disadvantages

B.   Creative thinking (poets and poetry)—songs of the sea: The sea is a mighty magnet, drawing explorers and the adventurers to its dangerous but exciting vastness. The world of the sea holds so many promises for those who look for the wild, gypsy life under the sail.

Many classic authors are also charmed by the exhilarating secrets of the sea. Stories such as *Moby Dick, Kidnapped,* and *The Old Man and the Sea* are only a few of the great sea tales. Poets such as Amy Lowell, Lillian Moore, James Witcomb Riley, Lord Byron, and Christina Rossetti are but a few who wrote of sea shells, ships, and life on the mighty oceans. Perhaps none describes the lure of the sea more beautifully than John Masefield in "Sea Fever." This poem tells why people are drawn to the dangers and the thrill of the tall ships and the lonely sea.

Research the poetry section of your library and list all the poems you find on the sea. Circle your favorite.

_____   _____   _____

_____   _____   _____

In how many categories can you think of to place your sea poems?

1.   animals_____   4.   _____

2.   _____   5.   _____

3.   _____   6.   myths_____

Think of all the things made from sea shells. There are picture frames, wind chimes, jewelry, lamps, animals, and houses, to name a few. Can you think of something original to make from sea shells?

Draw some simple shells below. What could you add to the drawing to expand it into something else? Could you create a shell girl, a butterfly, or, perhaps, a combination of all the shells in one new design?

Draw sea shells here:

Heidi, by Johanna Spyri. Watermill Press, 1980.

This is the classic story of "Heidi." *Heidi* is a story of the mountains and the girl who found love, happiness and home in her life in the Swiss Alps.

It is only after Heidi is transplanted to city life that she experiences the agony of homesickness and yearns to return to her mountain home. She misses her beloved grandfather, who is the only family she has. She misses her good friend Peter and the old, blind Grannie, who lived alone in her mountain hut. Who would care for Grannie now that Heidi was gone to the city? But above all, she missed the very sight of the majestic peaks and the spacious blue skies surrounding them.

Heidi dreamed and longed for home, but how could she leave the sick and crippled little girl, Clara, who depended on her? The story is filled with both happiness and sorrow.

Classic Author: Johanna Spyri

Johanna Spyri was born in Switzerland in 1829. She lived near the mountains and never lost her love for them.

Later in life, she married and moved to the city of Zurich. Her memories and dreams of her childhood home in the small village by the mountains motivated her to write the story of Heidi.

Johanna Spyri died in 1901, but her classic story of the little girl from the Swiss Alps will bring joy to all who continue to read it.

Activities

A. Brainstorming: Everyone is awed at the sight of tall, majestic mountain ranges, but mountains serve many uses in addition to providing us with spectacular scenery.

Working in groups of two or four, list as many things as you can that make mountains important to us. You may have to do some research. There are many good books on mountains.

Mountain Uses

1. <u>create rain forests</u>   6. _____

2. _____ 7. _____

3. _____ 8. _____

4. <u>ski slopes</u>   9. _____

5. _____ 10. <u>provide silver</u>

B. Analysis—synthesis: There are many important mountain ranges in the world. The famous mountains that most people recognize are listed below. Can you connect the mountain to the correct continent?

PART A:

1. Himalayas   ___ Africa
2. Alps   ___ Australia
3. Rockies   ___ Asia
4. Andes   ___ Europe
5. Atlas   ___ South America
6. Kosciusko   ___ North America

PART B:

Pick one of these mountain ranges. Find at least 10 facts about those mountains that make them unique and put them into clues. Make the first clues more difficult, but get easier as you get to number 10. Give your classmates the clues one at a time to see if they can figure out your mountain or range. See the example below.

Mountain Mystery

1. I am the longest mountain chain in the world.
2. One-third of all the people of the continent live on me.
3. I am the second highest mountain range in the world.
4. The capitals of four countries are found on me.
5. I am full of minerals.
6. I don't have much oxygen.
7. Alpacas, vicunas, and llamas live on me.
8. Many volcanoes, some active, are a part of me.
9. In me, you will find the mysterious city, Machu Picchu.
10. I was home to the Inca Indians.

ANSWER _____

Answer key: 1. Asia 2. Europe 3. N. America 4. S. America 5. Africa 6. Australia Part B: Andes

C. Character analysis—character study: Complete the patterns below to show what you know about the characters in *Heidi*.

If I were Grandfather

I would _____

And sometimes I would feel _____

And something I would do often is _____

And the thing I am most concerned about is _____

_____

But I wouldn't _____

Because Fraulein Rottenmeier does that.

If I were Fraulein Rottenmeier

I would _____

And sometimes I would feel _____

And something I would do often is _____

And the thing I am most concerned about is _____

_____

But I wouldn't _____

Because Grandmamma does that

If I were Grandmamma

I would _____

And sometimes I would feel _____

And something I would do often is _____

And the thing I am most concerned about is _____

_____

But I wouldn't _____

Because Heidi does that.

Add other pattern verses about other characters.

INTRODUCING SHAKESPEARE

Tales from Shakespeare: Seven Plays. Presented by Marcia Williams. Candlewick, 1998.

Part One: "Romeo and Juliet"

The Capulets and the Montagues had been forever at each other's throats, so imagine Lord Capulet's surprise when Romeo, in disguise, attends his party. It was at this party that Romeo fell in love with Juliet, Lord Capulet's 13-year-old daughter.

Synthesis: Organizing information in a new way. Re-create the party scene from the play as if you were the observer, using the pattern that follows:

The party was the color of _____ like _____

It sounded like _____

The overladen table of food smelled like _____

_____

And each taste was _____

The whole scene looked like _____

And made Romeo feel like _____

Part Two

At the party Romeo and Juliet fell deeply in love. When Juliet retires to her chambers she declares her love for Romeo. She knows that she will marry no one else.

Problem solving: How can Juliet persuade her father to let her marry Romeo?

Ideas	Fast	Maintain Harmony	Safe	Will Work	Total

Score each idea 1 = no 2 = maybe 3 = yes Total the scores for each idea.

The best idea is _____

Part Three

Romeo faces grave danger in visiting Juliet. They declare their love and decide to marry at once. It must be done in secret, however, because their families will object. Friar Lawrence, with some misgivings, agrees to marry them.

Evaluation: List the plus and minus elements of an object or situation. Suppose you are Friar Lawrence. List the reasons for marrying the couple and reasons for not marrying them.

Reasons to Marry	Reasons Not to Marry

Part Four

After the wedding the couple must part until the Friar can break the news to their families. On the way home Romeo intervenes in a fight and kills Tybalt, Juliet's cousin.

Attribute listing: List the basic qualities of a person, place, animal, plant, or object. On the lines that follow list:

The Attributes of a Master Swordsman	

These are just a few _____ , too.

From near and far,

Here they are

Attributes of a swordsman.

Part Five

Romeo is banished from Verona for fighting and he and Juliet have a sad parting. Paris, another suitor for Juliet's hand, receives permission from her father to marry her. Devastated at the idea and not knowing what to do, she seeks the help of Friar Lawrence.

Forecasting: Identify cause and effect. Complete these statements. Add others.

Cause	Effect
Juliet's father said Paris could marry her.	
Romeo killed Tybalt.	
Two families were feuding.	

Part Six

Before the wedding Juliet takes a drug to appear dead for 42 hours. She is carried to the burial vault, where Romeo is supposed to rescue her, but the friar's letter telling Romeo of the plan went astray.

Associative thinking: Identify similar attributes (see how things go together).

Power is to Lord Capulet as _____ is to Juliet.

Recklessness is to Romeo as _____ is to Friar Lawrence.

How many more can you add?

Part Seven

Romeo hears of Juliet's death and goes to her tomb, where he is attacked by and kills Paris. Believing that Juliet is dead, Romeo drinks poison and the friar arrives too late to save him.

Flexible thinking: Respond in a variety of areas and stretch your mind beyond the expected response. List all the ways Juliet might have avoided marrying Paris rather than taking the drug that made her appear dead.

Part Eight

When Juliet comes out of her drugged sleep, it is to discover that Romeo is dead. Not wanting to live without him, she kills herself with a dagger.

Fluent thinking: List all the words and phrases you can to describe caring deeply for someone that begin with the letters R O M E O. How many kinds of hugs can you name?

Part Nine

When the families of the two lovers realize what their feuding has done, they vow to end the feud and have statues built as a tribute to the two lovers.

Elaboration: Add to a basic product. What can you add to the golden statues to make sure the tragedy will not be forgotten?

A Vocabulary Contest

Rank order: Friar Lawrence is to choose eight citizens of Verona to take part in the dedication of a new cathedral. Suppose you are Friar Lawrence. Rank order the first eight applicants, giving a 1 to the first choice and an 8 to the last choice. Be ready to explain your rankings.

A.   The local mendicant.

B.   A corpulent centenarian.

C.   The capo of Verona.

D.   One who demonstrates capacious reverence.

E.   A 30-year-old carabiniere.

F.   The local merchant who owns a caroche.

G.   A person who raises kerrias.

H.   A woman who wears a peplos on her head.

Reviewing Shakespeare with Karaoke

A.   Tune: Herb Alpert's "What Now My Love?"

Hamlet

This is the tale
Of tragic Hamlet
Who lived at
Castle Elsinore
A ghost told him
His father's murder
Was done by one
Brother evermore.

To take revenge
Hamlet went mad
Made all around him
Sad, Sad, Sad
Proved Uncle's guilt
Put on a play
Watched Uncle cower
and run away.

Sent on a voyage
Across the great sea
The ship was wrecked
But his life was spared
He sailed back home
And killed his uncle
Then drank the cup
That they both had shared.

Thus Hamlet said
"Give me this cup"
I leave this world
With just one sup.
But you must live
And without fail
Tell the world
My sad sad tale

Good night, sweet prince
As angels hover
In restful skies,
Your young bones will lie
We'll tell your tale
To all the wide world
So that you may
Be at peaceful rest
(Repeat first stanza)

B.   Tune: "Tiny Bubbles."

Romeo and Juliet

Romeo and Juliet
It's too bad they ever met.
She was only a pretty child
When a party crasher saw her
And went very wild.
(Chorus)
Romeo
Why did you go
Climbing up the stone wall
No, No, No

They were married by the friar
From the frying pan to the fire
Tell the parents and do not tarry
Father says on Thursday
Paris she must marry.

Juliet she takes a draught
Pretends death, but all for naught
Romeo's not in on the scheme
Thinks she's dead, and kills himself
An awful scene.

(Repeat chorus)
Juliet she sees him stagger
Kills herself with husband's dagger
Both their parents
Became good friends
Now you know just how
This tragic story ends.

OCEAN VOYAGES: A THEMATIC UNIT BLENDING THE CLASSICS AND CONTEMPORARY LITERATURE

The True Confessions of Charlotte Doyle, by Avi. Orchard Books, 1990.

Thirteen-year-old Charlotte is the only passenger on a ship sailing from London to Boston in 1832. The cook gives her a dagger for protection, and she learns that mutiny is in the air. Should she stand with the captain or join the crew?

Activities

A.   Answer these questions about sailing ships. Guess if you do not know.

    1.   How many men were on a typical ship?

    2.   How many separate sails did a ship have?

    3.   *The Great Republic,* the largest clipper ship made, weighed how many tons?

    4.   How long was *The Great Republic?*

    5.   How long did it take a clipper ship to go from London to Boston?

Listen to the following to support or refute your answers.

> A typical sailing ship had a crew of 130 men. It had high masts with as many as 30 separate sails. In 1852 The Great Republic was the largest sailing ship in the world, weighing 4,555 tons and having a length of 325 feet. A trip from London to Boston took 12 days and 9 hours.

B.   Thirteen-year-old Charlotte is the only passenger on a sailing ship from London to Boston. She overhears talk of mutiny. Rank order what she should do.

    1.   Tell the captain.

    2.   Do nothing.

    3.   Join the crew.

    4.   Wait for more information

C.   Evaluation: At one point in the story, Charlotte incurs the wrath of the crew. Debate what she should do to make amends.

D.   Research—the "Mystery Person Report": List 10 clues about someone connected with the sea. One must be a "give-away" clue. Students pick numbers and guess.

20,000 Leagues Under the Sea, by Jules Verne. Raintree-Steck Vaughn, 1980. (Box 26015, Austin, TX 78755).

Professor Aronnax and friends discover the cause of many shipwrecks when they are taken on board the submarine, *Nautilus.* While aboard they have many adventures as Captain Nemo takes his revenge on society.

Activities

A.   Research: Captain Nemo was a pirate who was quite different from those who sailed the Spanish Main. Through *associative thinking,* how many words, beginning with the letter "B," can you associate with pirates? Create a book titled *B Is for Pirate.* Each association you make will be a separate page. Examples:

B is for Blackbeard—Edward Teach who died in battle. His head was nailed to the bow of a British ship.

B is for Booty—Treasure pirates stole from ships.

B is for Black Bart—A pirate who read to his crew from the Bible and never drank spirits.

B is for Bonney—An Irish girl named Anne who joined a pirate crew.

Treasure Island, by Robert Louis Stevenson. Raintree-Steck Vaughn, 1991.

This is the classic pirate story of all time. When Jim Hawkins comes into possession of a treasure map, he and his friends begin a perilous journey. They unknowingly hire a crew of pirates.

Activities

A.   Predict: Jim, hiding in an apple barrel, hears a conversation between two pirates. Predict what Long John Silver will say:

Pirate:

How long are we going to wait, Silver?

Silver:

_____

Pirate:

I've had my fill of Captain Smollett.

Silver:

_____

Pirate:

If you are a real leader, you'll take over this ship now!

Silver:

_____

Moby Dick, by Herman Melville. Raintree-Steck Vaughn, 1991.

This is a classic story about "men and whales." Ishmael is a young sailor on the *Pequod,* a ship captained by Ahab, who lost his leg to a great white whale named Moby Dick. Now the captain is out for revenge.

Activities

A.   Whale data bank:

Eats	Lives	Has
shrimp	in ocean	furry body
small fish	cold and warm climates	blowhole

What It Does	What It Looks Like	
migrates	a mountain in the sea	
spouts water	a prehistoric creature	

B.   A beautiful description of the whale is found in Joanne Ryder's *Winter Whale* (William Morrow, 1990). Use the information in your data bank to complete this pattern.

You are *changing, changing.*
You feel: *describe the atmosphere*
You are: *two adjectives*
You: *two verbs or verb phrases*
You are: *color*
The color of: *name an object the same color*
You are: *give size and shape*
And are: *use participle and prepositional phrase*
You do not: *what*
It is: *adjective to move like this*
So: *one adjective and one simile*
You are: *Name*

Whale Example
You are changing, changing
You feel the warm salt water slide over your bumpy skin
You are strong and furry
You sing to the moon and slide through the ocean depths without fear and without a map
You are gray, the color of fog

*You are 45 feet long from mouth to tail fins and are diving to the
ocean bottom toward a school of shrimp
You do not fear capture as you hunt for food, arch your mammoth
head and spout warm, moist air
It is wild to move like this
So free and secret like a dream
YOU are a California Gray Whale.*

C. Flexible thinking: List all the characteristics of the ocean that also apply to people (kind, cruel, can reach out, etc.) List all the things the ocean reminds you of. Example: a rolling prairie, a giant's bathtub, etc.

> Study the structure of this verse from *The Highwayman,* by Alfred Noyes. (Illustrated by Neil Waldman. Harcourt, 1990).

The wind was a torrent of darkness among the gusty trees,

The moon was a ghostly galleon tossed upon cloudy seas,

The road was a ribbon of moonlight over the purple moor

And the highwayman came riding, riding, riding,

The highwayman came riding up to the old inn door.

Use the same structure and words from your list to describe the ocean.

D. Personification

The ocean was a _____

(where) _____

The waves were _____

(How) or (where) _____

The ship was a _____

_____

And the white whale came _____

_____

The white whale came _____

(where) _____

The True Adventures of Daniel Hall, by Diane Stanley. Dial, 1995.

The reader can travel the world with Daniel. Whales migrate all over the world from cold to warm climates. This is the true story of a boy who left home at age 14 to go on a whaling voyage on the *Condor,* a whaling ship bound for Arctic waters in 1856.

Activities

A.   Evaluate: Rank order the dangers Daniel faced from the gravest to the least danger. (You may have to research the dangers before you can rank order them.)

1.   "Rounding the Cape"

2.   Eating meals with maggots

3.   Being dragged along in a small boat by a whale

4.   Being beaten with a knotted whip

5.   Walking 60 miles in the bitter Siberian cold

6.   Being attacked by a wounded bear

7.   Having your side cut open with a knife

8.   Being surrounded by 50 wolves

B.   Associative thinking: Choose one: spinning wheel, rusty spigot, empty bow, cat with no claws, tornado, locked safe, door hinge. Use the word you chose in this sentence and finish the sentence.

Injustice is like _____ because _____.

C.   For a fun book in which students can choose the character they want to be in an ocean disaster, share *Yikes,* by Alison Lester (Houghton Mifflin, 1995).

D.   Writing poetry—patterns from the masters: What can you do with a poem?

Choose a classic poem. (Example: *The Highwayman,* by Alfred Noyes.)

In collections of art books, find a painting that goes with the poem. Stand beside the painting and read aloud the poem.

Elaborate: Add words or sounds at the end of each line. Read the poem with these new additions.

Find a poem in the poem. Underline key words in each line. Rearrange the words and write them below the poem. Read aloud your new poem. Use the first verse of *The Highwayman,* by Alfred Noyes (Illustrated by Neil Waldman, Harcourt, 1990) or any poem from *A Child's Garden of Verses,* by Robert Louis Stevenson (Oxford University Press, 1966).

E.   Writing poetry—essential elements for poets:

1.   Observation:

Project a visual on the overhead for 30 seconds. Remove the visual. Ask students to list what they remember seeing. Show the visual again.

2.   Imagination (the ability to image): Read excerpts from well-known poems. Ask students what the poem is describing. Good sources of poems are:

The Dreamkeeper and Other Poems, by Langston Hughes (Knopf, 1992)

Eats: Poems, by Arnold Adoff (Lothrop, Lee & Shepard, 1979)

My Shadow, by Robert Louis Stevenson (Putnam, 1990)

Sunflakes: Poems for Children, by Lillian Moore (Clarion, 1992)

Words with Wrinkled Knees, by Barbara Esbensen (HarperCollins, 1986)

Zoomrimes: Poems About Things That Go, by Sylvia Cassedy (Crowell, 1987)

3.   Vocabulary:

Share poems with rich vocabulary. Ask students to underline words they don't know. Look them up! Read the poem again. Does it make more sense?

Challenge the students to write a paragraph telling what they know about the poet using the words they underlined in the poem.

Chapter FIVE

Exploring Diversity

Ask almost anyone in the United States from which state most new ideas come and the answer will be California. Why? The reason is simple. California probably has a more diverse population than any other state. Large groups of people from diverse backgrounds and cultures reside in that state, and when people work together in all fields of human endeavor, the diversity of backgrounds means a diversity of ideas are brought to the workplace. When people work together in harmony these ideas often bring about innovations that are designed to improve the quality of life.

Surely one of the greatest needs in the United States and in the world today is that of conducting human relations peaceably, of helping diverse groups to understand each other and to work in harmony. Nations find it hard to understand each other, as do their inhabitants. Books that can evoke an understanding of other peoples, of different racial and cultural backgrounds, are essential to the literary diet. The titles offered in this chapter are books about people facing real challenges and present real feelings to help children understand our common problems and fears.

A PICTURE BOOK FOR ALL AGES

Yo! Yes?, by Chris Raschka. Orchard Books, 1993.

This is an effective, unusual, 34-word story about the beginnings of a friendship, accompanied by wild and wonderful illustrations. Two boys parlay what could be a confrontation into a friendship. The meeting takes place between a stylishly informal, self-confident black boy and an anxious, overdressed white boy. The one- and two-word exchanges on each page spread lead to a tentative offer of friendship, and whether it is caution or prejudice that is overcome, the friendship is ultimately sealed as both boys jump in the air and yell, "Yow!" With beautifully balanced economical style the book illumines the peaks and pitfalls of getting acquainted.

Activities

A.   Questions to think about:

1.   Explain the significance of the way the boys are dressed.

2.   Compare the body language of either boy by looking at the first and the last page. What differences, if any, do you see?

3.   Do you believe it is caution or prejudice that is overcome by the end of the book? Why?

4.   Notice the changing placement of the boys on the pages as the story progresses. Why did the artist do this?

5.   Do you believe the book would have been more effective if more words were used? Why or why not?

6.   Every good book or story conveys a message. What was the message of this book?

B.   The world of art:

"An artist cannot fail. It is a success to be one."
—Charles Cooley, *Life and the Student* (Irvington Publishers, 1993).

1.   Which word best describes visual art?
   a.   incredible
   b.   boring
   c.   strange

2.   Which word best describes artists?
   a.   bizarre
   b.   ingenious
   c.   useless

3.   Which word best describes the imagination?
   a.   shallow
   b.   frivolous
   c.   rich

4.   Which word best describes a blank canvas?
   a.   daunting
   b.   exciting
   c.   open

5.   Choose the best word: Paintings should be
   a.   realistic
   b.   colorful
   c.   enigmatic

Use the dictionary if you do not know the meaning of every word.

Which of the 15 words above do you think best describes the art in *Yo! Yes?*

C. Making choices:

1. Predict how someone from another class you do not know would complete the following questionnaire. Write what you think his or her choices would be on a separate sheet of paper.

2. Ask the person to complete the questionnaire. Match your answers with his or her answers. How close did you come?

Would you rather:

    a. entertain or be entertained?

    b. take an ocean voyage on a sailing ship or stay home?

    c. be the ocean or an island?

    d. be the voyage or the voyage's end?

    e. be wealthy or know how to read?

    f. be marooned on an island or be the one searching for someone marooned?

    g. be unable to think or unable to move?

    h. be perfect or flawed?

    i. explore uncharted territory or follow a map?

    j. go with the crowd or go your way alone?

NATIVE AMERICAN FOLKLORE: PICTURE BOOK

The Girl Who Loved Wild Horses, by Paul Goble. Bradbury, 1978.

This is the story of an Indian girl whose people lived on the plains, moved from place to place, and kept horses to carry their belongings and hunt buffalo. The girl loved the horses and understood them in a special way. During a storm, she was carried away by the horses to a strange land where she and the horses were welcomed by a wild stallion. The girl became one with the horses. A year later, when hunters from the girl's tribe found her and took her home, she longed to return to her first love, the horses.

Activities

A. Questions to think about:

1. List all the words you can think of to describe the girl. From your list choose one word that best describes her. Tell why you chose that word.

2. Do you think the girl liked the storm or was she afraid of the storm? Tell why.

3. How do you know that the girl understood the horses in a special way?

4. Why do you think the hunters took the girl home when she wanted to stay with the horses?

5. Do you think this is a true story? Why or why not?

6. In this story, Paul Goble tells about an Indian girl who loved horses. What do you think the girl did to show her love for the wild horses? Make a list of loving things the Indian girl did for the horses.

B.   A wild horse chant:

This chant is fun to read with three groups. After group 1 reads the first verse once, group 2 begins reading. When group 2 completes one reading, group 3 begins reading. All groups should finish reading their verses at the same time and all read the last verse together.

Group 1: Repeat three times

Heads up, heads up, running without reins
Wild and free, wild and free, across the open plains
Heads up, heads up, running without reins
Wild and free, wild and free, across the open plains.

Group 2: Repeat two times

Strong and mighty, strong and mighty, nostrils snorting fire
His tail is high, his mane is long, a credit to his sire.
Strong and mighty, strong and mighty, nostrils snorting fire
His tail is high, his mane is long, a credit to his sire.

Group 3: Repeat one time

Ears up, nostrils flared and eyes opened wide,
Trampling hooves, trampling hooves with every mighty stride
Ears up, nostrils flared and eyes opened wide,
Trampling hooves, trampling hooves with every mighty stride

Everyone together:

His blood is hot and flows within his pounding, racing heart
Nature's creature, like a bullet, sky and earth to part
His blood is hot and flows within his pounding, racing heart
Nature's creature, like a bullet, sky and earth to part

Legend of the Indian Paintbrush, by Tomie dePaola. Putnam, 1988.

A very small Plains Indian boy longed to grow tall and strong and to join the brave warriors and hunters. But he was too small to keep up with the other boys and was not strong at all. He was not consoled by the wise shaman of the tribe, who told him that he would be remembered by the People for another reason. After a time, as the boy grew, he had a vision in which an old man and a young girl spoke to him, telling him that it was his task to paint the deeds of the warriors and the visions of the shamans. The boy then became the recorder of the tribe's history but was not satisfied with the dull colors with which he had to work. The vision came again and he was told where to find his colors. He followed the directions and found brushes filled with paint that allowed him to create the sunset in vivid color. When his painting was finished, he left the brushes behind and the next morning the hill was filled with color because the brushes had taken root in the earth.

Activities

A.   Questions to think about:

    1.   Why did being so small make Little Gopher unhappy?

    2.   What is a legend? How do you know this story is a legend?

    3.   What parts of this story could be true?

    4.   What parts of this story could not be true? Tell why.

    5.   Is painting the stories of the People as important as being a warrior? Why or why not?

    6.   Do you think the tribe gave Little Gopher a good new name? Why or why not?

B.   In response to the description of *The Legend of the Indian Paintbrush*, use the pattern below to write about the following things: (1) a teepee, (2) Little Gopher, (3) a flower, and (4) a sunset.

Little Gopher is just Little Gopher until _____ and then he becomes

a _____ . A _____ is just a

_____ until

_____ and then it becomes a

_____ . A _____ is just a

_____ until _____ and then it becomes a

_____ .

C.   Write a chant:

    After returning from a hunt, the warriors would often celebrate by dancing and chanting. Fill in the missing words in the following chant. Perform the chant for others. Study the pattern below. Use the same pattern in writing about the wild horses of the plains.

            Buffalo Chant
            I like buffalo
            Big ones
            Little ones
            Fat ones
            Skinny ones
            Round ones
            Short ones
            These are just a few.

On the _____

Under the _____

In the _____

Above the _____

Between the _____

Over the _____

Around the _____, too,

Truth to tell

Give a yell.

I like buffalo.

The Legend of the Bluebonnet, by Tomie dePaola. Putnam, 1983.

The rain had not come in a long time. The land was dry and the Comanche people danced to the Great Spirits. A small girl, who had no family, was cared for by the people. Clinging to her doll, she watched as the people danced and prayed for rain to come so that there would be grass. Without green grass, the buffalo would die and the people would have no food. One wise man of the people went to the mountains in hope of hearing the message of the Great Spirits. The Spirits told of how the Earth had been abused by the people. The young girl listened as he described how a sacrifice must be made so that the rains would come. It must be something of more value to the people than anything they own. What would satisfy the Great Spirits? What could the people give so that the rains would fall to the Earth? To find out, read *The Legend of the Bluebonnet.*

Activities

A.   Can you tell why these things happened in the story? Try to think of at least two reasons.

The drums sounded. Why? _____ or

_____

The people danced. Why? _____ or

_____

She sat by herself. Why? _____ or

_____

She remembered her grandparents. Why? _____ or

_____

They gathered in a circle. Why? _____ or

_____

She crept out quietly. Why? _____ or

_____

B. She-Who-Is-Alone's people prayed for rain. The famine and drought had brought much hardship. Plants would not grow without rain and the people were starving. Use the patterns below to write about rain.

> *Storms can be colored in many ways.*
> *The blackening sky warns of a*
> *coming storm. The purple sunset*
> *tells of fair weather to come.*
>
> *Thunder is brown.*
> *It sounds like a grumbling bear.*
> *It tastes like burned toast.*
> *It smells like an abandoned campfire.*
> *It looks like drab fallen leaves.*
> *It makes you feel like hiding.*

What color is your weather word? How might it affect the way you live? Be a word artist and write your poem.

Line 1   Tell the color of your subject
Line 2   Tell what it sounds like
Line 3   Tell what it tastes like
Line 4   Tell what it smells like
Line 5   Tell what it looks like
Line 6   Tell how it makes you feel

_____ is _____

It sounds like _____

It tastes like _____

It smells like _____

It looks like _____

It makes you feel like _____

NATIVE AMERICAN FOLKTALES: BROTHER EAGLE, SISTER SKY

Brother Eagle, Sister Sky: A Message from Chief Seattle. Paintings by Susan Jeffers. Dial Books for Young Readers, 1991.

When the last of the Indian tribes were defeated and the final treaties signed, Chief Seattle, head of the Northwest Nations, spoke to those who wished to buy the Indian lands. His message is as important today as it was 100 years ago: "How can you buy the sky?" he asked. "How can you own the rain and the wind? This we know, that all things are connected like the blood that unites us. We did not weave the web of life. We are merely a strand in it. Whatever we do to the web, we do to ourselves." These and many other words of this wise chief are brought to life with beautiful paintings by Susan Jeffers in *Brother Eagle, Sister Sky.*

Activities

A.   Thinking and writing activity: The Three Rs of keeping the Earth clean are:

REUSE
RECYCLE
REFUSE

Describe one way you can use each of the Three Rs to help keep the Earth clean.

I could REUSE _____

by _____

instead of throwing it away.

I could RECYCLE _____

by _____

instead of _____

I could REFUSE to _____

and the result would be _____

_____

NATIVE AMERICANS: NOVEL

Sing Down the Moon, by Scott O'Dell. Houghton Mifflin, 1970.

The spring that came to the Canyon de Chelly in 1864 was abundant, for the fields and orchards of the Navajos who lived there promised a rich harvest. The sheep were lambing and the sky was bright blue. But all was shattered when the white soldiers burned the crops, destroyed the fruit trees, and forced the Navajos out of the canyon to join their Indian brothers on the devastating long march to Fort Sumner.

Through the eyes of Bright Morning, a young Navajo girl, we see what can happen to human beings when they are uprooted from the life they know. She tells the story of the proud and able Tall Boy, the youth she expected to marry, who is maimed not only by a physical wound, but by a spiritual wound as well. And she tells of the other men of the tribe who on the march along the "Trail of Tears" lose their will along with their way of life. This is a story with tragic overtones, a story of the breaking of the human spirit. And yet, fortunately, then as now, there were a few possessed of inner strength based on hope; Bright Morning was one of these.

The Long Knives order the Navajos to leave the canyon. Tall Boy wants to fight but the elders lead the tribe to a hiding place in the hills. The soldiers destroy the village and wait for the starving tribe to come to them. Without food or water the Navajos surrender.

Activities

A.   Questions to think about:

1.   What does the title mean? Support your ideas with evidence from the story.

2.   Are there similarities between the treatment of the Navajos and the treatment of slaves in U.S. history? If so, what are they?

3.   Why do you suppose the author did not choose to end the novel by freeing all of the Indians?

4.   Who had the right to the Canyon de Chelly, the Navajos or the Long Knives? Explain.

5.   What advantages might Bright Morning receive staying with the cornsilk-haired woman? What disadvantages would she have?

6.   Who was the stronger, Bright Morning or Tall Boy? Why?

B.   A newspaper clipping report:

Find pictures, articles, ads, or anything else in the newspaper that deals with the topic of freeddom. Look carefully at the paper for several days.

Find and clip the items listed below. As you find other items that deal with freedom, list them on lines 9 through 15. Share your clipping report with the class.

KEEPERS OF FREEDOM!

Find and clip:

1.   A picture that symbolizes freedom

2.   A patriotic headline

3.   An article about loss of freedom

4.   An event that could take place only in a free society

5.   A statement concerning freedom of speech

6.   A controversial subject

7.   The name of one who can do something about injustice

8.   The name or picture of an Indian leader

9.   _____

10.   _____

11.   _____

12.   _____

13.   _____

14.   _____

15.   _____

Begin clipping!

Sort your clippings into major subject headings. This can be by date or by type of feature or other headings you choose. Display for others to see:

in a book
on the bulletin board
or other display

C. Both Bright Morning and Tall Boy changed from the beginning to the end of the novel. The free verse that follows describes the changes in Tall Boy. Use the same pattern to describe the changes in Bright Morning. Example:

Tall Boy

You are changing, changing
You feel the shackles of defeat like a vise around your neck
You are angry and grief-stricken
You clench your fist and shout to the sky
You are diminished in your tallness as the guns of the white soldiers are trained upon your people
You do not walk upright anymore as you hear women wailing, children crying and proud men bending under the Army's yoke.
It is demeaning to walk like this
As defeated as the wild buffalo
You are an Indian brave on the Trail of Tears.

Pattern: Bright Morning

You are changing, changing _____

You feel: describe the atmosphere _____

You are: two adjectives _____

You: two verbs or verb phrases _____

You: describe how change appears _____

You do not: what is different? _____

As you: three participle phrases _____

It is: adjective and simile _____

You are: Name _____

NATIVE AMERICANS TODAY: NOVELS

Following are two must-read novels about the Native American experience today. Both focus on what it means to be Indian today; how it feels to confront ignorance and racism, the struggle to reconcile traditional Indian views with the values of the non-Indian world, and the great pride there is in being Indian, coupled with the sadness for all that has been lost.

The Heart of a Chief, by Joseph Bruchac. Dial Books, 1998.

Sixth-grader Chris Nicola lives on an Indian reservation, where the issue of casino gambling has divided the people and endangered the island that is Chris's special place. When a school project on using Indian names for sports teams puts Chris in the spotlight, he finds himself taking his first steps toward leadership. But can one kid really make a difference?

The Talking Earth, by Jean Craighead George. HarperCollins, 1983.

Billie Wind looked into the dark dyes of the medicine man. "It is told," he said, "that you do not believe in animal gods who talk; or the great serpent who lives in the Everglades and punishes bad Seminoles; or the small people who live underground and play tricks on our people. We are disturbed by your doubts." Billie wanted to giggle but the faces of the tribal council were stern. "What do you think would be a suitable punishment?" the medicine man asked. Billie tried to think of something so dangerous and ridiculous that they would not let her do it. She looked at the medicine man. "I should go into the Everglades," she said, "and stay until I hear the animals talk, see the serpent and meet the little people who live underground." "Good," was the reply, much to Billie's surprise. And so begins a journey in which Billie must battle fire, wild animals, and her own prejudices before she discovers what her ancestors had long known, that the Earth does indeed talk to those wise enough to listen.

Activities

A. Questions to think about:

  1. Why are the customs and traditions of any group of people important?

  2. What traditions are important in your family? How would you feel if you could no longer take part in those traditions?

  3. List the difficulties you would encounter in adapting to a completely different society than your own. Consider differences in religion, foods, clothing, homes, etc.

AFRICAN-AMERICANS: PICTURE BOOK

The Wagon, by Tony Johnston. Illustrated by James E. Ransome. Tambourine Books, 1996.

On a Carolina morning a child is born into slavery. He grows, and is soon working for the master from dawn to dark. The boy admires his strong and proud father and resents deeply that he must work from dawn to dark and not be allowed to play like other boys. As he grows, he dreams that he is chopping wood with Abraham Lincoln and chopping became easier after that. He dreams, too, that the wagon he has helped build for Master is a glorious chariot to freedom. His dreams come true when the slaves are given freedom and he and his family depart in the wagon his father has built.

Activities

A.   What do you know about the life of a slave?

Directions: Work with a partner. Answer each question below yes or no. Guess if you do not know. Support or disprove your guesses by reading *The Wagon*. (While not every statement is mentioned in this book, you should understand enough about the life of a slave to support or disprove your guesses.)

1.   Many slaves had first names but no last names. _____
2.   Young children were expected to do a full day's work. _____
3.   Entire families lived in tiny one-room cabins. _____
4.   Slaves were forced to transport other slaves to be sold. _____
5.   A trusted slave could become a wagon boss. _____
6.   No light at night was allowed in the slave quarters. _____
7.   Whips were used by many overseers. _____
8.   Slaves were forced to watch the punishment of others. _____
9.   For punishment some slaves were whipped. _____
10.   Slave children did what they were told. _____
11.   Slaves who showed signs of anger were often punished. _____
12.   Secret schools were set up to teach slave children to read and write. _____
13.   Field hands often did not have enough to eat. _____
14.   A slave's working day could be sixteen or more hours. _____

Uncle Jed's Barbershop, by Margaree King Mitchell. Illustrated by James Ransome. Simon & Schuster, 1993.

Sarah Jean's Uncle Jed was the only black barber in the county. He had a kind heart and a warm smile. And he had a dream. Living in the segregated South of the 1920s, where most people were sharecroppers, Uncle Jed had to travel all over the county to cut his customers' hair. He lived for the day when he could open his very own barbershop. But it was a long time, and many setbacks—from the five-year-old Sarah Jean's operation to the bank failures of the Great Depression—before the joyful day when Uncle Jed opened his shiny new shop and twirled a now grown-up Sarah Jean around in the barber chair.

With James Ransome's richly colored paintings brimming with life, this is a stirring story of dreams long deferred and finally realized.

Activities

A.   Questions to think about:

1.   What reasons can you give for colored people in the South in the 1920s having to go 30 miles for a haircut? Why were they glad to see Uncle Jed arrive?

2. What was Uncle Jed's dream? Why did no one believe he would achieve his dream?

3. What kind of man was Uncle Jed? How do you know?

4. When Uncle Jed had just about enough money to open his barbershop, a bank failure took all his money away. Why do you suppose he still did not give up his dream?

5. When Sarah Jean was ill the doctors would not look at her until all the white patients were seen. How do you feel about this? What do you think Sarah Jean's family should have done?

6. Segregation meant separate rest rooms, water fountains, and schools. If you were Sarah Jean, how would you have felt about segregation? What do you think should have been done about it?

B. Comparing lives: Compare your life today with Sarah Jean's life on the sharecropper's farm in the 1920s.

You	**Sarah Jean**
1. Chores _____	_____
2. Family _____	_____
3. Pets _____	_____
4. Ambitions _____	_____
5. Neighbors _____	_____
6. Entertainment _____	_____

What conclusions can you draw about growing up as an African-American in the 1920s?

MORE PICTURE BOOKS TO READ

Crews, Donald. *Big Mama's*. Greenwillow, 1991.
    A family returns every summer to the homestead, making sure that nothing has changed.

Mathis, Sharon Bell. *The Hundred Penny Box*. Viking, 1975.
    A great-aunt has 100 pennies, one for each year of her life, as she recalls stories.

Amazing Grace, by Mary Hoffman. Illustrated by Caroline Binch. Dial Books for Young Readers, 1991.

Grace loved stories, whether they were in books or the kind her grandmother tells. After she heard the stories she would act out all the parts by herself. Sometimes she is Hiawatha, or Aladdin, or Joan of Arc. There is nothing that Grace enjoys more than acting.

Then one day the teacher announces that the class is putting on the play "Peter Pan." Grace raises her hand. She wanted to be Peter Pan. But a boy sitting next to her whispers that she can't be Peter Pan because she is a girl and she is black.

Grace is not discouraged. She practices dancing all around her house. She watches ballet dancers when her grandmother takes her to a matinee, then practices again. When the tryouts take place, Grace wins the part and learns that her mother's wise words are indeed true. "You can be anything you want to be if you try hard enough."

Activities

A. Characters alike and different: Read the description of *Amazing Grace.* Compare Grace's life to that of Sarah Jean in *Uncle Jed's Barbershop.*

B. Add the missing words to complete the song below. Sing it to the tune of "My Bonnie Lies Over the Ocean."

Amazing Grace

Grace was a girl who loved (1) _____,

It mattered not if short or (2) l_____,

She acted the part of (3) A_____,

And often would burst into (4) _____.

Chorus

Grace loved acting

She wanted to fly just like (5) P_____, P_____,

Mother told her

You'll do it if you think you (6) _____.

RECONCILING DIFFERENCES: NOVEL

The Cay, by Theodore Taylor. Doubleday, 1989.

Timothy WAS different. He was huge, and he was very old, and to Philip he seemed ugly. He ate raw fish and believed in JUMBIS. And he was the most stubborn man Philip had ever known.

But after the Germans torpedoed the freighter on which he and his mother were traveling from war-time Curacao to the United States, Philip found himself dependent on the old West Indian. There were just the two of them cast up on the barren little Caribbean island—three if you counted Stew Cat—and a crack on the head had left Philip blind. The story of their struggle for survival, and of Philip's efforts to adjust to his blindness and to understand the dignified, wise, and loving old man who was his companion, makes memorable reading.

Activities

A. Pre-reading: Choose a sentence starter to complete.

Chapter One:

    1. Living in a place without seasons …

    2. When submarines attack …

Chapter Two:

    3.   An island that depends upon ships for food and water …

    4.   Watching a large ship explode is like …

Chapter Three:

    5.   Drifting for days on the sea in an open raft …

    6.   Basic survival needs at sea are . . .

B.   Chapter projects:

Chapters One and Two

    Philip lives in the Dutch West Indies, where ships carrying oil from the Island of Curacao are attacked by U-boats. The year is 1942. Philip's father arranges passage for the boy and his mother on a ship to the United States.

    Activity: Answer these questions. Guess if you do not know. Support or disprove your guesses by finding out. Check articles on "World War II: Submarine Warfare" in *World Book* or *Encyclopaedia Britannica.*

    1.   How many tons did a U-boat weigh?

    2.   German wolf packs of ___ to ___ U-boats traveled together to attack Allied ships.

    3.   A U-boat could dive ____ feet in ____ seconds.

    4.   U-boats sank a total of _____ ships in World War II.

Chapters Three through Six

    Philip's ship is torpedoed. He awakens on a raft, blinded by a blow on the head. His companion is Timothy, a black man. Philip resents Timothy's efforts to conserve food and water. The raft is surrounded by sharks. Philip falls overboard and is rescued by Timothy.

    Activity: Complete a data bank on an ocean creature.

Lives	**Eats**	**Has**
warm seas	sea animals	rounded body
West Indies	bony fish	21-foot length
shallow water	turtles	pointed snout
near shore	seals	sharp teeth
Australia	tuna	warm body

Does	**Other Facts**
swims rapidly	dangerous to humans
opens jaws wide	top of ocean food
bites	prey chain
waits for blood loss	bites but rarely eats
	before eating humans

Use the data bank information in a "Mystery Report"

List 10 facts (clues).

Ask a classmate to give a number between 1 and 10.

Read the clue for that number.

The student can guess or pass.

The game continues until the mystery creature is guessed or all clues have been read.

Chapters Seven through Nine

Philip and Timothy arrive on a small island surrounded by high coral reefs. Timothy goes to explore and Philip becomes frightened to be left alone. Philip rebels when told he has to work and lashes out verbally at Timothy, who hits him.

Activity: Island analogies: How many can you write? Example: Coral is to island as claws are to bear. (Both protect themselves by ripping and tearing.) What can you do with sharks, palm trees, coconuts, grass hut, wild birds, fish, hurricane, palm fronds, tide pool?

Chapters Twelve through Thirteen

Timothy has a severe attack of malaria. His fever sends him running into the water. Philip pulls him out. Philip feels helpless to do anything about Timothy's illness. The boy learns to catch fish and volunteers to climb the trees for coconuts.

Activity: "Island Mystery Report": List 10 clues. One must be a "give-away" clue. A student gives a number from 1 to 10. Read the clue for that number. The student can guess or pass. The game continues until the answer is guessed or all clues are read. Example:

1. I am used in building houses.
2. Vinegar is made from part of me.
3. Part of me is used to make cups or bowls.
4. I am found in a tropical climate.
5. I can be used to make soap.
6. I can be as tall as 100 feet.
7. My fruit grows eight to ten inches long.
8. I have a thick husk around my fruit.
9. My shell has three eyes.
10. Palm leaves shade my fruit from the sun.

Chapters Fourteen and Fifteen

A hurricane hits the island. Philip and Timothy lash themselves to a palm tree. Timothy dies protecting Philip with his body. The storm passes, leaving Philip so sad that he is "beyond tears."

Activity I: Read the description of the hurricane by choosing mood music to play in the background as you read. This is called concert reading.

Activity II: A poetic description:

1. Choose one: The rain, the surf, the wind, the island. Example: *The rain.*
2. Place one or two descriptive words before the noun. Example: The *pounding* rain.

3. Tell what the (rain, wind, or surf) reminds you of. Example: The pounding rain *was a battering ram.*

4. Tell what your item does that a person also does. Example: The pounding rain was a battering ram *smashing its fist.*

5. Tell how or where the item does the action. Example: The pounding rain was a battering ram smashing its fist *against the angry sea.*

Chapters Sixteen through Nineteen

Alone, Philip buries Timothy and tries to rebuild his island home. He is attacked by wild birds and by a moray eel as he tries to fish. He hears planes overhead and sets the signal fire. A rescue party arrives and Philip is reunited with his parents.

Activity: Use the following pattern to write about the ways in which Philip changed from the beginning to the end of the novel.

Once he was _____

And believed that _____

A belief that was evident in every _____ he _____

His words echoed forth like _____

And no one could convince him otherwise,

But circumstances like wild horses thundered through his young life

Teaching him that _____

With lessons in humanness bringing _____

Discovering that one only has to _____

To discover the _____ in others.

His life is now filled with _____ and _____

His name is Philip.

AFRICAN-AMERICANS: NOVEL

Nightjohn, by Gary Paulsen. Delacorte, 1993.

To know things, for us to know things, is bad for them. We get to wanting and when we get to wanting it's bad for them. They thinks we want what they got . . . that's why they don't want us reading.—Nightjohn

I didn't know what letters was, nor what they meant, but I thought it might be something I wanted to know. To learn.—Sarny

Sarny, a female slave at the Waller plantation, first sees Nightjohn when he is brought there with a rope around his neck, his body covered in scars.

He had escaped north to freedom, but he came back—came back to teach reading. Knowing that the penalty for reading is dismemberment, Nightjohn still returned to slavery to teach others how to read. And 12-year-old Sarny is willing to take the risk to learn.

Activities

A.   Create an acrostic poem about the benefits of being able to read. Each line of this poem must begin with a letter in READING. The first line is done for you.

R   etrieve tons of information.
E
A
D
I
N
G

B.   Chapter projects:

Chapter Two

Sarny overhears Waller's wife complaining because he bought a slave for $1000.

Background: Some slaves were sold at slave auctions while others were taken from farm to farm by wagon, with the farmers making offers for one or more. Families were torn apart. Husbands, wives, and children were sold to different masters. The slaves knew terrible INJUSTICES.

Activity: Thinking about injustice: Complete the pattern below by choosing one of the items listed and writing about how the item you select is like injustice:

spinning wheel

a new pencil

an empty bowl

a rusty spigot

a cat with no claws

an alarm clock

a golf ball

a door hinge

a bubble

_____ is a symbol for injustice because _____

Chapters Three and Four

Nightjohn is brought to the farm with a rope around his neck and is immediately put to work in the fields. He trades Sarny letters for a piece of tobacco.

John teaches Sarny letters at night. He tells Mammy that he had escaped North to freedom but returned to teach slaves to read and write because "what they do to us has to be written."

Activity: Listed below are some famous African-Americans. All have spoken out for their race and worked to eliminate injustices. Choose one of the famous African-Americans listed below and find information about the person in the encyclopedia or a biography of the person's life. List 10 clues about the person. One must be a "give-away" clue. Ask a classmate to give a number between 1 and 10. Read the clue. The student can guess or pass. The game continues until the person is guessed or all clues have been read.

Bryant Gumble	General Colin Powell	Bill Cosby
Michael Jordan	Jackie Robinson	Satchel Paige
Aretha Franklin	Jesse Jackson	Martin Luther King, Jr.
Katherine Dunham	Langston Hughes	Paul Lawrence Dunbar

Chapters Five through Seven

Waller catches Sarny making words, punishes Mammy, and cuts off two of Nightjohn's toes. Nightjohn continues teaching Sarny letters and recovers enough to escape. Nightjohn returns to the farm to take Sarny to the pit school, risking his life once again so that slave children can learn to read and write. Nightjohn would have been good friends with William Wells Brown (see the next book) had they ever met. Both men believed in the power of the spoken and written word.

From Slave to Abolitionist: The Life of William Wells Brown, by Lucille S. Warner. Dial, 1993.

For 20 years William Wells Brown endured the pain of slavery. As a young man he was hired out to a soul driver—a dealer in slaves—and saw the worst evils of a brutal, inhumane system. He watched as families were torn apart, acts of violence committed against them, their bodies and spirits broken. He saw his own mother and sister shipped to the slave markets of New Orleans, the most terrible fate for a slave.

But on New Year's Day, 1834, William Wells Brown escaped to freedom. In the years that followed, his every spare moment was spent in educating himself; he then devoted his life to the abolition of slavery through his writings, lectures, and extensive travel throughout the United States and England. He was the first African-American to publish a play, a novel, and several histories.

Activities

A. Read the description of *From Slave to Abolitionist.* Can you discover at least four things Nightjohn and Brown had in common?

Roll of Thunder, Hear My Cry, by Mildred Taylor. Dial, 1976.

Set in Mississippi at the height of the Depression, this is the story of one family's struggle to maintain their pride and independence. It is a story of physical survival and of the survival of the human spirit. The characters—Cassie, Stacey, Little Man and Christopher-John—experience racial antagonisms and hard times, but learn from their parents the pride and self-respect they need to survive. Owning their own land meant much to the Logan family because it gave them freedom. But when Papa used his land to back credit for black families to shop in Vicksburg, that freedom was threatened. Live day by day with the Logan family in the turbulent year they experience in this moving novel.

Activities

A. Questions to ponder:

1. List reasons the Logan land was so important to Big Ma, Mama, and Papa. Which reason was the most important? Why?

2. What parts of the story might be different if it had taken place in 1998? Why do you think so?

3. Predict what might have happened if the field had not caught fire. Which prediction is the most likely one? Why?

4. Why do you think Papa wanted to give other black families credit when the Logans barely had enough money for themselves?

5. List specific incidents of prejudice in the story. What causes prejudice? What are some things that can be done to combat it?

6. Describe some characteristics of Cassie's personality. Choose one characteristic that BEST describes Cassie and tell why.

B. Connecting character and plot:

You are the director of a folk musical based on *Roll of Thunder, Hear My Cry.* Which character will you assign to sing the following songs? During which scene from the book will the song be sung?

Song Title	Sung by	During What Scene?
Just Before the News		
Leave Me Alone		
Angry Eyes		
For All We Know		
Walk On By		
My Way		
How Can I Be Sure?		
Fly Like an Eagle		
Long Time		

THE AFRICAN-AMERICAN HERO: NOVEL

The Righteous Revenge of Artemis Bonner, by Walter Dean Myers. HarperCollins, 1992.

In 1880 two important events took place: Catfish Grimes shot dead Ugly Ned Bonner, Uncle to Artemis Bonner, and Artemis headed west to avenge Uncle Ugly's death and find the gold mine left to him in his uncle's will. But Catfish wants to find the gold mine before Artemis does. Travels take the two from Mexico to Alaska and back again. Finally, they meet in a shootout in front of the Birdcage Saloon. The exciting finish to this romp through the Old West is one you won't forget.

Activities

A. Questions to ponder:

1. Define *stereotype.* Give examples of characters in this novel that are stereotypes. Tell why.

2. Why was Artemis so determined to avenge his uncle's death? Was it to uphold the family honor, help his aunt, or get the gold?

3. What role did Charlie play in the story? Would the story change if the character of Charlie were eliminated?

4. If you were to give this story another title, what would it be?

B. Chapter projects:

Chapters One and Two

Artemis receives word of the murder of his uncle by Catfish Grimes. He travels from New York City to Tombstone, Arizona, to avenge his Uncle's death. He finds his uncle's grave marker with the epitaph: "Here lives Ugly Ned Bonner. Once alive. Now a goner!"

Many lawmen and outlaws are associated with Tombstone: Wild Bill Hickok, Billy the Kid, Wyatt Earp, Colt Younger, Doc Holiday, and Charlie Siringo.

Activity: Research the life of one of these people. Design a grave marker with an appropriate epitaph. Include a paragraph telling why the epitaph is appropriate. Give the source(s) of your information.

Chapters Three and Four

Artemis chases Catfish to Albuquerque, and on the train trip there he is told he looks like one of the Buffalo Soldiers, members of the Tenth Cavalry.

Activity: Research this famous fighting unit. Write an acrostic poem about the B U F F A L O S O L D I E R S.

Chapters Five and Six

Artemis is tied to a cactus and left for coyotes to eat.

Activity: Research coyotes. Record your information in a data bank, putting as many items as possible under each of these headings: Lives, Eats, Has, Does, Looks Like. Use the completed data bank information to write a "Fact and Fable Book" about coyotes.

Chapters Seven and Eight

Artemis chases Catfish to Juarez, Mexico, where everyone speaks Spanish.

Activity: Prepare a Spanish/English dictionary for Artemis to help him get around. What would be important words for him to know?

Chapters Nine and Ten

Catfish's girlfriend, Lucy Featherdip, was a crack shot, as she proved when she shot a pistol out of Artemis's hand. Read about another woman sharpshooter of the Old West, Annie Oakley.

Activity: Report on her life as a bio-poem. Each number is a separate line:

1. First name
2. Four traits
3. Related to
4. Cares deeply about
5. Who feels
6. Who needs
7. Who gives
8. Who would like to see
9. Resident of

Chapters Eleven through Fourteen

Artemis travels by wagon train to San Francisco and by ship to Seattle.

Activity: Use the following model to write about either city.

Let's go to long-ago places

And see (Seattle's or San Francisco's) changing faces.

We will see:

(List six sights.)

_____

_____

_____

_____

_____

_____

But that's not all

(List six more sights.)

_____

_____

_____

_____

_____

_____

Where am I?

In _____, of course.

Chapters Fifteen through Eighteen

    Throughout the novel Artemis uses many colorful expressions. What does each mean?
1. He'd given up the ghost.
2. An Evil doer had forced the hand of cruel fate.
3. He had not enough decency to fill a thimble.
4. It was hot enough to steal the ice off a dead man.
5. He looked under the weather.

Chapters Nineteen and Twenty

    In freezing Anchorage, Artemis meets up with a teller of tall tales and sees the Inuit Indians.

    Activity: Describe Anchorage as Artemis saw it, using the following models:

Anchorage is the color of _____

It looks like _____

It tastes like _____

It smells like _____

It sounds like _____

It made Artemis feel like _____

If I visited Anchorage today I would see _____

And I'd _____

And _____

But I wouldn't _____

Because I could do that in Tombstone.

Cite the sources of your information.

Chapters Twenty-One through Twenty-Four

Artemis and Frolic had unique meals in each place they visited. Explain why food in Juarez would be different from food in Anchorage.

Activity: Prepare a menu for the President of the United States, who will be YOUR dinner guest. You can only serve foods and use ingredients found in your state.

Chapters Twenty-Five through Twenty-Seven

Activity: Trace the travels of Artemis on a map. Write a couplet about the most interesting place you think Artemis visited.

HISPANIC FOLKTALES: PICTURE BOOKS

The Blacksmith and the Devils, by Maria Brusca. Holt, 1993.

Juan Pobreza, the blacksmith, lived on the pampas. His name suited him perfectly because *pobreza* means poverty in Spanish. All day long he worked hard in his shop, often without being paid. But he never turned anyone away for lack of money. He was old and poor, but his life is about to change. One day as Juan is fixing the shoe of a gaucho's mule, the gaucho reveals himself to be Saint Peter and offers Juan three wishes. But Juan doesn't believe that the gaucho is truly Heaven's Gatekeeper, and squanders the wishes. When Saint Peter leaves Juan truly regrets wasting the wishes. So when a mysterious stranger appears and offers Juan 20 years of youth and a bag of gold, Juan readily accepts, kicking off a series of hilarious events in which the blacksmith outwits the underworld.

Maya's Children: The Story of La Llorona, by Rudolfo Anaya. Hyperion, 1996.

On a night when the wind howled through the trees and the rain cried tears in protest, Maya was born. Her smile was as beautiful as the sunrise but her face was flawed by a strange mark, which the priest knew to be a sign of immortality. As she grew to young womanhood, Maya was kind and loving and extended the hand of friendship to old and young alike. But Maya's gift of immortality drove Señor Tiempo, the god of time, wild with jealousy, for only he had the right to allot to the world's creatures their time on Earth. Although he could not control her destiny, Señor Tiempo used his powers to rob Maya of her heart's dearest treasure, her multitude of miraculous children raised from bowls of earth. Devastated, Maya wanders the countryside, forever wailing for the lost children and is known evermore as La Llorona, The Wailing Woman.

The Sleeping Bread, by Stefan Czernecki and Timothy Rhodes. Hyperion, 1992.

This is the tale of the village of San Pedro and of two men who were important to the life of the town. Beto was a cheerful baker who mixed bread dough every night and baked and sold the golden loaves by day. Zafiro was a ragged beggar who knew that when he was hungry kind Beto would have crusts of bread to share.

A festival was to be celebrated, with many visitors coming to San Pedro. Therefore the townsfolk decided that all beggars should be banished from the village. As Zafiro bade Beto a tearful good-bye a tear fell into the water jar used in mixing the bread dough. The next morning Beto was shocked to see the bread would not rise. Not even prodding or praying would help. Has the village lost more than just a beggar? Or is there a way to awaken the sleeping bread?

Activities

A.   List the elements of Hispanic culture found in each tale. Are the same elements found in more than one tale?

The Lizard and the Sun, by Alma Flor Ada. Illustrated by Felipe Davalos. Doubleday, 1998.

A long, long time ago, in ancient Mexico, the sun disappeared. Everything was dark, and the people were afraid. The animals decided to search for the sun through fields and forests, rivers and lakes. But the sun was nowhere to be found. At last the animals stopped looking, all except the lizard. This is the story of a brave little lizard who would not give up until she brought back light and warmth to everyone.

Activities

A.   Many tales are found in different cultures throughout the world. The tale of the search for the sun is told as an African tale by Verna Aardema in *Why Mosquitoes Buzz in People's Ears* (Dial, 1975). Compare these two tales using the following chart.

	Lizard	**Mosquito**
Setting		
Main character		
Reason there is no sun		
Language		
Way the sun is found		

HISPANIC AMERICANS: PICTURE BOOKS

Three Stalks of Corn, written and illustrated by Leo Politi. Scribner's, 1993.

Angelica and her grandmother live together in an early California house in Pico Rivera. At the corner of their home, near the vegetable and herb garden, grow three tall stalks of corn. "Qué bonito! How nice!," grandmother often whispers as she passes by, sometimes caressing the beautiful plants. Angelica wonders about the corn and why it is so cherished. Grandmother explains, "Corn is very precious to our people. No part is thrown away. Even the husk is used." As the days pass, Angelica learns the legends of the corn: about two children who took three kinds of corn with them as they escaped the great flood and about the great ruler of the Toltecs who transformed himself into a great black ant to find the sacred hill of corn. As Angelica helps her grandmother to make tortillas, plays with grandmother's collection of corn husk dolls, and makes her own brightly colored corn necklace, she begins to understand her grandmother's love for the corn plant.

Activities

A.   Fill in the missing letters in the diagram:

1.   Where Angelica lived.

2.   The person Angelica lived with.

3.   What grandmother made.

4.   What grandmother cherished.

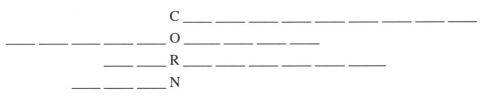

A Birthday Basket for Tia, by Pat Mora. Illustrated by Cecily Lang. Macmillan, 1992.

Cecilia has many happy memories of special times with her great-aunt, her Tia, baking cookies, having tea, or playing outside. So what can she give her on this truly special occasion, Tia's ninetieth birthday? With the help of her cat, Chica, Cecilia ingeniously finds just the right present for Tia. She gathers a basket of memories, a bowl, a teacup, and some flowers, each representing an activity she shared with her great aunt. Tia is enchanted by the birthday basket as well as her surprise party and ends up contributing a surprise of her own. This story pays tribute to a touching relationship between a child and Tia, an older person, as well as showing the details of daily life in one Mexican-American family.

Activities

A.   Write a song!

At Tia's surprise party there were many good things to eat. Complete the following pattern and sing it to the tune of "Skip to My Lou":

We had

	tortillas		
describing word		ing word	where?
	tacos		
describing word		ing word	where?
	rice		
describing word		ing word	where?

I Speak English for My Mom, by Muriel Stanek. Illustrated by Judith Friedman. Albert Whitman, 1989.

Lupé lives in the United States with her mother, who speaks only Spanish. At school Lupé speaks English but at home with her mother she speaks only Spanish. When strangers speak to her mother Lupé tells her what they said. At the doctor's office Lupé must also tell her mother what the doctor says. Lupé's mother keeps her pay from the dress factory where she works at home because she won't understand what the people at the bank say to her. She works hard to support herself and her daughter. Then the blow strikes. The business at the factory is not good and everyone receives a cut in pay. Mother knows she must find a better job, but how can she if she does not speak English? Lupé cannot go to work with her everyday. To discover the touching solution to this problem, read *I Speak English for My Mom.*

Activities

A.   Complete the following pattern:

If I were Lupé I would _____

And I'd _____

But I wouldn't _____

Because Lupé's mother does that.

HISPANIC AMERICANS: NOVELS

Elena, by Diane Stanley. Hyperion, 1995.

This is the true story of a brave woman who, after her husband is killed, saves the lives of her children during the Mexican Revolution. She overcomes many hardships and dangers to finally reach the United States safely.

Mama's Birthday Surprise, by Elizabeth Spurr. Hyperion, 1996.

"In hard times," Mama says, "we can ask Great Uncle who lives in Mexico for help." But times are always hard and it is difficult to believe mother when she never calls on Great Uncle. Other things are difficult to believe as well when mother tells them of her childhood and the big hacienda in which she lived. But mother's children are in for a big surprise when they make a trip to Mexico with their mother. Yes, Great Uncle has died these many years past, but the portrait hanging in the gallery can be no one else but Mother when she was a little girl.

Activities

A.   Questions to ponder:

1.   How did both Elena and Mama show courage?
2.   Are there different kinds of courage?
3.   If one is afraid does that mean that one does not have courage?

The Crossing, by Gary Paulsen. Orchard Books, 1987.

Manuel Bustos is the name he chose, but the life he leads no ordinary 14-year-old should have to choose: begging coins beneath the bridge between Juarez, Mexico, and El Paso, Texas; sleeping in a cardboard box; dreaming about crossing the Rio Grande to the United States to get work—and a belt with a silver buckle. Manny is an orphan. Across the river at Fort Bliss, Robert S. Locke is a sergeant, strictly Army issue, a veteran of Vietnam, a drunk.

Manny's place to be alone was under the bridge. The sergeant's place to be alone was in a bottle. A meeting of these two means death for the one and freedom for the other … or does it mean freedom for both? Find out in this brutal yet compassionate novel.

Activities

A.   Working alone or in a small group, decide which character in the description would be a lock and which would be a key. Tell why you think so. Support or disprove your initial guesses by reading *The Crossing.*

How God Got Christian into Trouble, by Maia Wojciechowska. Illustrated by Les Gray. Westminster Press, 1984.

Christian Wolny's grandfather warned him that someday he would hear a special voice. For generations the men in the family had heard voices. Still, it was a surprise when, in school, the voice said, "Christian, why do you worry so?" and told him that by next week Philomena Garcia will have forgotten all about him.

"How do you know?" asks Christian.

"That's part of my business," the voice says. "Knowing."

"Come on, only God knows everything," Christian says. He really doesn't want to be seen yakking with someone invisible.

"Would you like it better if I were seen?" the voice asks.

"I sure would," says Christian.

There is a tug on his sleeve and he looks down and there is this scrawny-looking Puerto Rican kid.

"I borrowed a body," says God the kid.

And that is how their friendship begins.

Activities

A.   From the brief meeting you have had with Christian in the description, choose two of the words below and complete the writing pattern to describe him. Defend your choice.

remarkable	courageous	honest	stubborn
deceitful	resentful	cowardly	rash
sincere	forlorn	enigmatic	angry
mighty	clumsy	weary	forgiving
greedy	jovial	jealous	unsure
lonesome	overwhelmed	gloomy	bored
inept	patient	stoic	self-reliant

_____ was _____ and _____ because

_____

_____

HISPANIC LITERATURE: NOVEL

The Black Pearl, by Scott O'Dell. Houghton Mifflin, 1967.

You could search all the pearling beds in the sea, but never would you find a better diver for pearls than I, Gaspar Ruis. You know of swimmers who can stay under water for two minutes? I jump in with the sinkstone to carry me down, and come up after three or four minutes; hardly needing a breath, with a fistful of baroque pearls. You think this fleet of Salazar's is big? I was the owner of a fleet twice as large once. If wasn't for that storm which dashed my boats against the underwater reef, I'd be a rich man still. How could I afford it? On one dive in the Gulf of Persia, I came up with a pearl larger than the egg of a hen. Twice the size of that "big one" you all dream of finding, weighing more carats than a coconut and not a flaw to mar its beauty. The Shah paid a pretty price for it, as you can imagine.

People call me the Sevillano because I came here to La Paz from Seville in Spain. Ah, the times I had in Spain. Do you see this tattoo here on my arm? That's me sending the most vicious bull in the ring to his death. And this one, on the other arm? That's me crushing the life out of an octopus larger than any you'll ever see. And here, on my chest, it took me less than five minutes to strangle that lion with my bare hands.

What! You dare to doubt me? I'll tell you only once what I told that spoiled, worthless son of Salazar's: Guard your tongue. Tangle with me and you'll wish you'd angered the Manta Diablo instead! You'd rather snatch the Heavenly Pearl from that stingray sea monster and face his wrath than have to deal with mine! You'd rather your arm was in the grip of a burro clam than up against my knife. You'd rather be in a black lagoon with no harpoon to defend yourself against the devilfish and needlefish than to be up against me!

Activities

A.   Pre-reading activity: Look at the following list of words. Working with a partner, decide on a definition for each. Guess if you do not know the meaning of a word. Then listen to the booktalk and see whether it supports or contradicts your predictions about the words.

harpoon _____	lagoon _____
flaw _____	sinkstone _____
manta _____	devilfish _____
reef _____	burro _____
carat _____	baroque _____
pearling bed _____	needlefish _____

B.   Post-reading discussion questions:

1.   Were you surprised by the ending? Why didn't Ramon give the pearl back to the Manta Diablo? At the end, do you think Ramon was sorry he had ever taken the pearl from the ocean? Was it his fault that his father had died?

2.   The villagers believed that the Manta Diablo was a supernatural monster. Was it? Do you think it was "evil?" Did Ramon think so?

3.   Why did Ramon's father give the pearl to the church? Do you think he used good judgment?

4.   Does this story about Ramon's quest for the Heavenly Pearl remind you of any others? How?

5.   The story is told from Ramon's point of view. How would it have been different if Salazar had been the narrator?

6.   Do you agree that the main conflict in the story is between "man" and "nature?" Explain yourself. What other kinds of conflict do you find in this story?

C.   Post-reading activities:

1.   Create a collage that captures your impression of the most terrifying moment in the story. Write a descriptive caption.

2.   Make a five-frame cartoon strip showing the events leading up to Ramon's securing of the pearl.

3.   Write an interior monologue that tells the boy's thoughts as he returns the pearl to the Madonna at the end.

4.   Retell part of the story from the Sevillano's point of view.

5.   Write the story that Ramon thinks up to tell his mother at the end.

D.   Research model: Following are statements about "mantas" (rays) and sharks made in *The Black Pearl*. Read a non-fiction book that provides information about the undersea animals called "rays" ("mantas" in *The Black Pearl*). A good resource is *Dangerous Sea Creatures* (Time-Life Books, 1974). Based on the TV series, *Wild, Wild, World of Animals,* this informative book covers sharks, rays, skates, sawfish, octopuses and squids, among other true-life (and not-so-true-life) sea monsters. Color photographs are plentiful throughout this book.

Discover which statements are fact and which are fiction.

Create a "Fact and Fiction Book of Rays" using the statements. On one page write "True or False" and one of the statements. On the next page tell whether the statement is true or false and why.

1.   There are small mantas no larger than 10 feet from one wingtip to the other when they are full grown.

2.   Some mantas weigh almost three tons.

3.   Some mantas grow to 20 feet.

4. Mantas swim through the water with a regular upward and downward beat of their flippers.

5. A manta has a mouth so big a person could easily put his or her head into it.

6. On either side of the manta's maw are large lobes like arms.

7. The manta uses its arm-like lobes to capture its prey.

8. Mantas eat shrimps and crabs and small things.

9. Some mantas have a pilot fish, which swims in and out of its mouth.

10. The Manta Diablo has seven rows of teeth.

11. A manta can break a person's neck with a flick of its tail.

12. A manta can wreck the strongest boat with one flipper.

13. A manta has the intelligence to pursue someone it dislikes.

ASIAN-AMERICANS: PICTURE BOOKS

My Father's Boat, by Sherry Garlan. Illustrated by Ted Rand. Scholastic, 1998.

Early one morning, a boy and his father ride to the docks and climb into their fishing boat. This father and son are Vietnamese Americans, the father an immigrant, the son born here. All day, they work the boat that provides their family's livelihood. Soon the father's thoughts drift to his own father, who plies the same trade, half a world away. And he hopes that someday they might fish together—grandfather, father, and son—on a beautiful boat out on the quiet water.

Angel Child, Dragon Child, by Michele Maria Surat. Illustrated by Vo-Dinh Mai. Raintree Publishers, 1989.

Ut, who has come to America from Vietnam with her father, misses her mother terribly. The first day at her new American school a red-headed boy pointed at her, shouting "Pa-jaa-mas!" The same boy led the laughter when she did not understand what the teacher was saying. She consoles herself by opening the tiny box she carries with her mother's picture. "Angel child," her mother seems to whisper to her. With the first snowfall, Ut and the red-headed boy end up in the principal's office for fighting. "You will write each other's stories," he said. How could they do that if they do not speak to each other? Then Ut sees a tear slide down the boy's face. Gently she tugs at his sleeve. To discover two young children who are far more alike than different, you will want to read *Angel Child, Dragon Child.*

I Hate English, by Ellen Levine. Illustrated by Steve Bjorkman. Scholastic, 1989.

Mei Mei was a very good student in school, in Hong Kong, where everyone spoke Chinese. But her family moved from Hong Kong to New York City, where everyone at school spoke English. Mei Mei hated English … such a lonely language where every letter stands alone, not like Chinese. Writing the stiff English letters was no fun either, not like the fast, short, long strokes she made with the brush when writing Chinese. Every day Mei Mei became more determined that she would speak and write only Chinese. And then one day a terrible thing happened. A teacher came to the Learning Center to help Mei Mei with ENGLISH! The teacher is very kind but Mei Mei is very determined not to learn English. What do you suppose will happen? To find out, read *I Hate English.*

Activities

A.   Immigrants who do not speak English often have trouble with English idioms. Introduce three books of idioms by Fred Gwynne: *A Chocolate Moose for Dinner* (Simon & Schuster, 1976), *The King Who Rained* (Simon & Schuster, 1970), and *A Little Pigeon Toad* (Simon & Schuster, 1988).

      Put together a class book of popular idioms (a chip on the shoulder, etc.) with each child illustrating a page.

ASIAN LITERATURE

Sadako and the Thousand Paper Cranes, by Eleanor Coerr. Illustrated by Ronald Himler. Putnam, 1977.

      Sadako Sasaki was only two when the atom bomb was dropped on her city in 1945. Ten years later the first signs of leukemia appeared. This story of Sadako's twelfth year is filled with life, longing, fear, hope, love, and inevitability. During the long days abed Sadako folded paper cranes, for legend holds that a crane lives a thousand years and if a sick person folds a thousand cranes the gods will grant her wish and make her well again. This story speaks directly of the tragedy of Sadako's death and, in its simplicity, makes a universal statement for peace in the world.

Activities

A.   Questions to ponder:

1.   List as many words as you can to describe Sadako. From your list choose the one word that you think best describes her. Explain your choice.

2.   Do you think Sadako really believed that folding 1,000 cranes would make her well? Why or why not?

3.   Chizuko had no faith in good luck charms, yet she brought Sadako a paper crane. Why do you suppose she did this?

4.   Suppose that Sadako had recovered from her illness. Would this change the message of this book in any way? Why or why not?

5.   Why do you think the author wrote this story? What was she trying to tell young people all over the world?

      If you find *Sadako and the Thousand Paper Cranes* interesting reading, you will want to read another Eleanor Coerr book about the effects of the bomb on a Japanese child, *Mieko and the Fifth Treasure* (Putnam's, 1993), which tells of a young girl who has four treasures for painting Japanese word pictures: a fine sable brush, an inkstick, an inkstone shaped like a lily pond, and a roll of rice paper. In the old days, her art teacher told her, "Mieko, you are one of the lucky few who are born with the fifth treasure: beauty of the heart. With practice, you will surely become a great artist." But the bomb that fell on Nagasaki changed all of that. Mieko's village was turned into ruins, and her hand was badly hurt. She longs to be able to paint as she once did, but can barely hold a paintbrush. It takes time and patience to bring about both healing and wisdom for Mieko. Only then does she begin to understand what the fifth treasure really is.

B. Chapter projects:

Chapter One

Sadako, who ran everywhere, is excited about Peace Day. To her it means music, fireworks, and cotton candy. To her parents it is a day to remember those who died when the atom bomb was dropped on Hiroshima nine years earlier. Sadako believes in good luck signs like a cloudless sky or seeing a spider.

Activity: Check with friends, family or members of your class to see how they would finish the following common superstitions:

1. Breaking a mirror is _____
2. If you spill salt you should _____
3. Walking under a ladder is _____
4. If you don't always stir the batter in the same direction _____
5. Bubbles in coffee mean _____
6. Looking at the new moon over your left shoulder will _____
7. A black cat crossing your path means _____
8. Opening an umbrella indoors is _____
9. Stepping on a sidewalk crack brings _____
10. Carrying a rabbit's foot will bring _____
11. Finding a four leaf clover is _____
12. A ring around the moon means _____
13. A number thirteen is _____
14. Eating walnuts is supposed to be good for _____
15. Friday the thirteenth is _____
16. An itchy nose means _____
17. A blister on the tongue means _____
18. Wearing squeaky shoes means _____
19. The gift of a knife _____
20. Wearing a peacock feather will bring _____

Chapters Two and Three

Sadako enjoys the sights and sounds of Peace Day, except for seeing those who had scars from the bomb. She turns away quickly from the bomb victims. Lanterns carrying names of the relatives who died from the blast, including Sadako's grandmother, float on the river.

Activity: The "Lanterne Poem." *Issun Boshi, the Inchling*, another Japanese folk tale, tells the story of an old couple whose prayer for a child was answered. Only the size of a thumb, Inchling remains small, even though he grows older. Determined to seek his fortune, he arrives at the home of a great lord, who hires him to be a companion for his daughter. After rescuing her from three demons he is granted one wish. Magically, he grows and becomes a full-sized man and marries the beautiful princess. Using the lanterne poem pattern, write a poem about their adventure.

Following is the tale retold as a Lanterne Poem

Line One	One syllable Child
Line Two	Two syllables Thumb-sized
Line Three	Three syllables Hired by Lord
Line Four	Four syllables Saves his daughter
Line Five	Five syllables Marries the Princess

Use this poetry pattern to describe Peace Day as Sadako saw it.

Line One	One syllable	_____
Line Two	Two syllables	_____
Line Three	Three syllables	_____
Line Four	Four syllables	_____
Line Five	Five syllables	_____

Use the same pattern to describe Sadako.

Line One	One syllable	_____
Line Two	Two syllables	_____
Line Three	Three syllables	_____
Line Four	Four syllables	_____
Line Five	Five syllables	_____

Chapters Four through Six

Sadako becomes ill at school and is taken to the hospital, where she is diagnosed with leukemia. When her family leaves for the night, she is lonely and miserable. Chizuko shows Sadako how to make paper cranes and tells her the legend that says that when a sick person makes 1,000 cranes she will be well. The cranes remind Sadako's mother of a familiar poem. Sadako meets Kenji, another leukemia victim, and the two strike up a brief friendship until Kenji dies. Sadako continues to make the cranes.

Activity: When the atom bomb was dropped, the radiation absorbed by the people who were not killed in the blast usually resulted in sickness and death. Children who received radiation from the bomb often did not show signs of illness until years later. When Sadako becomes ill she feels both lonely and miserable. List 10 different feelings people have. What feelings did other members of the family show before Sadako became ill?

1. Father felt _____ when

_____

2. Mother felt _____ when

_____

3. Masahiro felt _____ when

_____

4. Chizuko felt _____ when

_____

5. Sadako's family felt _____ and _____ when she became ill.

Chapters Seven through Nine

Mother brings Sadako's favorite foods to the hospital, but she cannot eat. Then mother reads to her from a book of poems. Sadako makes another crane but is too tired to make more. Sadako has a brief visit home to celebrate a holiday. She returns to the hospital and mother gives her a beautiful kimono she has made. Sadako grows weaker. Her family gathers around her and are with her when she dies. Later, her class collects her letters and publishes them. A Peace Monument is built to her and to all children killed by the bomb.

Activity: The Nobel Peace Prize. Alfred Nobel, the inventor of dynamite, established a fund to award monetary prizes for outstanding accomplishments in many fields. One of these awards is the Nobel Peace Prize, first awarded in 1901.

Following are some U.S. winners of the Nobel Peace Prize. Choose one and discover what he or she did to win the prize.

1906	Theodore Roosevelt	1912	Elihu Root
1919	Woodrow Wilson	1929	Frank B. Kellogg
1931	Jane Addams	1945	Cordell Hull
1946	Emily G. Balch and John R. Mott	1950	Ralph J. Bunche
1953	George C. Marshall	1962	Linus Pauling
1964	Dr. Martin Luther King, Jr.	1970	Norman Borlaug
1973	Henry A. Kissinger	1986	Elie Wiesel

1. Name _____

Awarded the Nobel Peace Prize for _____

_____

_____

_____

2. If you were to award the prize today, who would you nominate for the prize and why?

CLASH OF CULTURES

The Eternal Spring of Mr. Ito, by Sheila Garrigue. Bradbury Press, 1985.

Sent from London to live with relatives in Canada during World War II, young Sara becomes friends with the Japanese gardener, Mr. Ito. He explains the meaning of the bonsai tree to Sara and shows her how to grow her own. Pearl Harbor is attacked and Sara's cousin's fiancé is killed. Her uncle is in charge of rounding up all Japanese and sending them to camps. Mr. Ito takes refuge in an isolated cave, going there to die. As hostility toward the Japanese increases, life at Sara's aunt's house becomes tense. Mr. Ito dies and Sara promises to pass his bonsai tree on to his family. But how can she when the camps are far away and anyone helping the Japanese is branded a traitor? Here is the story of a courageous young girl told with the background of real history—a story in which all participants learn the power of understanding.

Activities

A.   Questions to ponder:

1.   What evidence shows Uncle Duncan was not fond of the Japanese even though it was Mr. Ito who once saved his life?

2.   Explain how the title is related to the theme of this novel.

3.   How did Sara receive comfort from the messages of the bonsai?

4.   List as many injustices as you can that Japanese who were Canadian citizens suffered during World War II. Which do you think was the greatest injustice?

5.   What brought about Duncan's change of attitude toward the Japanese at the end of the novel?

B.   Chapter projects:

Chapters One through Four

Sara's cousin and a friend go aground at a place where dangerous currents and quicksand threaten. A trawler manned by Mr. Ito's son saves the boys. A letter from Sara's mother tells of the nightly bombing in England. Sara's cousin, Mary, is excited about her coming wedding to a young serviceman.

Activity: Discover what your class has in common with the characters in this novel. Find a different name for each line. The student finding all 10 names first is the winner! Find someone who:

1.   Can find Vancouver on a map. _____

2.   Likes to grow plants. _____

3.   Can draw a sketch of a bonsai tree. _____

4.   Can name the date Pearl Harbor was bombed. _____

5.   Has moved from one city to another. _____

6.   Has visited or lived in Canada. _____

7.   Has been unjustly accused of something. _____

8. Has camped in the mountains. _____

9. Knows what *discrimination* means. _____

10. Has explored a cave. _____

Chapters Five through Eight

The family goes to church, where David and Mary's wedding banns will be read. The service is interrupted with news of the bombing of Pearl Harbor. The Ito home and other Japanese businesses are attacked by a mob. Mary receives word that David has been killed.

Mary tries to deal with her grief, and the rest of the family shares her anger and her sorrow. Duncan fires Mr. Ito and in a fit of rage, Duncan destroys all of the bonsai. Later Sara rescues and replants hers. Sara misses Mr. Ito working in the yard. Duncan is appointed to a commission on security. He tells the family that all Japanese in Vancouver are to be shipped to camps in the mountains. Sara goes to visit Mrs. Ito without her aunt's knowledge. Mrs. Ito tells her that rather than face the shame of the camps, Mr. Ito has gone away to die.

Activity: Time for skills—homographs. Homographs are words that are spelled the same but have different meanings. Example: It was *fine* with me that he had to pay the *fine*. Choose from the pairs of homographs below. Write four sentences about a character or the setting from *The Eternal Spring of Mr. Ito,* using a pair of homographs in each sentence.

arms (body parts)	date (day, year)	jar(container)
arms (weapons)	date (fruit)	jar (rattle)
ball (dance)	down (move lower)	lean (stand slanting)
ball (round object)	down (feathers)	lean (not fat)
bark (tree covering)	duck (bird)	lock (fasten door)
bark (sound of a dog)	duck (lower suddenly)	lock (hair)
bat (club)	fair (pretty)	miss (fail to hit)
bat (mammal)	fair (just)	miss (unmarried girl)
bear (animal)	fast (speedy)	mum (silent)
bear (carry)	fast (go without food)	mum (flower)
can (able to)	fly (insect)	pitcher (container)
can (container)	fly (with wings)	pitcher (baseball player)
clip (cut)	grave (burial)	seal (close)
clip (fasten)	grave (serious)	seal (mammal)
content (things inside)	ground (soil)	sock (to hit)
content (satisfied)	ground (did grind)	sock (foot covering)
count (1, 2, 3)	hide (conceal)	steer (guide)
count (nobleman)	hide (animal skin)	steer (male cattle)

1. _____

_____

2. _____

_____

3. _____

_____

4. _____

_____

Chapters Eleven through Eighteen

Ernie learns his mother was killed in a London bombing. Walking alone, Sara finds Maggie and shows her the bonsai. She chases the dog and finds Mr. Ito's hiding place. They have a long talk about beliefs of Christians and Buddhists. Mr. Ito dies and Sara rescues his bonsai to keep safe for his family. The children go to spend a week on a farm that is near the camp where the Ito family lives. Sara takes the bonsai with her, disguises herself, and joins a group of Japanese who are returning to the camp. She finds the Ito family and delivers the bonsai. Duncan arrives while Sara is with the Itos and is ashamed of their living conditions, for which he is partly responsible. He is further embarrassed when Mrs. Ito greets him warmly. A change of heart brings new understanding.

Activity: A book review—words of history. A challenge: The words listed below are often used in writing about history. In the novel *The Eternal Spring of Mr. Ito* the reader learns much about the history of World War II in Canada. Write a brief review of the novel. In your review use as many history words that apply as you can. Underline in your review the words you use.

abolish	absolute power	alien
alliance	ally	amnesty
ancestor	ancient	artifact
assembly	barter	blockade
boycott	bureaucracy	cabinet
candidate	charter	civilization
colony	compromise	Congress
debate	delegate	democracy
dictator	discrimination	election
exile	expedition	feudal
foreign	freedom	frontier
generation	government	heritage
immigrant	independence	invention
justice	law	legal
medieval	migrant	military
minority	official	patriot
pioneer	possession	refugee
renaissance	republic	revenue
rule	settlement	slavery
taxation	trade	traitor
tolerance	treason	tyranny

ASIAN-AMERICANS

The New Immigrants: Early 1900s

Dragonwings, by Laurence Yep. HarperCollins, 1975.

Moon Shadow was eight when he sailed from China to join his father Windrider in America. Windrider lived in San Francisco's Chinatown and worked in a laundry. Moon Shadow had never seen him. But soon he loved and respected his father, a man of genius, a man with a fabulous dream. And with Moon Shadow's help, Windrider was willing to endure the mockery of the other Chinese, the poverty, and the longing for his wife and his own country to make his dream come true.

Inspired by the account of a Chinese immigrant who made a flying machine in 1909, this novel beautifully portrays the rich traditions of the Chinese community as it made its way in a hostile new world.

The World War II Internment and Release of Japanese-Americans: 1940s

Journey Home, by Yoshiko Uchida. A Margaret K. McElderry Book. Atheneum, 1978.

Twelve-year-old Yuki and her parents have just been released from Topaz, one of the many concentration camps in which all West Coast Japanese were imprisoned during World War II. Although they are welcomed by a loyal friend, Mrs. Jamieson, returning to Berkeley is not easy. There are no houses to rent, Papa cannot find a job, and former friends have changed. In the climate of fear and distrust created by the war, many people had come to hate the Japanese, as Yuki and her family painfully learn.

Yuki's best friend, Emi, and her grandmother join them in trying to start a new life; so does old Mr. Oka, whom they meet in their makeshift lodgings. Their joint venture is almost destroyed by anti-Japanese violence, however, and, even the return of Yuki's brother, wounded in the war, brings another disappointment. But eventually they find new hope and strength in themselves, and Yuki discovers that coming home is a matter of the heart and spirit. Here is a sensitive glimpse into a tragic episode in our country's history.

Immigrants from Cambodia: 1980s

Children of the River, by Linda Crew. Delacorte, 1989.

Sundara fled Cambodia with her aunt's family to escape the Khmer Rouge Army when she was 13, leaving behind her parents, her brother and sister, and the boy she had loved since she was a child.

Now, four years later, she struggles to fit in at her Oregon high school and to be a "good Cambodian girl" at home. A good Cambodian girl never dates; she waits for her family to arrange her marriage to a Cambodian boy. Yet Sundara and Jonathan, an extraordinary American boy, are powerfully drawn to each other. Haunted by grief for her lost family and for the life she left behind, Sundara longs to be with him. At the same time, she wonders, are her hopes for happiness and a new life in America disloyal to her past, and to her people?

Here is a novel of moving contrasts: between Sundara's Cambodian past and her vivid insights into American life, between cultures, and between loss and hope.

Yang the Youngest and His Terrible Ear, by Lensey Namioka. Illustrated by Kees de Kiefte. Joy Street Books, 1993.

After four years of violin lessons given by father, Yingtao, the youngest in the Yang family, still has a terrible ear and can't hear his own mistakes. When he moves with his family from China to Seattle, Yingtao not only is faced with the struggle to learn English and make new friends, he is also supposed to play a quartet with his talented siblings at an important recital Father is hosting. Convinced he'll bring shame to the Yang name, Yingtao concocts a plan to save the recital. But what if it doesn't work? And how can he ever explain to his musical family that he's finally found his true talent: baseball? For a story of the experiences of a young Asian immigrant meeting challenges and finding his place in his family as well as in the New World, read *Yang the Youngest and His Terrible Ear*.

Wingman, written and illustrated by Daniel Pinkwater. Dodd Mead, 1975.

At school Wing was called Donald, and he hated the name and the school. His teacher didn't understand about family pride when she sent a charity basket home with him. For the first time Wing saw his father cry, before he threw the food away. Wing escaped from the world with his comic books, almost 2,000 of them that he got from money he earned. He also began skipping school, until the truant officer caught him. Wing didn't mind being caught, but he felt awful knowing that his father was now ashamed of him. Then a new teacher arrives and Wing discovers that he is the best reader in the class. Not only that, but the teacher helps Wing discover and develop a uniquely individual talent. School, perhaps, won't be so bad after all.

Activities

A.   Select two characters from the descriptions you have heard:

Moon Shadow from *Dragonwings* (or his father)

Yuki from *Journey Home* (or Jonathan)

Sundara from *Children of the River*

Wing or Donald from *Wingman* (or his father, the old teacher or the new teacher)

Yang from *Yang the Youngest and His Terrible Ear*

Complete the pattern below. Example:

<u>Sundara</u> was a "<u>good Cambodian girl</u>" until she <u>fled Cambodia to America</u> and then she became <u>confused as to whether her hopes for happiness with Jonathan are disloyal to her past and her people</u>.

_____ was _____ and then he/she became

_____.

Learning from the Past

Reading is not a vicarious experience. The laughter and tears that are evoked by the pages of a finely written book are very real indeed. Through literature children learn of the common needs of all of humanity regardless of time or place and are able to walk in the shoes of those who trod the Earth long before them. The child who loses a pet will empathize with Johnny, who knows he must give up *The Biggest Bear*. One who has ever been lost will know how homeless Brat feels in *The Midwife's Apprentice*. A remembered injury will allow the reader to feel the pain of Johnny Tremain's injured hand. Historical fiction can build bridges across time to help children understand, and perhaps learn from, the past and apply the lessons learned to building a more peaceful and rewarding future.

THE MIDDLE AGES

The Door in the Wall, by Marguerite deAngeli. Doubleday, 1945.

In this book of historical fiction, we meet Robin, son of a nobleman and destined to become a knight of the king. However, destiny has a way of playing cruel jokes on one's hopes and dreams, especially when you live during the Middle Ages.

Robin had to be brave when his father left to fight the Scots and when his mother was called away to care for the Queen. He was brave when he became sick and his legs would no longer hold him up and he couldn't even feel them. But when the servants deserted him and he was left alone, he began to doubt how long he could hold on.

Brother Luke saves his life, but Robin must face many problems and dangers. Is his father dead on the battlefield? Will his mother ever return and find him? What is to become of him without the use of his legs? How could he ever serve his king?

All these questions were answered when the castle came under attack and Robin had to find a way to save it. It was then that Robin found his "door in the wall."

Activities

A.   Questions to ponder:

    1.   Do you think Robin was justified in feeling bitter? What happened to change his attitude from the beginning to the end of the story?

    2.   Of all the skills Robin learned, which do you think was the most valuable and why?

    3.   How was life in the Middle Ages different from your life today? Name as many differences as you can.

    4.   At which point in the story did you think the tension or excitement was highest? Why?

    5.   How is this statement related to the theme of the story? "When you come to a stone wall, if you look far enough, you will find a door in it."

B.   Abstract thinking:

In this story, Robin finds there are many doors leading to beauty, courage, freedom, and love. These are abstract concepts and are sometimes hard to define or evaluate. Look at the questions below. Work alone, in pairs, or in groups, and try to find answers.

What are some examples of courage that you can think of?

_____

_____

What are some examples that seem to be a lack of courage?

_____

_____

When you are courageous, you can or will do what?

_____

_____

Is fear the opposite of courage or is it a part of courage?

_____

_____

Do you know anyone who is truly courageous? Who?

_____

_____

Are there different kinds of courage? What kinds?

_____

What is the most courageous thing you have ever done?

_____

Is there a difference between being courageous and being foolhardy? Give an example of each.

_____

_____

What kinds of courage are these?

physical courage _____

mental courage _____

ethical courage _____

Can you now give a definition for courage?

The Castle in the Attic, by Elizabeth Winthrop. E. P. Dutton, 1981.

William is the smallest kid in the class, without much confidence in himself. Mrs. Phillips, who has taken care of William for a long time, is moving back to England. William has grown too old to need a nurse. But William is very fond of Mrs. Phillips and does not want her to leave. He is determined to find some way to make her stay. As a farewell present Mrs. Phillips gives him a wooden and stone model of a real medieval castle, complete with a Silver Knight. She tells William that the Silver Knight was thrown out of his kingdom by an evil enemy and one day will come back to life and return to reclaim his lands. Then one night William creeps up to the attic and takes the Silver Knight from its box.

To his surprise the Knight feels soft and squishy and even warm. And then it moves!

Activities

A.   Questions to ponder:

   1.   Do you approve or disapprove of William's plan to keep Mrs. Phillips with him? Why?

   2.   List many words to describe Sir Simon. What one word from your list best describes him? Why?

   3.   Look at the rules for a knight on page 98 of the book. Would these be good rules for your classroom? Why or why not?

   4.   Give as many reasons as you can why William got safely past the dragon when no one else could.

   5.   What did Mrs. Phillips mean when she said she was only William's spotter and therefore he didn't need her anymore?

   6.   What changes did you see in William from the beginning to the end of the novel? What caused these changes?

B.   A research project:

1.   Two castles are very important to the story: the castle in the attic and Alastor's castle. After reading this chapter see if you can tell the purpose of each of these rooms, places, or objects:

GREAT HALL _____

ALLURE _____

BUTTERY _____

ARMORY _____

PORTCULLIS _____

MOAT _____

BELFRY _____

DRAWBRIDGE _____

CROSSBOW _____

COURTYARD _____

2.   Life in Sir Simon's time was different in many ways from life today. List as many differences as you can.

Sir Simon's Day	Today

Knights of the Kitchen Table, by John Scieszka. Illustrated by Lane Smith. Viking, 1991.

Hold on, adventure-lovers: The Time Warp Trio's about to make history as it's never been made before! But from the way that a knight in black armor is bearing down on them with the giant shish-kebab skewer, they may not live to tell about it. How did they end up at King Arthur's court, anyway?

It all started with *The Book*, a birthday present from Joe's magician uncle. One minute they're looking at pictures of knights, the next minute they're battling fire-breathing dragons and vile-smelling giants. Will Joe, Fred, and Sam escape death, destruction, not to mention life with none of the modern conveniences of home? Read on if you dare!

Joe, Sam and Fred encounter a fierce Black Knight from the days of King Arthur and can't convince him that they mean no harm. The knight moves forward on his horse with his lance pointed directly at them.

About King Arthur

King Arthur was a hero of many legends and stories of the Middle Ages. According to most of these, he ruled the Britons in the sixth century A.D.. With his wife, the lovely Guinevere, King Arthur lived at Caerleon-on-Usk in Wales and had a castle at Tintagel in Cornwall. In some legends, his court is at Camelot, which has been variously located in Somerset and at Winchester in England, and in Wales and Scotland. The knights at his court sat with him around a table called the Round Table. King Arthur was assisted by Merlin, a magician.

About the Round Table

The Round Table was a famous table in the legend of King Arthur. Merlin, a magician, supposedly created it. According to legend, the table was made of marble, but it could be folded magically and carried in a coat pocket. The table was round so that no one could argue over the order in which Arthur's knights should be seated. According to legend, the Round Table remained at Camelot, the location of Arthur's court.

Activities

A.   Questions to ponder:

1.   If you could go back to another time in history, what would it be?

2.   List all the differences you can between life in the Middle Ages and today.

3.   When finding yourself in a dangerous situation, is it better to use your wits or fight?

4.   Suppose that Bleob didn't care what Smaug said about him. How would this change the story?

5.   Do you think the boys really time-traveled to the Middle Ages, or did they just imagine the trip?

B.   Create a story about knights and knaves:

There were many, many people, places, and things that made up what we call the Middle Ages. The place where this story occurred was the continent of Europe. Of all the kinds of people and things that made up the medieval times, the two most interesting seem to be knights and castles.

In the pages of this book you will read about, and see, the fortress homes called castles, with their great halls and their dirty dungeons. You will find out what a knight wore into battle and how knights competed with each other in a joust.

Protecting a castle under siege and joining a crusade were only two of the dangerous tasks that knights were called on to perform. Life was not easy during the Middle Ages, and, many times, this life ended much too soon.

C.   Originality—story starter: Think of all the things you can that have to do with knights and castles. Make a list of them. It might help to work with a partner or in a group. When you have a long list, pick out the five or six things you would like to have in your story. Perhaps it will be a wizard, or a magic ring, a dungeon, or a castle mouse. Answer the question, "WHO?" (the story is about), "WHERE?" (the main character is going), "WHAT?" (the problem is), "WHEN?" (the problem is solved), and "HOW?" (it is solved), and your story will be written.

Starter: One dark night, as I explored the cold and lonely room in the castle tower, I discovered a small door hidden behind the tapestry …

(Remember: who-what-where-when-how.)

Catherine, Called Birdy, by Karen Cushman. Clarion Books, 1994.

"What follows will be my book—the book of Catherine, called Little Bird or Birdy, daughter of Rollo and the lady Aislinn, sister to Thomas, Edward, and the abominable Robert. Begun this 19th day of September in the year of Our Lord 1290. … Picked off twenty-nine fleas today."

Catherine's mother wants to teach her the skills of the lady of the manor and to prepare her to be a gentle and patient wife. Her father wants only to see her married off, and profitably. Catherine herself hopes to become a painter, a Crusader, a maker of songs, a peddler, a minstrel, a monk, a wart charmer. … Of all the possibilities, she has ruled out only one: being sold like a cheese to the highest bidder.

Against a vivid background of everyday life on a medieval English manor, Catherine's earthy, spirited account of her fourteenth year is a richly entertaining story with an utterly unforgettable heroine.

Birdy discovers that a hanging is not a joyful affair. She sees a funeral procession for the queen and is punished for losing her temper and discouraging another suitor. Christmas is celebrated with many guests at the manor. When the guests depart Birdy is bored and makes a list of all the things girls can't do. A winter storm keeps her indoors. She is restless and unhappy.

Activities

A.   Questions to ponder:

1.   Describe Catherine's relationship with her father. Why do you think she disliked him so?

2.   List all the words you can to describe Birdy. What one word from your list best describes her? Why?

3.   At one point in the story Birdy compares herself to the bear at the fair. Was it a good comparison? Why or why not?

4.   Which of her ambitions do you think Birdy will realize? Why?

5.   Which was more important to Birdy's father? His daughter or money? Why do you think so?

B.   Use the diamante pattern that follows to describe Birdy:

Diamante

_____

noun

_____ _____

two adjectives that describe it

_____ _____ _____

Three verbs that tell what the noun does

_____ _____ _____ _____

Two nouns relating to first line   Two nouns relating to last line

_____ _____ _____

Three verbs that tell what the noun does

_____ _____

Two adjectives to describe it

_____

Noun

The Midwife's Apprentice, by Karen Cushman. HarperCollins, 1995.

One frosty evening, a girl who knows no home, no parents, and no name but Brat finds shelter and warmth in a farmer's dung heap. There Jane the village midwife finds her. So it is that Brat, now called Beetle by her new mistress, begins her career as a midwife's apprentice.

It is not a safe life. Jane is a hard woman with a sharp glance and a sharper temper. Still, Beetle makes a place for herself, adopting a cat and befriending one of the village boys. By secretly watching Jane work. she learns some of the skills the midwife greedily tries to hide. Beetle even gives herself a real name at last: Alyce.

Then one day she fails at an important assignment. Alyce runs away, believing she is too stupid to be of use to anyone. Is she truly Brat, a know-nothing who belongs nowhere? Or is she Alyce, the midwife's apprentice, a person with a name and a place in the world?

Activities

A.   Questions to ponder:

1.   Do you believe that reasons for being homeless in the Middle Ages were different from reasons for being homeless today? Were the people of the Middle Ages less caring for others than people today?

2.   List the various events that led to Alyce gaining self-confidence and self-esteem. Rank order the events on your list from the most to the least important.

3.   Why do you think Alyce made the hoofprints around the village? What was the effect of the footprints on the villagers?

4.   Do you think that a closer relationship will develop between Alyce and Will Russet, perhaps leading to marriage?

5.   Would the villagers' treatment of Alyce be judged differently by standards in the Middle Ages than by today's standards?

6.   What advantages did Alyce gain from her meetings with Magister Reese? Could these same advantages be gained today? Why or why not?

B.   Descriptive writing: When keeping a journal, many people try to write interesting descriptions of the people and places they encounter. One way to do this is to use the simile. Suppose you were Magister Reese keeping a journal of his journey. What things would you see along the way (example: the Inn, river, village, manor house, etc.)? Use at least 10 of the similes below to describe 10 things Magister Reese might have seen on his trip.

1.   As fat as a _____   Describes _____

2.   As light as a _____   Describes _____

3.   As cold as _____   Describes _____

4.   As lovely as _____   Describes _____

5.   As smooth as _____   Describes _____

6.   As hard as a _____   Describes _____

7.   As soft as _____   Describes _____

8.   As strong as _____   Describes _____

9.   As worn as _____   Describes _____

10.   As dark as _____   Describes _____

11.   As busy as _____   Describes _____

12.   As happy as _____   Describes _____

13.   As hungry as _____   Describes _____

14.   As sweet as _____   Describes _____

15.   As quiet as _____   Describes _____

16.   As stubborn as _____   Describes _____

17.   As tall as _____   Describes _____

U.S. HISTORY

I Sailed with Columbus, by Miriam Schlein. Illustrated by Tom Newson. HarperCollins, 1991.

Twelve-year-old Julio has lived a quiet life. Starting out as an orphan and raised in a monastery, he has been safe and sheltered, until now. Suddenly, he is offered a chance to sail as a ship's boy on a most unique voyage to discover a new route to the Indies! This voyage will take them to places no one has ever seen before! Julio can hardly wait! Soon he finds himself waving good-bye to the Brothers at the monastery. He watches the shoreline of the land he calls home disappear as they set sail for unknown seas.

Aboard ship, Julio writes as much as he can about the events of the voyage. Oh, the challenges of becoming a gromet! Budding friendships with fellow ship boys are a great comfort to Julio when rough sailing sets in. The mounting fear that they will never find land is something that Julio has to struggle with also. But his personal encounters with Captain General, Christopher Columbus, restore his faith in finding land. And when they do reach land, the real adventure begins for Julio.

At last, "Tierra, tierra!" they exclaim. The captain, the interpreter, the gift bearer, and Julio lower the batel and approach the island. Upon encountering naked islanders and realizing a language barrier, the crew is eager to search for gold and claim land for Spain.

Activities

A.   Questions to ponder:

1.   What risks did Julio take when he went on this voyage?

2.   Would you consider making a voyage like Julio did? Why or why not?

3.   Do you feel Julio did the right thing by not telling anyone when he discovered that Columbus was lying about the logging entries? What else could he have done?

4.   How did Julio's friendship with the other ship boys help him when he became discouraged?

5.   What do you think Julio will remember the most about this adventure and why?

6.   What do you think are some reasons Julio decided to turn down the offer Columbus made to him about going on a second voyage?

B.   Use the words below to complete the island description that follows.

translate	gifts	island	naked
shore	friends	explore	understand
possession	language	clasp	exchange
claim	chief	captain	motion

I am an island green and _____

A growing place where _____

Within the shade of my palm trees I shelter _____

and _____

I am strong, stronger than _____ that

try to wear me down. I am an island looking on as man approaches with _____

Feeling fear as _____

Yet, harboring hope as others _____

My name is The West Indies.

Related Reading

Brenner, Barbara. *If You Were There in 1942.* Bradbury, 1991.

Readers take a trip back in time to learn about the culture and civilization of fifteenth- century Europe and Spain.

Clare, John D. *The Voyages of Christopher Columbus.* Harcourt, Brace, 1992.

This book describes the four voyages of Columbus to the New World and his activities there.

Dyson, John. *Westward with Columbus.* Photographs by Peter Christopher. Scholastic, 1991.

An account of the 1990 voyage in a replica of the *Niña,* across the Atlantic, by some Spanish students.

Fradin, Denis Brindell. *The Niña, the Pinta, and the Santa Maria.* Franklin Watts, 1991.

A biography of Christopher Columbus, focusing on his voyage aboard the three famous ships.

The Sign of the Beaver, by Elizabeth George Speare. Houghton Mifflin, 1983.

Twelve-year-old Matt shook his head in disgust. The disgust was with himself. It was his carelessness that let the stranger in the house … the stranger who took off in the night with Matt's gun, his only means of getting food. It was his carelessness that left the cabin open to a hungry bear who destroyed everything in sight and took the little food Matt had left.

When Matt's father left to get the rest of the family he trusted Matt to care for himself for the few weeks he would be alone. And Matt had let him down. Fish was still plentiful and he had his hook and line. It looked like a steady diet of fish was ahead. Then Matt remembered … the bee tree! A taste of honey sure would be a treat.

It was an easy tree to climb and the bees didn't even seem to notice as he pulled himself higher and higher. Peering in a small hole he could just glimpse far inside the golden mass of honeycomb. The bark around the hole was rotted and crumbling. He put his fingers on the edge and gave a slight tug. A good-sized piece of bark broke off in his hand.

With it came the bees. The humming grew to a roar, like a great wind. Matt felt a sharp pain, and another and another. The angry creatures swarmed along his hands and bare arms, in his hair, on his face.

Matt's only hope was to make it to the icy cold water of the river. This was the most careless thing he had ever done and he'd live to regret it; if, that is, he lived.

Activities

A.   Questions to ponder:

1.   Matt was only a boy. Why didn't his father take him back East with him when he went to get the rest of the family?

2.   When people of different cultures meet, why are they often suspicious or cautious around each other?

3.   What did Attean mean when he said, "No one can ever own the land?"

4.   Matt had a difficult choice to make. Before reading the last chapter, evaluate his choice. What were the positive things about his choice? The negative?

5.   In what way is *The Sign of the Beaver* like one of these books: *Island of the Blue Dolphins* by Scott O'Dell (Houghton-Mifflin, 1960), *Hatchet,* by Gary Paulsen (Bradbury, 1987), or *Robinson Crusoe,* by Daniel Defoe (repr. Scribner's, 1920)?

B.   The first non-Indian explorers of land in the New World were fur traders and trappers, who blazed trails through the wilderness. At the time Matt and his father settled the land in Maine, Daniel Boone was exploring the rich prairie lands of Kentucky. Others who followed in later years, blazing trails beyond the Mississippi, were George Rogers Clark, Davy Crockett, and Jim Bridger.

Research statement:

1.   Write a song about the adventures of one of the early trappers. Sing it to the tune of "Oh, Susannah":

> *Oh, a hunter and a trapper,*
> *A fur trader and a guide,*
> *Yes, he crossed the rocky mountains*
> *With his rifle at his side.*
>
> *Chorus*
> *Built Fort Bridger*
> *So folks could find their way,*
> *Oh, Jim Bridger was a mountain man*
> *Always on his way.*
>
> *Oh, for forty years moved onward*
> *Leaving mountains in his wake*
> *Was the first to gaze upon it*
> *The magnificent Salt Lake.*

2.   Tell about the life and work of a famous fur trapper as a bio-poem.

Line 1	First Name	Daniel
Line 2	Four Traits	Inquisitive, brave, restless, leader
Line 3	Related to	Rebecca
Line 4	Cares deeply about	Making the land safe for settlers
Line 5	Who feels	Reluctant to take human life
Line 6	Who needs	A wilderness home
Line 7	Who gives	A trail to follow
Line 8	Who fears	Civilization
Line 9	Who would like to see	Peace with the Indians
Line 10	Resident of	Boonesborough

YOUR TURN!

My Brother Sam Is Dead, by James Lincoln Collier and Christopher Collier. Four Winds Press, 1974.

"We've beaten the British in Massachusetts! The Minutemen hid in the fields along the roads and massacred them all the way back to Boston!"

When Tim's brother Sam burst in with the exciting news, everyone in the little crossroads tavern sat silent and shocked. Most people in that part of Connecticut were Tories or people who thought the colonies had some legitimate complaints against England, but nothing serious enough to shed blood over.

Tim's father and mother, who ran the tavern, felt the same way. But not Sam. At sixteen, just a few years older than Tim, he was bull-headed. Sam was convinced that the rebel cause was just—and worth fighting for.

Tim was eager to hear more about what had happened, but he dreaded what he knew would be a bad argument between Sam and his father. Tim wondered if there was any way their disagreement would ever be settled.

A few days later, when Sam stole his father's gun and, despite Tim's efforts to stop him, went off to fight the British, Tim's fears were confirmed. To find out what happens to Sam and Tim and their mother and father, as even the peaceful Tory town of Redding Ridge is caught up in the bitter turmoil, read *My Brother Sam Is Dead.*

Activities

A.   Look at the list of words below. If you think a word is a person, put a "P" on the line; if a place, put "PL"; and if an action, put "A" on the line. Guess if you do not know. Then support or disprove your guesses by listening to or reading the description of the book.

1. _____ minutemen
2. _____ massacre
3. _____ crossroads
4. _____ Tories
5. _____ complain
6. _____ burst
7. _____ tavern
8. _____ rebel
9. _____ disagree

B.   Questions to ponder:

1.   Why do you think Tim's father acted toward Sam the way he did?

2.   Draw a map of how you think the different settings in the town of Redding Ridge were located. How did the design of the town influence the story?

3.   Do you believe that Tim was able to almost shoot his brother Sam? Why or why not?

4.   Why do you think Sam joined the Patriots? Give reasons Sam didn't want to return home when his enlistment was up.

5.   Name another time in American history when families have been divided by political issues. Do you believe that Sam and his father could have "agreed to disagree" for the sake of family harmony? Why or why not?

C.   Mind stretchers: Following are four kinds of thinking that are exercises for the mind.

Fluency: The ability to make many responses. How many different words can you use to describe George Washington?

Flexibility: The ability to respond in a variety of areas. Select two famous people from the Revolutionary period. List as many ways as you can that these two people are alike.

Originality: Responding in new or unique ways. Suppose a new boy suddenly shows up in your neighborhood. He looks like all your other friends, but you suspect he has been transported from another period of history. What behavior would give him away? How could you discover what period he was from?

Elaboration: Adding to basic ideas. Tales of George Washington and the cherry tree and Honest Abe have made these men legends of honesty. Legends about famous people are often elaborations of simple incidents. Find a recent news incident about a famous person. Elaborate on it to create a legend about that person.

Johnny Tremain, by Esther Forbes. Houghton Mifflin, 1943.

Clever and gifted Johnny Tremain is apprenticed to a silversmith in the year 1773. Johnny sees a great future ahead until the day that carelessness causes his hand to be so badly burned that his dreams of being a silversmith are destroyed. Johnny becomes bitter and feels useless until he becomes a dispatch rider for the Committee of Public Safety and gets to know the leaders of the Revolution. With the rapid events that follow leading to independence, Johnny fills a valuable role in securing the nation's freedom from English oppression. Live through two years of history with Johnny Tremain and watch through his eyes as the Revolution unfolds.

Activities

A.   Questions to ponder:

   1.   List words to describe Johnny at the beginning and the end of the novel. Are the word lists very different? Why?

   2.   How were Lavinia and Priscilla different? At the end of the novel, were they alike in some respects? How?

   3.   Why did the members of the Sons of Liberty take such chances when they knew if they were caught they would be shot as traitors?

   4.   The tea tax was very small and did not affect the price of tea of Bostonians. Why then did the Rebels dump the tea in the harbor?

   5.   At what point in the novel do you think Johnny realized that war was not an adventure, but a killing of people?

   6.   Of the real historical figures mentioned in the novel, which do you think played the most important part in the Revolution? Defend your choice.

B.   Use the patterns that follow to write about the famous men in this book.

If I were <u>Sam Adams</u>

I could _____

And I'd _____

And _____

But I couldn't _____ because

<u>Paul Revere</u> does that.

If I were <u>Paul Revere</u>

I could _____

And I'd _____

And _____

But I couldn't _____ because

<u>Dr. Warren</u> does that.

Name the character:

Where found? (setting)

One thing the person would do for someone else.

A second thing he would do.

Repeat the first line.

Example:

If I were George Washington

At home in Mount Vernon

I would feed you a rich dinner

And tell you how you got your freedom

If I were George Washington.

I am <u>James Otis</u>

Hear me _____

_____

_____

See me _____

_____

_____

Watch me _____

_____

_____

But watch out! I may be watching you.

George Washington's Socks, by Elvira Woodruff. Scholastic, 1992.

Five children are members of the Adventure Club. They try to recreate George Washington's crossing of the Delaware River, experiencing some exciting adventures along the way.

Activities

A. Elaboration—adding to a basic product. What can you add to this booktalk script to make it livelier?

Narrator One:	Matthew was president of the Adventure Club and planning
Matthew:	the first all night camp out in Tony's backyard
Narrator One:	when disaster struck. Matthew couldn't go unless little sister Katie went along!
Narrator Two:	So that night, the boys, with Katie tagging along, decide to take a walk along the river bank and find an old row boat.
Matthew:	"This is too good a chance to pass up,"
Narrator One:	Matthew thinks, as the children climb into the boat.
Narrator Two:	Before long the children are lost in a velvety darkness, moved along by a strong current in a river choked with ice. And then it happened.
Matthew:	The boat tipped and Katie went overboard.
Narrator Two:	After a frantic search, another boat appears. In the center stands George Washington holding a wet and sleeping Katie in his arms.
Washington:	"Arrest the Tory spies,"
Narrator Two:	the General calls out, pointing to Matt's boat.
Narrator One:	The boys were speechless. Was this some TV show gag, or had they somehow gone back in time?

B. Associative thinking—identifying similar attributes (seeing how things go together). Group or match as many of these words as you can or use all the words in one column in one sentence to describe the cover of the book. Add other words as needed.

Katie	Matthew	Tony	George Washington
adventure	Delaware River	Revolutionary War	disgusting
desperate	research	incredible	allegiance
inexperienced	ominous	disappearance	emphatic
transfixed	vessel	tautness	iridescent
horrified	overboard	visibility	disbelief
ice floe	commander	muskets	underestimate
ingenuity	marbleheader	expedition	Hessians
mercenaries	maneuver	treacherous	casualties
detachment	imagination		
Continental Army			

C. Chapter projects:

Chapters One and Two

Matthew, Quentin, Hooter, Tony, and Matt's little sister, Katie, camp out as members of the Adventure Club. Their first adventure will be to explore Washington's crossing of the Delaware River to capture the Hessians at Trenton.

Activity I: Fluent thinking—many responses. List all the words you can to describe Matthew.

Activity II: Flexible thinking—responding in a variety of areas. Describe the American Revolution using the "Only One" pattern. Example: There were many ships in the Boston Harbor but ONLY ONE hosted the Boston Tea Party.

Chapters Three through Five

The boys and Katie hike through the woods to the lake. Tony recalls his grandpa's tales of strange disappearances. The woods seem threatening as the children hear strange noises and think about the night animals that will be watching them.

Activity: Attribute listing—listing the basic qualities of a person, place, animal, plant, or object. Prepare a data bank about a forest animal. Use the headings in the example that follows for the raccoon.

Eats	**Lives**	**Looks Like**
frogs	dens in ledges	gray, furry
crayfish	North and South America	face like a fox
turtles	in hollow trees	weighs 25 lbs.
berries & fruits		32 inches long
What It Does	**What It Has**	
climbs trees	long coarse hair	
sleep during winter	tail with black rings	
ruin crops	black patch around each eye	
wash food	long legs, strong claws	

Use the information to write a raccoon sale ad. Follow the pattern given below.

Descriptive Pattern

Hey kids! I have a _____ for sale. It's the handiest thing you will ever want to own since it can _____ and _____ and _____ and the greatest thing about it is _____.

Chapters Six through Eight

The boys join Katie in the boat and are suddenly surrounded by freezing rain and snow. Katie falls overboard and is rescued by George Washington, who takes the boys into his boat as well. Matthew notes that Washington has "the face of a leader. The face of a determined man."

Activity: Analyze: Taking apart—identifying relationships. Read the acrostic poems about Washington and Jefferson. Compare the two men in the model that follows.

Thomas Jefferson

J   ustice was important to him
E   ducated man
F   ounded the University of Virginia
F   elt that the Colonies should be free
E   xplorer
R   ealized his dream of freedom from England
S   erious minded inventor
O   ne of the writers of the Constitution
N   ever gave up his ideas on the dignity of man.

George Washington

W   as over six feet tall
A   rgued that the Colonies should be free from taxation
S   howed courage in battle
H   e married Martha
I   naugurated as President in 1789
N   ation's first President
G   eneral in the army
T   ook Cornwallis to task
O   bituary written 1799
N   otable American

> *If I were George Washington*
> *I'd be the first President of the United States*
> *I'd live at Mount Vernon*
> *I'd have wooden false teeth*
> *But I wouldn't be the second President from Virginia*
> *For I would be Thomas Jefferson*

Model:

If I were _____

I would _____

And _____

And I'd _____

But I wouldn't _____

Because _____ does that.

Chapters Nine through Twelve

Matt is not allowed to return to the boat after returning the General's cloak. He makes friends with another soldier, Israel, who helps him. Matt feels lost and wonders how many will be killed in the coming battle.

He is amazed to see that Henry Knox is one of the officers; he has always admired accounts of Knox's bravery.

Activity: Decision making—identifying the problem. List possible solutions. Judge solutions with specific criteria. Make decisions: If you could time-trek back to 1776, what one thing could you share to improve the quality of life?

Ideas	Possible?	Help many?	Accepted?

Score 1=no; 2=maybe; 3=yes Total scores

Chapters Thirteen and Fourteen

Israel's wounds are too severe for him to travel any longer. He falls and Matt is determined to stay with him. Israel dies and Matt is found by a farmer, who takes him home. When Matt awakens in the farmhouse he is fascinated by the things he sees there.

Activity: Evaluation—Listing the plus and minus elements of an object or situation. List the advantages and disadvantages of living in colonial times.

Advantages	Disadvantages

Chapters Fifteen and Sixteen

The farmer loans Matt a mule to take him back to the river. He meets up with Hooter, Tony, and friendly Indians. Hooter tells Matt that the Hessians have Q and Katie.

Activity: Forecasting—identifying cause and effect. Complete the following statement. Add others.

Cause	Effect
Because Matt had to take Katie camping	

Chapters Seventeen and Eighteen

The Indians stop the boys from eating poison berries. Matt, Tony, and Hooter plan to sneak up on the Hessians and rescue Q and Katie.

Activity: Generalizing—form a rule that explains a number of situations. List personality traits of several well-known leaders: Washington, Jefferson, Lincoln. What generalizations can you make about the qualities of a leader?

Chapters Nineteen and Twenty

The Hessians capture the boys, who make friends with one young Hessian soldier, only to see him shot. The Patriots think the children are spies. George Washington intervenes and promises safe passage across the river.

Activity I: Make a collage representing some of George Washington's favorite things. Under this collage, you will add one extra feature. Write a rhymed couplet about George Washington.

Activity II: Analogy—comparing two things different in other respects.

1. George Washington is to ___ as General Grant is to ____.

2. The Boston Tea Party is to ___ as the Dove is to ____.

Add others related to the American Revolution.

Chapters Twenty-One through Twenty-Three

George Washington gives Katie a pair of socks. She helps the boys find the rowboat and they make it safely back into the twentieth century. Katie tries to relate the great adventure to her parents and they smile at her vivid imagination.

Suppose you could time travel to the FUTURE! What might you find there?

Activity: Synthesis—organizing information in a new way. Re-create one scene from the novel as if you were the observer.

Jericho's Journey, by G. Clifton Wisler. Puffin Books, 1995.

It was October 1852, and Jericho Wetherby and his family were finally on their way to Texas. Jericho had lived his whole life in County, Tennessee, never traveling more than 50 miles away from home. For years he had heard the stories his father had told about the battle of the Alamo and Texas winning independence from Mexico. Now, after all these exciting stories along with the letters Uncle Dan had written telling about the wonders of Texas, Jericho and his family, along with Eli Grady, the cousin of a neighbor "up river," were on their way to Texas. Pa even wrote in the family Bible, "Gone to Texas, 1852." The Wetherbys built a chicken coop and tool box and attached them to a covered wagon, then loaded their plow and water barrels and set off.

Jericho knew winter would be setting in soon and time was of the essence, but traveling with one wagon, some animals, and three young boys on foot would be slow. Would they get to their new home in Texas before winter set in? What hardships would they have to endure on their trip through Tennessee and Arkansas?

Will Jericho and his family make it all the way to Texas or will they turn around and go home as so many others have done? To take part in Jericho's adventures, read *Jericho's Journey*.

Activities

A. Questions to ponder:

1. Did the Wetherbys have valid reasons for uprooting the entire family and traveling hundreds of miles to a new home? Explain.

2. Find six colorful expressions used in the story. Why do you think the author used these expressions?

3. Along the way the family was often charged money to travel on certain roads. Do you think the people should have charged travelers? Why or why not?

4. Jericho's father said that living out in the open "toughens a man." Give examples from the story to show how Jericho toughened.

5. How did the Wetherbys' late start affect their journey?

6. People use various techniques to overcome their fears. Find passages in the story to show how the Wetherbys overcame their fears.

7. The family passed a number of deserted wagons and possessions left behind. Why do you think people took so much on such an arduous journey?

B. Read each statement below and decide if you agree or disagree with the statement. When you have finished this novel, read the statements again and examine your opinions. Did you change your mind about any of the statements?

1. Battles in war can be exciting.	Agree	Disagree
2. Children look forward to moving to a new home more than their parents do.	Agree	Disagree
3. The greatest distance a covered wagon can cover in a day is five miles.	Agree	Disagree
4. Being afraid of high places is foolish.	Agree	Disagree
5. A horse colic cure is for horses.	Agree	Disagree
6. Those who traveled west in the 1850s either made it or died.	Agree	Disagree
7. It is okay to charge people to travel on a road you own.	Agree	Disagree
8. Wild animals should not be killed.	Agree	Disagree
9. A Prairie Chicken is a bird.	Agree	Disagree
10. People who leave home to travel to unknown places are foolish.	Agree	Disagree

C.   Using the information you have read so far in *Jericho's Journey*, how many different sentences can you write using the following pattern?

1.   A raccoon is just an animal until it invades your camp and then it becomes a very scary intruder.

2.   A wagon is just a wagon until _____

and then it becomes _____

3.   A bridge is just a bridge until _____

and then it becomes _____

4.   A house is just a house until _____

and then it becomes _____

5.   A _____ is just a _____ until _____

_____ and then it becomes a _____

The Slave Dancer, by Paula Fox. Bradbury Press, 1973.

While walking home late one night through the French Quarter in New Orleans, Jessie Bollier is kidnapped by two members of the crew of *The Moonlight.* He is wrapped in a canvas cloth and forced to walk across a bayou, all the while afraid that a cottonmouth snake is going to attack him. His captors force him onto the ship because they want him to play the fife for Captain Cawthorne. Thinking that he has been abducted to entertain the crew members, Jessie is shocked to learn he will be playing his fife to "dance the slaves." The slaves are being illegally transported from Africa to Cuba aboard *The Moonlight.* During the journey, Jessie befriends a young slave boy named Ras. While trying to escape an American patrol ship during a violent storm, everyone on board dies except for two people. To find out who survives and what happens to them, read *The Slave Dancer.*

Activities

A.   Pre-reading activity: Before each word below, write the number of the heading under which you think it belongs. Guess if you do not know. Then read the description of the book to support or disprove your answers.

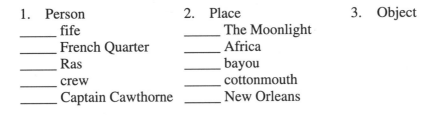

1.   Person
_____ fife
_____ French Quarter
_____ Ras
_____ crew
_____ Captain Cawthorne

2.   Place
_____ The Moonlight
_____ Africa
_____ bayou
_____ cottonmouth
_____ New Orleans

3.   Object

B. Questions to ponder:

1. In the first chapter of the novel, Jessie's mom says to him after he heard a black woman called Star by her master, "Might as well call someone 'shoe'. It's not a human name." How does this quote foreshadow what happens in the novel?

2. Why did Jessie decide to save Ras instead of letting him drown?

3. At the end of the novel, Jessie is a grown man with a child of his own. He says he is unable to listen to any music at all. Why do you think this is so?

4. Why do you think the author, Paula Fox, named this novel *The Slave Dancer*? Can you think of another name for the novel?

5. At first glance there seems to be no similarity between this novel and the children's classic by Beatrix Potter, *The Tale of Peter Rabbit* (Warne, 1987). However, there are many similarities. How many can your group list?

6. Could this same tale have been told in any other setting? Why or why not?

7. How many ways does Jessie change from the beginning to the end of the novel? Can you give a reason for each of the changes?

C. Responding to *The Slave Dancer:* Some people like to pretend that fortunes can be told by looking at a hand of cards. There is no scientific basis for this, of course, but just for fun, suppose that Jessie had had his fortune told before he was kidnapped and taken on board *The Moonlight*. Draw the cards listed below to tell what will happen to Jessie.

Card	Clubs	Hearts	Diamonds	Spades
Ace	wealth, fame	important event at home	something important received	misfortune
2	someone opposes you	success	serious encounter	change of location
3	changes	problems from rash actions	quarrels	bad luck
4	collapse of a favorite project	long delay	clashes with friends	misunderstandings
5	happy relationship	complications	honor won	success in friendship
6	success	dangers	end of a relationship	failure of a project
7	good fortune	fear of others	loss of something	loss of a friend
8	troubles caused by money	happy event	unexpected news	much need for caution
9	bad luck, arguments	getting one's wish	travel	illness or handicap

The House of Dies Drear, by Virginia Hamilton. Macmillan, 1968.

The Small family leases an old Ohio house reportedly haunted by the runaway slaves who died there during the days of the Underground Railroad. Thomas Small, the son, is afraid of and resents old Pluto, the caretaker. Strange shapes appear at night and warning signs are left on doors. The family is not welcomed in the community and Thomas becomes more and more unhappy. Then a series of events leads to the discovery of a treasure trove deep in a cave underground, guarded for many years by Pluto. The Darrow boys want to run Pluto out and get the treasure for themselves. Pluto's son, with the help of the Smalls, foils their plan and the House of Dies Drear finally gives up its secrets.

Activities

A.   Questions to ponder:

1.   Thomas had very negative feelings about the huge old house. What caused these feelings?

2.   How can you explain the many odd things about Pluto? For example, he seemed ill at one moment and well the next.

3.   Why wasn't the Small family welcomed at the church? Was there more than one reason?

4.   Why did Pluto refuse to use any of the treasure, especially when he was so poor?

5.   Give as many reasons as you can why Mayhew hated the town and the people in it.

6.   What do you think should have been done with all of the treasure in the cave?

B.   Thomas thinks he has heard a ghost and goes exploring, only to disturb Pluto, who chases the boy through the woods. Thomas is very frightened but reaches the house safely. Thomas, sleeping downstairs, does not see a dark figure emerge from behind the mirror. It wanders around the house putting something on the door frames.

Design a warning poster the figure might leave to frighten the Small family into moving.

Mr. Lincoln's Drummer Boy, by G. Clifton Wisler. Scholastic, 1995.

Willie enlisted in the Union Army at the age of eleven. He left his ma, two brothers, and the place he called home in Vermont, and boarded a train with his pa to fight in a war. Since he has learned to play drum rolls he knows his job will be to wake the troops in the morning as well as to carry out commands to advance or retreat in battle. The battles did not start immediately; Willie and Pa spend three months at Camp Griffin with little to occupy them. When the battles do begin, there is more suffering and death from the mosquito-ridden swamp in which they find themselves than from battle wounds. Working as a stretcher bearer as well as a drummer boy, Willie becomes ill and after a brief meeting with President Lincoln he is sent to a hospital to recover. Eventually he receives the Congressional Medal of Honor for his valiant service during the battles known as "Seven Days." What an extraordinary accomplishment for an eleven-year-old!

Activities

A.   Questions to ponder:

    1.   Willie and Jeb were on opposite sides in the conflict. List all the ways the two boys were alike.

    2.   List the natural elements that were an enemy to both sides in the war. Rank order your list from the most to the least dangerous.

    3.   Describe the character of Willie. Would he have served the South as honorably as he did the North? Explain.

    4.   Why do you think so many soldiers deserted the camp before the fighting started?

    5.   Would the story have changed if Willie had lost or abandoned his drum? If so, how?

    6.   Other than defending their homes, what reasons did young boys have for joining the military? Were these good reasons? Why or why not?

    7.   Suppose your family had religious beliefs opposing the war. Would you consider yourself a coward for not fighting? How else might you help in the cause?

    8.   How were the women involved in the war, whether on the side of the North or the South?

B.   Willie Johnston and his family live in St. Johnsbury, Vermont. Willie is eleven years old. The year is 1861 and the Civil War has just begun. Find out what members of your class know about the Civil War. Put a classmate's name on any item where he or she can give the correct answer. You can only use a name one time and you can only put your name on one line (even if you know more than one answer). The student who first finds a different name with a correct answer for each line is the winner. Find someone who knows:

    1.   The year the Civil War began. _____

    Name _____

    2.   The year the Civil War ended. _____

    Name _____

    3.   The number of states that formed the Confederacy. _____

    Name _____

    4.   The chief crop of the South in 1860. _____

    Name _____

    5.   The year John Brown raided Harper's Ferry. _____

    Name _____

6.   The President of the Confederacy. _____

Name _____

7.   The year Lincoln became President of the United States. _____

Name _____

8.   The state in which Fort Sumter is located. _____

Name _____

Little House in the Big Woods, by Laura Ingalls Wilder. HarperCollins, 1955 (Originally 1932).

Six-year-old Laura lived in the Big Woods in a nice, cozy log cabin with Ma and Pa and big sister Mary and baby sister Carrie. Ma and Pa worked very hard providing the family with food, shelter, and protection. Laura was happy in the log cabin. She really tried to be good, but never seemed to be as perfect as her blonde-haired sister, who never got dirty and never misbehaved. Sometimes Laura wished she was a boy who could hunt and go sledding. At times things did get exciting. Like the time her mother accidentally slapped a bear, and the time Laura saw the wolves. She especially liked it when Pa would tell stories, like the one about how he was coming home from town and thought he saw a bear, and started hitting it with a big stick, then realized it was a huge tree stump! And there was the wonderful Christmas, the sugar snow, and the dance at Grandpa's. To experience life in pioneer days, read *The Little House in the Big Woods*.

Activities

A.   Questions to ponder:

1.   Compare the noises you hear at night with the noises Laura heard. Which would you rather hear? Why?

2.   Compare the jobs you do at home with the jobs Laura and Mary did. Which seem easier? Why?

3.   List five things that the pioneer family used that we do not use today. Why don't we need these things anymore?

4.   Name instances in which children misbehaved in the story. What happened to the children for misbehaving?

5.   How were the holidays alike and different from the way you celebrate the holidays?

6.   List all the good things about pioneer life. List all the things you think were not so good about pioneer life.

B. Use the following chart to tell how the story of *The Little House in the Big Woods* and *Caroline and Her Kettle Named Maud,* the next book, are alike and different.

	Little House	**Caroline**
Main characters		
Setting		
Main problem		
Daily life		

Caroline and Her Kettle Named Maud, by Miriam Mason. Macmillan, 1951. Grades 2–4.

Caroline was a pioneer girl living on the frontier in the 1830s. Instead of wanting a doll for her birthday, all she really wished for was a bright new shiny gun. Caroline had 17 uncles, some younger than she, and they all had guns. Caroline longed to do brave and dangerous things. However, because she was a girl during the pioneer days, she was expected to grow up, marry, and take care of a family and a home. Caroline's birthday came and much to her anguish she received not a bright new shiny gun but a bright new shiny copper kettle from grandfather. Caroline decided to accept the kettle graciously and even gave it a name, Maud, which means "mighty in battle."

Caroline's family decided to move and live in a wild new country called Michigan. Caroline just knew that she could use a gun in this untamed land because Michigan was known to be the land of vicious animals such as wolverines and wolves. While her uncles took their guns with them, Caroline took her kettle named Maud. However, as Caroline soon discovers, sometimes a kettle is better protection than a gun.

Grasshopper Summer, by Ann Turner. Macmillan, 1989.

Safe. We were safe. We got the land from the government and it was ours as long as we planted 10 acres, built a house, and stayed for five years. That didn't sound so hard. No Northerners could come and take it away. We wouldn't look out one day and see our bottomland all shrunk to nothing, the way Grandpa did after the war.

Sam White likes Kentucky. He likes fishing and joking with his friends; he likes the cool shade under the trees in summer; he likes his grandmother's peach pies and his grandfather's soldierly ways. But Sam's father is restless, still haunted by the bloodshed of the Civil War, and resolves to make a new life for himself and his family in the Dakota Territory. Sam can't stand the idea of leaving behind his grandparents and the orderly, familiar life of their farm.

The journey west is long and hard, and when the White family finally reach the Dakotas, things are harder still. To Sam the sod house they are building feels like a grave, and the endless prairie sky seems empty and unwelcoming. But he does his best to stop missing Kentucky and begins to look forward to their first harvest. Then the grasshoppers come, eating every green thing in sight.

How Sam and his family meet the challenge of this harsh land makes an engrossing story of love and courage in the face of tremendous odds.

Activities

A.   Questions to ponder:

   1.   Pa and Grandpa both fought in the war, yet both had very different ideas about it. How did they differ in their attitudes toward war, and why do you think this was so?

   2.   Ma had to give up some of her ideas about socializing with people and about the behavior she expected from Sam and Billy. How did Ma's thinking change and why do you think it changed?

   3.   If you were Pa, would you want to start all over again after the grasshoppers destroyed your crop? Why or why not?

   4.   Sam changed his opinion of prairie life from the beginning to the end of the novel. What was this change and what do you think caused it?

   5.   Do you think accepting help from the government was charity? Or did the government need the settlers? Give reasons for your answer.

B.   Sam's family packs the wagon with essential items and starts the journey to the Dakota Territory. Pa sings "Oh Susannah" to keep their spirits up. Complete the missing words and sing this song to the tune of "Oh Susannah":

Oh we come from old (1) K _____

And our (2) w _____ is packed full

There's a (3) s _____, an (4) a _____ ,

and Ma's (5) c _____

And some (6) b _____ made of wool.

Chorus:

Grandpa, Grandma, they stood and waved good-bye

Now our home's the open prairie

And our roof's the clear blue sky.

(7) S _____ and (8) B _____ they were brothers

They thought farm life was the best

But their (9) P_____ thought something different

So the family headed (10) W _____ .

A big smile was hard to come by

And their (11) M _____ she shed a tear

But their (12) P _____ said in the future

There was nothing there to fear.

After you have read the entire book, write another verse telling about the grasshoppers.

_____

_____

_____

_____

Old Yeller, by Fred Gipson. HarperCollins, 1956.

The big, ugly, yellow dog showed up out of nowhere one night and stole a whole side of hanging pork, and when Travis went for him the next morning that dog started yelling like a baby before he was touched. Then he got into the spring water with five-year-old Arliss. Travis took an easy hate to Old Yeller, as they started to call him; in fact, he would have driven him off or killed him if it hadn't been for brother Arliss's loud and violent protest. So Yeller stayed, and Travis soon found he couldn't have got along without him.

Pa and Ma and Travis and Arliss lived on Birdsong Creek in the Texas hill country. It wasn't an easy life, but they had a snug cabin that Pa had built himself, they had their own hogs and their own cattle, and they grew most of what else they needed. The only thing they and the rest of the settlers lacked that year in the late 1860s was cash, so the men decided to get together and drive all the cattle up to the new market in Abilene, Kansas, more than 600 miles away.

Travis was only fourteen, but he was proud of his new role as man of the family and determined to live up to his responsibility. It was hard work, too: plowing until his legs ached, chopping wood until his hands were raw and his head was spinning, weeding the garden in the hot sun, toting the heavy buckets up from the spring, and trying to keep his mischievous little brother in line.

But there were pleasant moments, too: his Ma treating him like a man, and deer hunting in the early-morning stillness, and hot summer nights out in the corn patch under the stars with Old Yeller, trying to keep the coons and skunks out of the winter food supply. And there was plenty of excitement, like the fight between the two bulls, and the time Arliss nearly got mauled by the bear, and trying to catch and mark the new hogs. At this point in the story the suspense and excitement reach a peak, only to be topped a few pages later when the crazy-sick loafer wolf goes for Ma. Both times it is Yeller who saves them, only the second time it is not lucky for Yeller, as Travis comes to find out. And in finding out, Travis learns just how much he has come to love that big ugly dog, and he learns something about the pain of life, too.

Activities

A. Questions to ponder:

1. List the responsibilities Travis was expected to carry when his father left on the cattle drive. Rank order your list from the most to the least difficult.

2. Why do you think Mama allowed Travis to do very dangerous jobs like marking the hogs when she knew he could be injured or killed?

3. Travis had mixed feelings about Arliss. What were these feelings?

4. What did Travis learn about life?

B. Pa leaves on a cattle drive and Travis becomes the man of the family. At fourteen he plows, weeds, hunts, chops wood, and tries to keep his little brother, Arliss, in line. He wants no part of the ugly yellow dog that shows up one day and steals the meat.
    Write about the story setting:

Old Yeller takes place in the hill country of Texas in 1860. This setting is essential in the story

since _____

_____ .

The author uses the phrase _____

_____

to help the reader actually see the setting.

Use the pattern below to create a five senses poem about _____

_____ .

Use the most descriptive words possible to help year reader see _____

_____ .

Use the pattern below to describe the hill country.

The Hill Country

The hill country is the color of _____

It sounded like _____

_____

It smelled like _____

_____

It tasted like _____

_____

It looked like _____

_____

It made me feel like _____

_____

A Family Apart, by Joan Lowery Nixon. Bantam Books, 1989.

The Orphan Train saga begins in 1860 in New York City, where the Kelly family lives in dire poverty. When Mrs. Kelly, a young widow, realizes that she cannot give her six children the life they deserve, she makes the ultimate sacrifice of love and sends them west on the orphan train to begin again with new families. The children—Petey, 6; Peg, 7; Danny, 10; Mike, 11; Megan, 12; and especially 13-year-old Frances Mary—feel that their mother has betrayed and abandoned them. Their mother's comfort and love has made hunger and poverty easier to bear; now it seems as if Ma doesn't feel the same way about them.

After a long journey to St. Joseph, Missouri, the children find they will be separated not only from their mother but also from one another. One by one they are adopted by Western families, some looking for children to love, others only seeking cheap farm labor. Some of the families come from as far away as Kansas, and it looks as if the Kellys may never be reunited.

Frances, the oldest of the children, records in the Orphan Train Quartet how the Kellys face these separations and the adventures they encounter in their new lives. This novel, the first of the quartet, tells of Frances's decision to masquerade as a boy to protect her youngest brother. Frances's adventure eventually involves her in the activities of the Underground Railroad and helps her to learn the true meaning of her mother's sacrifice.

Activities

A. Questions to ponder:

1. Did Ma have other ways to see her children were well cared for?

2. If a law hurts people, should it be broken?

3. Give reasons people gave up comfortable lives in the East to go West to a life of hardship.

4. Was it Mike's fault the children were sent west? Why or why not?

5. How did Frances come to understand her mother's sacrifice?

B. Danny and Mike shine shoes to help out. Frances Mary follows Mike one day and catches him stealing. She tries to convince him that stealing is wrong; a policeman shows up, grabs Mike, and takes him away.

Writing about scary things: Use your imagination to complete each sentence below:

1. Not having enough food in the house to eat is scary but _____

_____ is terrifying.

2. Being pushed in front of a horse and carriage is scary but _____

_____ is terrifying.

3. Watching your brother knock into a man to take his money is scary but _____

_____ is terrifying.

4. Seeing your brother grabbed by the police is scary but _____

_____ is terrifying.

5. Not having any money is scary but _____

_____ is terrifying.

6. Losing your job is scary but _____

_____ is terrifying.

WORLD WAR II

Number the Stars, by Lois Lowry. Houghton Mifflin, 1989.

Ten-year-old Annemarie Johansen and her best friend Ellen Rosen don't run home from school anymore. Anyone running in the streets of Copenhagen is suspicious in the eyes of the Germans, who have occupied the country since 1940. It is now 1943 and life for the girls is filled with school, rationing, food shortages, and the ever-present Nazi soldiers marching in their town.

Tiny Denmark, with its kindly King Christian and no army, had no choice but to surrender early in the war. The beloved king still rode his horse through the streets each day, bringing courage to the hearts of the Danes, and he was never touched by the soldiers. Then, in 1943, a difficult life became unbearable. Jewish leaders in Denmark received word from a high German official who was sympathetic to their cause that all Jews were to be "relocated." How could the Johansens hide their friends the Rosens in their tiny apartment? The only one who could be hidden was Ellen, who became the Johansen's third daughter. What reprisals there would be if Ellen were found! Yet the Johansens remembered the courage it took for the Danes to sink their own navy to keep it from the Germans. Could they show less courage to protect an innocent child? Before Ellen and her family can make the dangerous boat trip to Sweden and freedom, Annemarie must undertake a mission filled with peril. Somehow she must find the strength and courage to save her best friend's life. There is no turning back.

Activities

A. Pre-reading activity: Before reading the novel, decide if these statements are fact or fiction:

1. Rationing of sugar, coffee, meat, and many other goods was a daily reality in Denmark during World War II.

2. Denmark surrendered to the Germans without a fight because it was a small country with no army.

3. King Christian was the leader of Denmark before the Germans occupied the country in 1940.

4. The Germans controlled the newspapers, rail system, government, schools, hospitals, and day-to-day experiences of the Danes but they never controlled King Christian.

5. The Danes sank their entire naval fleet in Copenhagen harbor to keep the Germans from using it.

6. A man named G. F. Duckwitz, who held a high position in Germany, warned Jewish leaders in Denmark of the coming relocation of Jews. Because of this early warning, most of Denmark's Jews escaped.

B. Questions to ponder:

1. In how many different ways was bravery demonstrated in the story?

2. If you were a member of the Rosen family, what might you have done when word of the Jewish "relocation" was received?

3. What might have happened if the German soldiers had not allowed Annemarie to get to her uncle's boat?

4. What do you think the title means?

5. How many other stories can you name in which bravery plays an important part? How are any of these stories and *Number the Stars* alike?

C. You can give a reader insight into a book character with a cinquain. A cinquain is a short, five-line poem that follows a definite pattern, but does not require any rhyme. Example:

Line 1	one word	David
Line 2	two words, descriptive	Gentle caregiver
Line 3	three words, action	Healing sick animals
Line 4	four words, phrase/thought	Actions like soothing medicine
Line 5	synonym for line 1	Veterinarian

Select one of these characters from *Number the Stars*:

Lise Johansen   Annemarie Johansen
Inge Johansen   Uncle Henrik
Peter Neilsen   Ellen Rosen

Brainstorm the character. Try to capture something special about the character you select, something that makes the character stand out as unique. Then create a cinquain about that character.

D. The "Mystery Person Game":

1. Read a biography about a person from Denmark or a person connected with World War II.

2. List 12 facts about the person. Do not put the facts in any kind particular order.

3. Ask: "Who would like to play the mystery person game?" Tell your classmates that (one at a time) they may give you a number between 1 and 12. You will read the clue for that number. The person selecting the number can then guess who the person is or pass. Classmates continue giving numbers and hearing the clues until the mystery person's identity is guessed or all clues have been read.

4. Be sure to tell those playing the game that if they think they know the mystery person's identity and it is not their turn, they should please *not call out* the answer. Simply raise your hand to select the next number.

WHO AM I ?????

1. I always wanted to be an actor and spent some time on the stage.

2. I am not a citizen of the United States.

3. My writings have been translated into more languages than any other book except the Bible.

4. A statue of me is located in Lincoln Park in Chicago.

5. I left home to seek my fortune at the age of 14.

6. I have often met with failure.

7. I consider my plays to be my best work.

8. I was often an honored guest of kings.

9. I was a lonely child and spent a lot of time on the docks with the fishmongers.

10. My father supported us by mending shoes.

11. I was born in 1805.

12. My works, including "The Ugly Duckling" and "The Little Mermaid," were first translated into English in 1846.

Answer: Hans Christian Andersen

Snow Treasure, by Marie McSwigan. Illustrated by Andre LaBlanc. Scholastic, 1958.

Hitler's troops had been relentlessly moving across Europe, and in this early spring of 1940, they were poised to invade Norway. The people of Norway were not sure they could fend off the Nazi troops, but they were resolved that if they were overrun, the Germans would not use Norway's resources against them. Their main concern was 40 million Kroner in gold bullion.

The decision was made to smuggle the gold out of the country, and the only way they could do that once the Germans were there was to send it to the coast with the sledding children. The gold would be sent out from Peter's home town, and he and the other children would be the ones to smuggle it on sleds past the Germans.

The children bravely agreed to the task, but questions remained. How would they respond physically to the almost daily 12-mile sled runs over six weeks' time? What would they do if they were bothered by the soldiers or if the German commandant ordered them to stop? Read this exciting tale to discover that giant-sized heroes and heroines can come in small packages.

Activities

A. Pre-reading activity:

1. Examine a map of Europe in the 1930s that shows the countries that Germany invaded and when each was invaded. (Familiarize the reader with the setting.)

2. Small groups:

Create a list of the qualities of a hero.

Discuss what it takes for an adolescent to be a hero.

What is the difference between being brave and being a hero?

List adolescents you consider to be heroes and be prepared to tell why they are on your list.

Share with the class.

3. Answer these questions in groups:

What does a fiord have to do with Norway?

Why might someone who works with bullion know the term Kroner?

Why might a child be afraid of a commandant? A long winter with good snow for sledding should make children's days filled with carefree fun. That is, if times are normal. In Norway of 1940 times were anything but normal.

B. Questions to ponder:

1. Contrast Jan's reasons for saving Peter with Peter's reasons for his action that caused him to get put into jail (heroism vs. bravery).

2. Analyze the relationship shown between these adolescents and the adults of Riswyk.

3. Discuss the particular features of Norway that enabled the people to save their gold from the Germans.

4. Evaluate the adults' decision to involve their children in the saving of the gold bullion.

C. Creative thinking:

Fluency: The ability to make many responses. Name many possible ways to smuggle bags of money past the enemy soldiers who are watching you.

Flexibility: Finding new categories; stretching the mind beyond the expected response. How can you group the items you named under fluency?

Originality: Responding in new or original ways. What group and/or items did you name that no one else named?

Elaboration: Adding details to make a product more complete. Add features to a basic sled to make the sled more useful or attractive.

Planning: Determining a task to be done, the steps to take, materials needed, and possible problems. Plan an exciting way to present the book *Snow Treasure* to another class. Assume that the students in the class have not read the book and you want to get them excited about reading it.

Forecasting: Determining cause and effect. What might cause a country to smuggle its gold out of the country? What effect would enemy troops have on the daily lives of the people in an occupied country?

D.   Responding to the novel—comparing attitudes: For each pair of statements, below choose the one that you believe is closest to the truth. Then choose the one that Peter, in *Snow Treasure*, would choose.

MY Choice	Peter's Choice
1.	1.
2.	2.
3.	3.
4.	4.
5.	5.

1.   a.   Often the negative things in people's lives are caused by bad luck.

   b.   Often the negative things in people's lives are caused by their mistakes.

2.   a.   People who are prejudiced are not at fault; it is their parents who taught them their prejudice.

   b.   People who are prejudiced have chosen to accept the prejudice of their parents.

3.   a.   There have always been wars, and there will always be wars, regardless of some people's efforts to prevent them.

   b.   If people made more effort to be aware of current events, they could see the power of their vote to prevent future wars.

4.   a.   No matter how much many people have, they will usually want more, and will go to any lengths to get it from others.

   b.   Many people are quite satisfied with what they have, and are not often jealous of those who have more.

5.   a.   Often I have found that "what will be, will be."

   b.   Often I have found it is better to plan my actions than to trust to fate.

Are there any choices where you and Peter disagree? Explain why you think the two of you would not agree on at least one choice.

The Big Lie, by Isabella Leitner. Scholastic, 1992.

This is the story of a Jewish Hungarian family and their sufferings under the Nazis during World War II.

Activities

A.   In March 1944 the Nazis took over Hungary. If you were a Jewish child in that place at that time you would not be allowed to:

___ Own or listen to a radio
___ Ride a bicycle
___ Go to school
___ Talk to a non-Jew in public
___ Walk outside with your parents after 7:00 P.M.

Rank order these from the restriction you would find most difficult to the least difficult one.

B.   Vocabulary: Use as many words as you can in one sentence to describe what life in Hungary would be like for a Jewish child in 1944 (Add other words as needed): Hungary, ancient, Nazi, invaded, rumors, Jews, unimportant, shopkeepers, threatened, ally, broadcast, overturned, confusion, orders, obeyed, previously, mistake, punishment, bicycle, celebrate, separated, fearful, gendarmes, bayonet, terrified, courtyard, ghetto, disappeared, protection

C.   Sentence starters: Write for five minutes on the one you choose from the following list. Share orally with a small group.

1.   Having four sisters and one brother ...

2.   Rumors can be alarming when ...

3.   Discrimination means ...

4.   Reasons not to celebrate a birthday ...

D.   Chapter projects:

Chapter One

In March 1944, Isabella's family hears rumors of persecution of the Jews by the Nazis, but all seems quiet in her small town until Sanyi, a friend, arrives with news that the Germans have invaded Budapest.

Activity: Create a dialogue between Sanyi and Isabella. How will she reply?

S: Let me in! Let me in, please!

I: _____

S: The Germans invaded Budapest yesterday. They are seizing all the Jews.

I: _____

S: I was in the library when Nazis with guns rushed in.

I: _____

S: I escaped through an open window. Please hide me until sunset. I'll be gone after dark.

I: _____

S: Your family must leave now while you can.

Chapters Two and Three

Many restrictions are placed on all Jews in Hungary. Finally they are sent to the ghetto, marched from the ghetto to a cattle car, and travel by train for two days to Auschwitz, with no food or water.

Activity: Describe the ghetto in a five senses report.

The ghetto is: _____

It sounds like: _____

It tastes like: _____

It smells like: _____

It looks like: _____

It made Isabella feel like: _____

Chapter Four

At Auschwitz, the German doctor, Josel Mengele, separates the weak from the strong. Isabella and her older sisters are separated from her mother and baby sister. Their hair is cut off. Philip tells Isabella they must eat to survive. Isabella shows many feelings in these first four chapters.

Activity: Choose four different feelings and explain when Isabella had that feeling and why.

brave	cautious	foolish
scared	impatient	upset
helpless	wicked	happy
caring	unhappy	confused
optimistic	terrified	

Chapter Five

Thousands are put to death in the camp. Others look like walking skeletons. Prisoners are shot for little or no reason. A message on a carved piece of wood comes from Philip: "You must live. You simply must. I love you."

Activity: Create a message Isabella might send in reply. Send the message in a code you devise.

Chapter Six

Late in 1944 the girls are forced on a three-week death march. They escape in a blizzard and take shelter in an empty house. They then see Russian tanks and trucks on the road.

Activity: Describe Isabella in a bio-poem:

> *Name*
> *Four traits*
> *Related to*
> *Who has*
> *Who needs*
> *Who fears*
> *Who gives*
> *Who would like to*
> *Resident of*

Chapter Seven

The girls make their way to a railroad station and a train that takes them out of Germany. With help they finally arrive in America and have a bittersweet reunion with their father.

Hitler's "Big Lie" was that the Jews caused Germany's unemployment problems. He put to death nearly six million Jewish people. This was called the Holocaust.

Activity: Create a time line of events that led to the Holocaust.

Journey Home, by Yoshiko Uchida. Atheneum, 1978.

Twelve-year-old Yuki and her parents have just been released from Topaz, one of many concentration camps in which all West Coast Japanese in the United States were imprisoned during World War II. Although they are welcomed by a loyal friend, Mrs. Jamieson, returning to Berkeley is not easy. There are no houses to rent, Papa cannot find a job, and former friends have changed. In the climate of fear and distrust created by the war, many people had come to hate the Japanese, as Yuki and her family painfully learn.

Yuki's best friend, Emi, and her grandmother join them in trying to start a new life; so does old Mr. Oka, whom they meet in their makeshift lodgings. Their joint venture is almost destroyed by anti-Japanese violence, however, and, even the return of Yuki's brother Ken, wounded in the war, brings another disappointment. But eventually they find new hope and strengths in themselves, and Yuki discovers that coming home is a matter of the heart and spirit.

This warm and authentic story gives a sensitive glimpse into a tragic episode in our country's history. Yuki and her family and friends will remain in the reader's mind as immensely likable and courageous people.

Activities

A. Questions to ponder:

1. Do you think Emi's grandmother was foolish to refuse to leave the camp without her husband's bones? Why or why not?

2. How did Mrs. Henley show prejudice in the conversation she had with Yuki?

3. Yuki's dream of returning to California came true but did not at first bring happiness. Why?

4. Why would an adult say cruel things to a child of a different race? How can prejudice be eliminated in a society?

5. What was the role of the Olssens in the story? How did their loss help Ken?

6. How does the title, *Journey Home,* reflect the theme of the book?

B.   Thinking like Uncle Oka: For each pair of statements, choose the one that you think Uncle Oka would agree with. Briefly state why you think he would make that choice. Then decide what your choice would be. Do you think like Uncle Oka?

1.   a.   Often the negative things in people's lives are caused by bad luck.

     b.   Often the negative things in people's lives are caused by their mistakes.

     _____

2.   a.   People who are prejudiced are not at fault; it is their parents who taught them their prejudice.

     b.   People who are prejudiced have chosen to accept the prejudice of their parents.

     _____

3.   a.   There have always been wars, and there will always be wars, regardless of some people's efforts to prevent them.

     b.   If people made more effort to be aware of current events, they could see the power of their vote to prevent future wars.

     _____

4.   a.   No matter how much many people have, they will usually want more, and will go to any lengths to get it from others.

     b.   Many people are quite satisfied with what they have, and are not often jealous of those who have more.

     _____

5.   a.   Often I have found that "what will be, will be".

     b.   Often I have found it is better to plan my actions than to trust to fate.

     _____

SEVEN

Heroines and Heroes

To find role models for the gifted child, visit the biography shelves in any library. Here are accounts of the lives of human beings, both men and women, who displayed extraordinary courage in reaching their life goals. Read about Kate Shelley, a young farm girl who risked her life to save the lives of passengers in an oncoming train; Neil Armstrong, the first man to set foot on the moon; Pocahontas, who gave up the world she knew to live and die in a foreign land; Susanna, the heroic survivor of the Alamo; Bob Lemmons, who runs with the wild mustangs day and night until they accept his presence; and Mary Breckenridge, who saved more lives with her Frontier Nursing Service than Clara Barton and Florence Nightingale combined.

Among fictional heroines and heroes who can serve as role models for the young are courageous Caddie Woodlawn, who singlehandedly stops an uprising; Robin, from *The Door in the Wall,* who, despite his handicap, saves the castle from attack; Charlotte Doyle, who climbs the mast of a pitching sailing ship; and Karana, who survives alone on the *Island of the Blue Dolphins*. These and many more heroes and heroines are introduced in this chapter, along with activities to foster greater understanding of the literature and to provide for creative responses.

HEROINES: PICTURE BOOKS

Heroines do not necessarily have to perform brave deeds or save the lives of hundreds of people. One can become a heroine by following a passion for the one thing that a person does best. Arizona was a teacher and followed her passion all of her life to better the lives of those she taught, even at the cost of giving up other dreams she might have pursued.

My Great-Aunt Arizona, by Gloria Houston. Illustrated by Susan Condie Lamb. HarperCollins, 1992.

Arizona was born in a log cabin her papa built. She grew into a tall girl who liked to sing, square-dance, and—most of all—read and dream of the faraway places she would visit one day.

Arizona never did make it to those places. Instead she became a teacher, helping generations of children in the one-room schoolhouse that she herself had attended. When Arizona married and had a daughter, the baby went to school with her. For 57 years Arizona taught not only reading, writing, and arithmetic, but also how to make dreams come true even if they aren't exactly the dreams one started with.

Activities

A.   Questions to ponder:

1.   Was Arizona's life a happy one even though she did not travel to faraway places? Why or why not?

2.   Which of the things Arizona and her brother did to have fun as children would you like to do? Can your group agree on the one thing you would like most to do?

3.   In the blab school all the children read their lessons aloud at the same time. Do you think this is a good idea? Why or why not?

4.   Arizona rode a mule through the snow to get to school. Would it be more fun to go to school this way than on a school bus? Why or why not?

5.   Why do you think Arizona brought a Christmas tree to school in a pot instead of having one cut down?

6.   How would your life be different if everyone had to travel in a wagon pulled by horses?

7.   Would you have liked to be a pupil in Miss Arizona's school? Why or why not?

B.   Play the "Mystery Game": Use the following clues to discover the mystery word. One student selects a number. The clue for that number is read. The student can guess the mystery word or pass. The game continues until the word is guessed or all clues have been read.

1.   You can do it alone.

2.   You can do it with someone.

3.   You can wear special shoes to do it.

4.   Some people wear costumes to do it.

5.   Some are slow and some are fast.

6.   Children do it.

7.   Arizona liked to do it.

8.   You can take lessons to learn it.

9.   Music is an important part of it.

10.   You need a beat

C. Arizona loved the changing seasons. In summer she went barefoot and caught tadpoles. In the fall she climbed mountains. In the winter she made snow cream and helped Papa tap the maple trees. Arizona might have described winter this way:

> *Winter is white like freshly washed sheets*
> *It sounds like bells as icicles touch in the wind*
> *It tastes like maple syrup candy*
> *It smells like warm wood-burning fires*
> *It looks like a Snow Queen's ice palace*
> *It makes me feel like making snow cream.*

Use the same pattern to describe summer or fall as Arizona might have seen it.

_____ is _____

(Season)   (Color)

like _____

It sounds like _____

It tastes like _____

It smells like _____

It looks like _____

It makes me feel like _____

_____

Mystery word: Dance.

Rose Blanche, by Roberto Innocenti. Harcourt Brace, 1985.

Rose Blanche, who lives in Germany during World War II, watches from school windows as the trucks roll by. She wonders where the trucks are going and what they contain. One day a truck stopped and a little boy jumped from the truck and tried to run away but was quickly caught. Rose wanted to know where the little boy went, so on foot she followed the trucks. She was stopped by barbed wire. Behind the wire were children who said they were hungry. Rose gave them the bit of bread she had with her, then day after day she saved what she could of her meals and took the food to the children. It was a dangerous trip because if she were caught the consequences would be grave. Then one day as Rose made her way to the hungry children, the people left the town and new trucks with soldiers with different uniforms rolled in. Rose was at the camp and did not know of Germany's defeat. A shot rang out, for the new soldiers saw the enemy everywhere, and Rose gave her life for the hungry children.

Activities

A. Create a dialogue between Rose and her mother. How will Rose reply to Mother's questions concerning her "lack of appetite?"

MOTHER   Rose, are you ill? Why aren't you finishing your meal?

ROSE   _____

_____

MOTHER   You know how hard the war has made it to get decent food. You must eat every bite.

ROSE   _____

_____

MOTHER   I don't understand why you are taking more to eat at school than you do at home.

ROSE   _____

_____

_____

_____

Although Rose did not expect to lose her life in her quest to feed the hungry children, she did know the dangers in the daily trips she made. Had her kindness been discovered, punishment would have been swift and severe. To survive her many trips to help the hungry children, Rose had to show great courage. Write about the courageous things she did. The first letter of each sentence will begin with the letters in COURAGE.

C _____

O _____

U _____

R _____

A _____

G _____

E _____

Miss Rumphius, by Barbara Cooney. Viking, 1982.

Some heroines work in their own quiet way to make the world a better place. This is true of Miss Rumphius, who left the world a more beautiful place than she found it.

Miss Rumphius's first name was Alice. When she was small she dreamed of traveling to faraway places and living by the sea. Her grandfather told her that she must also make the world a more beautiful place in which to live.

Miss Rumphius *did* travel to faraway places and saw coconuts and cockatoos on tropical islands, lions in the grasslands, and monkeys in the jungle. On a hillside she found lupine and jasmines growing and rode a camel across the desert to meet a kangaroo in an Australian town.

Yes, Miss Rumphius did almost everything she wanted to do. In her later years she even lived by the sea. But what could she do to make the world a more beautiful place? She decided to plant the seeds gathered in her travels and cover the land by the sea where she lived with beautiful lupines. Indeed, she became known as "The Lupine Lady."

Activities

A.   Pre-reading activity: Before hearing the description, put a "J" in front of any word below that would be found in a jungle, a "D" in front of things found in the desert, an "I" in front of things found on a tropical island, and an "M" in front of things found on a mountain.

_____ 1. lupine	_____ 2. lions	_____ 3. coconut
_____ 4. cockatoos	_____ 5. jasmine	_____ 6. mother-of-pearl
_____ 7. kangaroos	_____ 8. camels	_____ 9. monkey

What ideas do you have to make the world a more beautiful place?

B.   A writing activity: In this book you will discover that Alice's favorite flower is the lupine. Following is an acrostic poem that describes the lupine. Choose your favorite flower and write an acrostic poem about it.

L   *upines are beautiful flowers that bloom*
U   *p after you*
P   *lant the seed*
I   *n the ground. One day you*
N   *otice their beautiful rose and purple colors, but*
E   *ventually they will begin to wilt.*

Susanna of the Alamo, by John Jakes. Illustrated by Paul Bacon. Harcourt Brace, 1986.

"Remember the Alamo!" is a cry that evokes memories of Davy Crockett, Jim Bowie, and William Barrett Travis, three of the many heroes who died there. But few remember Susanna Dickinson, the woman of quiet courage and unwavering resolve who survived the massacre to tell its story. Were it not for Susanna, the Alamo might have been forgotten.

Susanna was spared death at the Alamo by Mexico's General Santa Anna so that she could bear witness of his might to Sam Houston's rebel Texas army. But Susanna scorned the general's attempt to make her his emissary. Her chilling story instead provoked a rage and inspired a memory that fired the strength of Houston's badly outnumbered Texans. They decisively defeated Santa Anna at San Jacinto and their victory assured Texas's independence from Mexico.

Activities

A. Pre-reading activities—pre-reading journal sentence starters: Before reading *Susanna of the Alamo*, choose one of the open-ended sentence starters below. Complete the sentence and write about the topic for 10 minutes. Write from your own experience with the topic. Be prepared to share what you have written with a small group.

1. Leaving a place where you have always lived and settling in a new area would be ...

2. Not being able to read or write would not be a handicap for a pioneer woman because ...

3. Freedom is worth defending because ...

4. Living in one place with a large group of people would be difficult in some ways ...

5. Living in one place with a large group of people would be desirable when ...

6. When a person knows he or she cannot win a disagreement, the best thing to do is ...

7. Being offered a reward not to report an injustice ...

8. Bravery in the face of an enemy can be shown by ...

9. Other stories where people face an overwhelming enemy are ...

10. A "larger-than-life" super hero would possess these qualities ...

11. Strength can be shown in quiet ways when ...

12. Losing a loved one in battle is ...

13. A non violent way to solve a disagreement between nations would be to ...

14. Revenge can never be rewarding because ...

15. Historic buildings should be preserved for future generations to see because ...

B. A legend—creative writing: Susanna Dickinson was a *legendary* heroine. While she was a real person, so many stories have been told about her and others at the Alamo that it is difficult for historians to tell fact from fiction. We know that Susanna refused Santa Anna's offer to educate her child and provide her with a life of ease in Mexico, but throughout the rest of her life she refused to talk about her experiences at the Alamo. Create a legend about her and her bravery at the Alamo.

Title: _____

    Here is an account of one incident in the life of Susanna Dickinson. It is not clear whether this incident actually occurred, but knowing what history tells us about the life and adventures of this brave woman, it could possibly be true.

It happened _____ _____

when where

_____ that _____

name

was _____

_____

_____

_____

_____ .

The reaction of the folks around was _____

_____

_____

_____

Kate Shelley: Bound for Legend, by Robert D. San Souci. Dial Books, 1995.

Once in a while an ordinary person performs a deed so brave and unexpected that we remember it long afterward. Kate Shelley was such a person. In the midst of a torrential storm in the summer of 1881, a dreadful train wreck occurred near 15-year-old Kate's Iowa farm. Instantly Kate knew she must go for help and warn an oncoming train of the danger up ahead. Risking her life, she set out through the treacherous night to find the survivors of the wreck, then crawled over the slippery tracks of a 700-foot railroad bridge on her rescue mission. This is the tale of an unforgettable young girl whose great courage and humanity are still remembered today.

Activities

A.   Create a Kate Shelley data bank:

Lived	**Description**	**Has**	**What She Did**
Iowa—1881	15 years old	little schooling	plowed and planted
near Honey Creek	dark hair	love of railroads	ran the family farm
by train tracks	work-worn hands	determination	shot hawks
on a farm	courageous	sense of duty	rode bareback
near Des Moines River	responsible	inner strength	read a lot
clapboard house	hard working	a bridge named	prevented a train
		after her	wreck saved lives
			of two men
			made a dangerous
			journey alone

Related to
deceased father (railroad man)
invalid mother
sister Mayme, brother John
deceased brother James

Remembered for
making dangerous journey
alone at night in a storm to
stop trains from crossing a
bridge that was out.

B. What Ever Happened to …:

   Read the information in the data bank about Kate Shelley. Use the information to write about her using the following pattern:

What ever happened to _____

Did she _____

Maybe she _____

Or could it be that _____

_____

Was there _____

Maybe someday we will know the truth that _____

_____

Fortunately Kate Shelley was a responsible, hard working girl. Unfortunately she had to do most of the work on the farm where she lived. Continue the pattern to tell about Kate's life.

HEROINES: NOVELS

Adventures with a Female Indiana Jones!

The Drakenberg Adventure, by Lloyd Alexander. Dutton, 1988.

   The Grand Duchess of the proud but poor Kingdom of Drakenberg invites 18-year-old Vesper Holly and her aunt and uncle to the Diamond Jubilee celebration … but alas, it may be the final year of existence for Drakenberg. The country is so poor that it is about to be overtaken by a larger country.

   Unfortunately, the sinister Dr. Helvitius also arrives in Drakenberg, with two objectives: to kill Vesper and her guardians and to bleed tiny Drakenberg of any treasures it might own. Vesper is determined to prevent Helvitius from stealing anything from Drakenberg and to find a way to save the small country from oblivion.

Activities

A. Clue cards:

   1. Work in groups of four. Each group member gets one clue card.

   2. Clues must be shared orally. Notes can be taken.

   3. By sharing clues can your group discover:

      a. What treasure did Dr. Helvitius find?

      b. How did he plan to get it out of the country?

      c. How did Vesper thwart Dr. Helvitius's plan?

      d. How did Drakenberg find income to survive?

CLUE CARD

In the Duchy of Drakenberg those
who commit a crime must forfeit all
of their property to the Duchy.
Schwanfeld Castle's lands are rich in
bauxite (aluminum)
Dr. Helvitius has a special cheese
barrel made with a false compartment.

CLUE CARD

Dr. Helvitius takes a barrel of cheese to the
train station and pays to have it shipped to
Carpathia, a neighboring kingdom.
Dr. Helvitius is an art lover who would risk
anything (even commit a crime) to own a
valuable painting.
Schwanfeld Castle and Drakenberg Palace
are both located in the Duchy of Drakenberg.

CLUE CARD

Dr. Helvitius tricked the owner into selling him
Schwanfeld Castle.
The baggage handler switched the barrels.
Vesper Holly bought a real cheese in an
ordinary cheese barrel on the morning the
train was to depart for Carpathia.

CLUE CARD

A fifteenth-century Da Vinci painting was stored
away in the cellar of Schwanfeld Castle and forgotten.
It is a crime to remove art treasures from the Duchy
of Drakenberg.
Vesper Holly has a friend who is a train baggage
handler.

Answers: a.) A fifteenth-century Da Vinci painting; b.) He planned to smuggle it out on a train hidden in a cheese barrel; c.) Vesper got her friend, the baggage handler to switch cheese barrels; d.) Selling the bauxite from the land taken from Helvitius.

The Jedera Adventure, by Lloyd Alexander. E. P. Dutton, 1989.

Vesper Holly needs to return a library book that is 15 years overdue. This seems like a rather simple task; however, this undaunted and determined young lady lives in Philadelphia and the library is in the rugged North African country of Jedera. The postal system of 1874 could not be trusted with the undertaking of returning the valuable book, so with her trusted and long-suffering guardian, Brinnie, Vesper embarks on a great escapade that will lead her right into the teeth of a desert war. Will she be able to match her wits with the cunning and evil Dr. Helvitius and will the mysterious blue-skinned warrior, An Jalil Es Siba, be her savior or her destroyer?

Activities

A. Questions to ponder:

1. Find three examples of rarity in the book and explain in your own words why they had value.

2. Find an example of a natural resource that was useful in helping Vesper to return her book.

3. For Vesper to return the library book and defeat her enemies, what resources were needed? Natural? Human? Capital?

4. What resources were missing that made Bal-Saaba such a terrible place to live?

5. How does the story show how Vesper uses her resources to produce good?

6. How does the story show how Dr. Helvitius uses his resources for evil gain?

B. "Mystery Country Report": While the country of Jedera is fictional, many African countries have come into existence in the past century, while others have existed for hundreds of years. Select one country of Africa and read about it. List 10 things you discovered. One of the ten should be a "give away" clue, one that reveals the name of the country in some way.

Play the "Mystery Country" game with your class. A student selects a number between 1 and 10. You read the clue for that number and the student can guess the name of the country or pass. If the student does not guess correctly, then another student chooses a number and you read the clue for that number. Continue until the country is guessed or all clues have been read.

Here are clues for the country Egypt:

1. The official language of this country is Arabic.

2. This country is almost square in shape.

3. The Mediterranean Sea forms the northern boundary of this country.

4. The Nile River runs through this country.

5. The capital of this country is Cairo.

6. This country has a very dry climate and rain seldom falls.

7. The Great Sphinx can be found in this country.

8. This country was granted independence from Britain in 1922.

9. This country was invaded by Germany in 1940.

10. The name of this country begins with an E and ends with a T.

The Double Life of Pocahontas, by Jean Fritz. Putnam, 1983.

Pocahontas, an Indian princess, daughter of Chief Powhatan, befriends the English settler, John Smith, who is adopted into the tribe. When fire destroys Jamestown, the English settlement, she visits often, bringing food. But a series of poor leaders cause the settlers and the Indians to war with each other. During one winter, most of the settlers starve, but more arrive. Hostilities increase and Pocahontas is kidnapped. Christian beliefs are forced on her and she eventually marries an Englishman. Caught between two worlds, she journeys to England with her husband and son, where she dies, never resolving the conflict of identity that was her life.

Activities

A. Questions to ponder:

1. Why do you think John Smith was the only Englishman able to get along with the Indians?

2. Did Pocahontas truly accept Christian beliefs? Why or why not?

3. List reasons for the early failure of the Jamestown settlement. Which do you think was the most important reason, and why?

4. Why do you suppose John Smith waited such a long time to visit Pocahontas in London?

5. Would it be true to say that after three years of marriage, John Rolfe did not really understand his wife? Why or why not?

6. In what ways does Pocahontas symbolize the problems faced by North American Indians today?

B. A Pocahontas time capsule: List things that were very important to Pocahontas.

_____   _____

_____   _____

_____   _____

_____   _____

_____   _____

Now select five of the things that Pocahontas might place in a time capsule for people to find a hundred years in the future. Attach a note to each one telling why this person thinks the item would have lasting significance.

1. _____   _____
2. _____   _____
3. _____   _____
4. _____   _____
5. _____   _____

C.   Contemporaries:

In the ovals below, list four famous people who lived at the same time in history as Pocahontas (one is done for you).

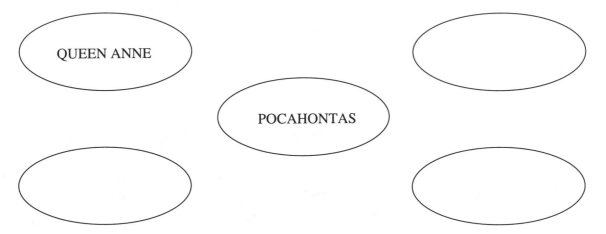

Write a brief conversation between Pocahontas and one of these people.

_____
_____
_____
_____
_____
_____
_____
_____

Caddie Woodlawn, by Carol Ryrie Brink. Little Brown, 1976.

In 1864 on the Wisconsin frontier it was hard to tell which of the Woodlawn family were boys. Caddie could run and jump and climb trees as easily as her brothers Tom and Warren, and much to the dismay of her mother and sister, Clara. But because of Caddie's adventurous spirit, a conflict with the neighboring Indian tribe (with whose leader, Indian John, Caddie has become friends) is avoided. Here is a tale of pioneer life as it was lived and of a spirited young girl whose parents despair of her ever becoming ladylike.

Activities

A.   Questions to ponder:

1.   Suppose Caddie had not made the ride to Indian John's camp to warn him. Predict what might have happened.

2.   The author shows two sides of Obediah, the bully and the hero. Why do you suppose she did this?

3.   What is courage? In what way did the different characters in this novel display courage?

4.   Compare Caddie's frontier life with your life. What would be the positive aspects of living on the frontier? The negative aspects?

5.   If the family had decided to go to England their life there would have been very different. Do you think Caddie would adapt to the life of being the daughter of a lord? Why or why not?

B.   The frontier people used many quaint expressions or idioms that did not really mean what the words said. Caddie was often told to "hold your tongue," which simply meant to be quiet.

Idioms are colorful words used to convey a description or an idea. The words do not actually mean what they say. For example: "We're in hot water" has nothing to do with water. It simply means we are in trouble.

Choose four of the common idioms listed below. Who in the novel would have used the idiom, and when?

Stop pulling my leg.
It's a dog's life.
You could have knocked me over with a feather.
It's just chicken feed.
We're up a creek.
That's the way the cookie crumbles.
It's in the bag.
Go fly a kite.
Cat got your tongue?
He has a green thumb.

1.   (Character) _____ would have said (idiom)

_____ to or about

_____ when

_____ .

2.   (Character) _____ would have said (idiom)

_____ to or about

_____ when

_____ .

3.   (Character) _____ would have said (idiom)

_____ to or about

_____ when

_____ .

4.   (Character) _____ would have said (idiom)

_____ to or about

_____ when

_____ .

C.   Famous firsts for women:

Caddie was "ahead of her time"; that is, she wanted to do things that were not an accepted part of her society. Following is a list of women who were the first to do things that were once considered to be activities for men only. Choose one of the women to find out more about. Complete the bio-poem model about the woman you choose.

First woman elected to the United States House of Representatives: JEANETTE RANKIN
First woman doctor with medical degree in the United States: ELIZABETH BLACKWELL
First woman to pilot a plane alone across the Atlantic Ocean: AMELIA EARHART
First woman three-time Olympic gold medal winner: WILMA RUDOLPH

Bio-Poem

Line 1   First name only _____

Line 2   Four traits _____

Line 3   Related to _____

Line 4   Cares deeply about _____

Line 5   Who feels _____

Line 6   Who needs _____

Line 7   Who gives _____

Line 8   Who fears _____

Line 9   Who would like to see _____

Line 10   Resident of _____

What similarities can you find between the woman you chose and Caddie Woodlawn?

_____

_____

_____

Island of the Blue Dolphins, by Scott O'Dell. Houghton Mifflin, 1960.

　　Karana, a young Indian girl, lived with her family on an island in the Pacific Ocean. As she and her brother Ramo gathered roots and herbs, they were ever-watchful for the enemy Aleut ships and the fierce warriors that were a threat to her peaceful tribe. When danger threatened, Karana would hide in the ravine behind the thick toyan bushes. After the death of Karana's father, Chief Chowig, a large ship came to the island to take the people away. When Karana realized that Ramo was not on the ship she jumped into the water and swam back to the abandoned island. Ramo is killed by wild dogs and Karana must survive alone. She makes crude weapons and gathers shellfish, abalones, and water. She builds a house on the headland and constructs a fence held together by strands of bull kelp and sinew. But strangely enough, as the years pass Karana slowly makes friends with the leader of the wild dog pack, Rontu. And then the day came when the Aleut ship approached once again!

Activities

A.　Below is a list of words from the story *Island of the Blue Dolphins*. Guess whether you think the word is a person, place or thing. If you guess it is a person put "P" on the line. If you guess it's a place put "PL," and for a thing put "T." Read the description to support or disprove your guesses.

1. _____ Aleut	5. _____ abalones	9. _____ rontu
2. _____ ravine	6. _____ sinew	10. _____ karana
3. _____ toyan	7. _____ ghalas-at	11. _____ chowig
4. _____ kelp	8. _____ headland	12. _____ ramo

B.　Questions to ponder:

　　1.　Predict what would have happened if Tutok had shown the rest of the Aleuts where Karana was hiding.

　　2.　Design a floating device that Karana could have made from things on the island to get from the island to the white man's land.

　　3.　Hypothesize what would have happened to Karana if she had not made friends with the wild dog that she later named Rontu.

　　4.　Create a new article of clothing or item of jewelry that Karana or someone on an island can make using items on or around the island.

C.　Pattern poem: Using the pattern provided, complete the poem by choosing a place to live. List at least four things a person would do there. Finally, pick another place and list something you could do only if you were there. Example:

If I lived on the Island of the Blue Dolphins
I'd have to make my own weapons and tools, I would
travel by foot or by boat, I would gather my own food
and I'd make friends with the animals.
But I wouldn't visit the Eiffel Tower
Because only people in Paris can do that.

D.   Newspaper article:

ARCHAEOLOGISTS MAKE TRUE CONNECTION WITH THE PAST THROUGH YOUNG EYES.

SAN DIEGO, California (AP)—Two American archaeologists from the Museum of Lost Islands in San Diego, California today made known some findings on a small island approximately 75 miles southwest of Los Angeles. Maps dating back to the 1600s cite this island as La Isla de San Nicolas, but Marvin Richards and Lema Wilson call their find the Island of the Blue Dolphins because "dolphins play in the waters surrounding this land form which itself resembles that of a dolphin lying on its side."

Using sophisticated equipment, Richards and Wilson were able to completely excavate in near perfect condition a grave-like area in rock on the headland. Uncovered was the skeleton of a large dog, multi-colored pebbles, a gnawed stick, sand flowers, and a log. Carbon-14 tests show that these objects date from approximately 1835. This is presently being confirmed by scientists deciphering the found log.

"What we have here," explained an excited Wilson, "is a journal of a young girl who lived a solitary life on this ancient land for nearly 20 years! To be able to read what she saw and did—and more importantly, felt—is a dream. We can actually step back into time with an actual eye witness."

Additional information on the findings is due to be released within the next three to four months, when journal entries have been more fully deciphered.

Obviously, these journals were written by Karana and buried with Rontu. Select one incident from Karana's life story and write what you think she would have said at the time about the happening. Remember, you are Karana and you not only recount the event but also your feelings about it. You may need to write three or more entries about the event.

_____

_____

_____

_____

_____

_____

Sarah Bishop, by Scott O'Dell. Houghton Mifflin, 1980.

My name is Sarah Bishop. My home is a dark cave in the wilderness. I am a fugitive and I hear the roar of the muskets and firelocks although the mountain has its own silence. At night when I close my eyes the terrible moments return. I see our home aflame and our barn burning and the monstrous figure of my father staggering toward me. The Skinners did their work well. Not so much as a chowder bowl was left in the blackened ashes.

My father paid with his life for his Tory beliefs. Yet it was the British he defended who killed my brother. It was the British who falsely accused me of setting a fire and who would have taken me prisoner had I not escaped. No apothecary alive has a medicine for the sickness I feel at this moment.

Listen! There is a shadow against the rock, a shuffling sound of heavy footsteps coming toward me. Is it the green-eyed Hessian with the twisted, cruel mouth, who tracks me? No, the sound has faded, 'twas only a wild creature trying to survive as I am trying to survive.

I ration my small store of russets and maize, which must last the winter. I carefully store the gunpowder, molasses, salt, and tea bought at the Quaker store before my exile, keeping them hidden from the vermin that share my shelter. I shall survive the coming winter. My light is deer tallow, my bed, fur pelts; my food is mostly fish caught on lines made of deer sinews. Yes, with the coming snows I shall be fed and warm, but nothing made by either man nor nature will ever again warm my heart.

Activities

A. Pre-reading activity: Following are some numbered categories:

      (1) things needed for wilderness survival
      (2) loyal to King George
      (3) patriots
      (4) food
      (5) other (does not fit categories 1-4)

In front of each word below write the number of the category in which it belongs. Guess if you do not know the word. Then listen to the description from *Sarah Bishop* and support or disprove your choices.

_____ musket	_____ Tory	_____ vermin	_____ pelt
_____ maize	_____ Skinners	_____ tallow	_____ chowder
_____ Quaker	_____ Russet	_____ apothecary	_____ firelock
_____ sinew	_____ Hessian		

B.   Concert reading: Select music that fits the mood of the description above. Two appropriate pieces might be Wagner's "Prelude to Lohengrin" or Samuel Barber's "Adagio for Strings." Read the description with the mood music in the background. Reading to mood music helps to get the words off the page to get to the images and feelings underneath.

C.   Questions to ponder:

1.   What similarities are there between prejudice in Sarah Bishop's day and prejudice today?

2.   Suppose that Sarah had not run away to the wilderness. What might her fate have been?

3.   If you were Sarah, would you have helped those who wronged you? Why or why not?

4.   What was the significance in the story of the white bat? The copperhead?

5.   Name any other book with a female main character. How many ways are Sarah Bishop and that character alike?

D.   Problem solving: Read the story up to the problem. Example: Sarah must evade the British who want to put her in prison. How shall she do this? Set up a problem-solving grid:

Ideas	Fast	Low Cost	Effective	Total
Go to a neighbor for shelter	1	1	3	5

Score 1 = no 2 = maybe 3 = yes

E.   Acting-out vocabulary: Two teams are given separate word lists from the story. Examples from *Sarah Bishop*: list 1 would be pelt, cave, snake, Quaker, Tory; list 2 would be Skinner, candle, girl, maize, gun. Each team has three minutes to guess the words as they are acted out (not spoken) by a team member. The team that gets the most words in the shortest period of time is the winner.

F.   Debate: Each team has a set period of time to debate an issue. An example from *Sarah Bishop* would be: The Colonists had a right to revolt against British rule. The class votes for the team with the best arguments. Or list pros and cons (an equal number of each) on an issue.

The True Confessions of Charlotte Doyle, by Avi. Orchard, 1990.

Thirteen-year-old Charlotte Doyle is the lone passenger on the *Sea Hawk,* bound from London to New York. The cruel Captain Jaggery has Charlotte's friend, the ship's cook, beaten to death on the deck of the ship. Charlotte realizes that the captain is not her friend but has no friends among the crew either because it was her tattling to the captain about the grumblings of the crew that brought about the cook's death. Will Charlotte survive the rest of the trip without a single person to protect her? To find out, read *The Tru Confessions of Charlotte Doyle.*

Activities

A.   Topic focusing: Answer the following questions from your experience. Guess if you do not know. Support or disprove your guesses by reading about sailing ships in the *World Book Encyclopedia.*

   1.   How many separate sails did a clipper ship have? _____

   2.   *The Great Republic,* the largest clipper ship ever made, weighed how many tons? _____

   3.   How long (in feet) was *The Great Republic?* _____

   4.   How many days did it take a typical clipper ship to sail from London to New York? ___

   5.   How many men made up a typical crew? ____

   Answers: 1, 30; 2, 4,555; 3, 325; 4, 12 days 9 hours; 5, 130.

B.   Rank order: It is 1830. You are the only passenger on a sailing ship from London to New York. You hear the crew grumbling and the word. "mutiny." It is four days until the ship reaches land. Number the actions below in the order in which you would do them:

   1.   Tell the captain what you have heard

   2.   Say nothing

   3.   Ask crew members for more details

   4.   Agree with the crew and join the mutiny

   5.   Wait until the ship reaches port and tell someone in authority

C.   Responding to the novel: In how many ways is the tale of Charlotte Doyle like the story of Rapunzel?

D.   Pick a project: Decide how you will respond to the novel. Choose a topic, choose a verb and choose a product. Make a task statement. See the example below.

Verb	Topic	Product
Compare	Titanic disaster	poem
Create	Famous pirates	song
Describe	Charlotte Doyle	interview
Record	Famous person	journal
Judge	connected with	mystery
Summarize	with the sea	report

Sample statement: I will describe a famous person connected with the sea in a mystery report.

E.   Who am I?:

1.   Choose a famous person connected in some way with the sea.

2.   Read about that person's life and list 10 things (clues) about the person that you would like to share with others.

3.   One of your clues must be a "give-away" clue.

4.   Ask a volunteer to give you a number between 1 and 10. Read the clue for that number. The volunteer can guess who the person is or pass.

5.   The game continues with other students guessing additional clues until all clues have been read or the mystery person is revealed.

Example:

1.   I was born in Hannibal, Missouri.

2.   I used a school atlas as a map in my travels.

3.   I once lived in a town with 93 saloons, 54 boarding houses, 23 restaurants, and 2 sausage makers.

4.   I liked to tell stories but I never became a writer.

5.   In Honolulu I learned to play the ukulele.

6.   One goal in my life was to help other people.

7.   I was a world traveler.

8.   I claimed to have been born in a cyclone on the Mississippi River.

9.   I once helped to save the lives of 23 people.

10.   I was known as "unsinkable" and as the heroine of the *Titanic* disaster.

Answer: Molly Brown.

The Heroine of the Titanic, by Joan W. Blos. Macmillan, 1982.

Here is a tale both true and otherwise of the life of Molly Brown. She is remembered for saving the lives of 23 people during the *Titanic* disaster. Part of her story is told here in a "To Test the Truth" script. This can be used as a model to report on any famous person or event.

Activities

A. "To Test the Truth" show: Three people pretend to be the same famous person. Only one tells the truth. The class votes on who the real person is.

HOSTESS: LORETTA BORE: Welcome everyone to our show. Only one eyewitness is telling the complete truth. It is up to you to guess which it is. Now let's meet our guests.

EYEWITNESS #1: My name is Molly Brown and I was an eyewitness to the sinking of the *Titanic.* I was reading in my stateroom when I felt a terrible jolt. We had hit an iceberg.

EYEWITNESS #2: My name is Molly Brown. I was traveling with my husband, James, when there was this terrible crash. James pushed people aside so I could get into a boat.

EYEWITNESS #3: My name is Mrs. James J. Brown and I was a passenger on the *Titanic* when it began to sink. I made it to a lifeboat manned by a drunken sailor.

BORE: What else can you tell us?

EYEWITNESS #1: There was such panic and since I had never learned to read, I could not read the instructions given us as to what to do in an emergency. I was so frightened.

EYEWITNESS #2: I had no one to depend on but myself so I grabbed my mink coat and made it to a lifeboat before the *Titanic* went under.

EYEWITNESS #3: The sailor in our boat did nothing to help the frightened people so I took charge. I got them to rowing and singing to keep their spirits up.

BORE: Now it is time to decide who is the real eyewitness to the sinking of the *Titanic.* We will vote by a show of hands. Is it #1? (Wait for show of hands.) Is it #2? (Wait for show of hands.) Is it #3? (Wait for show of hands.). Now for the moment you have all been waiting for. Will the real Molly Brown step forward?

HEROES: PICTURE BOOKS—REAL LIFE HEROES

Following one's passion or beliefs can often be heroic, especially when others ridicule you or put obstacles in the way. Following are three heroes who had huge difficulties to overcome before they achieved greatness.

Anton Leeuwenhoek

The Microscope, by Maxine Kumin. Harper, 1984.

This is the tale of a forgetful storekeeper who was so fascinated with glass lenses that he ignored other responsibilities. The townsfolk laughed at him and called him "Dumkopf," but nothing could dampen Anton's curiosity as he investigated the power of glass lenses. He finally became known as the inventor of the microscope.

Activity: Told in verse, this is fun to read to rhythm music.

Abraham Lincoln

Young Abe Lincoln: The Frontier Days, 1809–1837, by Cheryl Harness. National Geographic, 1998.

Lincoln overcame poverty and a lack of formal education to become a sought-after lawyer and finally President of the United States. This book shows the many obstacles that he had to overcome.

Activity: To introduce this book ask students to vote on which statements are true:

1. My home in Indiana was a three-sided shelter with a fire on the fourth side that kept us from freezing to death.

2. My mother taught me to read at home until I was 15. I learned to read between hunting and chores.

3. I saved wages earned from cutting wood and doing farm work to buy books.

Share the book to support or disprove guesses.

Elijah McCoy

The Real McCoy, by Wendy Towle. Scholastic, 1996.

This is the story of African-American inventor Elijah McCoy who was the son of slaves. His inventions were used throughout the railroad industry, but getting them accepted at first took heroic effort.

Activity: Write about his life as a bio-poem, using the following model:

Name
Who fears
Four traits   Who gives
Related to   Who would like to see
Who has   Resident of

Bob Lemmons

Black Cowboy, Wild Horses: A True Story, by Julius Lester and Jerry Pinkney. Dial, 1988.

As lightning blazes through the night sky, Bob Lemmons sees the wild mustangs galloping across the open plains. Bob has tracked the horses for days, reading their hoofprints on the ground. Now he and his horse, Warrior, will run with the mustangs day and night until they accept his presence. Then Bob and Warrior will challenge the stallion leader to a fight to take over the wild herd and bring it back into the corral.

This is the true story of Bob Lemmons, a former slave whose tracking ability was legendary. He could look at the ground and "read what animals had walked on it, their size and weight, when they had passed by, and where they were going." When he finds the wild herd, one of the colts is bitten by a rattler and the leader of the herd has trouble getting the colt's mother to leave it and run with the herd. Bob decides that this is the time to challenge the leader and take over the herd, but a wild mustang is not easy to challenge. Only bravery and know-how will help Bob to succeed.

Activities

A. Questions to ponder:

1. Bob Lemmons never learned to read words but he could read the land. Which skill was most important in his work? Why?

2. List 10 words that describe Bob Lemmons. Rank order your list from the one that best describes him to the one that least describes him. Explain your rankings.

3. When a rattlesnake struck a colt and killed it, Bob did not kill the rattler. Why?

4. Bad weather didn't seem to bother Bob. Do you think he would have preferred a soft feather bed to sleeping upright on his horse? Why or why not?

B. Questions to guess:

Guess the answer to these questions about mustangs. Then support or disprove your guesses by studying the following data bank. Answer yes or no:

1. A horse can weigh more than one ton. _____

2. A horse has 32 teeth. _____

3. A horse can see both sideways and behind. _____

4. Long ago horses were used to pull railroad cars. _____

5. Horses were very important to both the Indians and the settlers. _____

Horse

Used For
Carried soldiers
Pulled wagons and carriages
Hauled trains on short railroads
Pulled plows

Eats
corn
hay
grass
oats

Does
gallops, trots, walks
grows thick coat of hair every fall
Never sheds the hair of a tail or mane
Can see sideways & a little behind
Has a good memory

Looks Like
weighs 300–2,600 lbs.
has rippling muscles
has long slim legs
has 36–40 teeth

C. Create a FOR SALE poster for Warrior that Bob Lemmons might have seen that convinced him that he must have this horse. What qualities would be listed on the poster that would appeal to Bob?

Neil Armstrong

One Giant Leap: The Story of Neil Armstrong, by Don Brown. Houghton Mifflin, 1998.

While the pioneers who headed west were the heroes of early days, the pioneers of space are the heroes of today. Read about a modern space hero in this book.

As a young boy, Neil Armstrong had a recurring dream in which he held his breath and floated high above people, houses, and cars. He spent his free time reading stacks of flying magazines, building model airplanes, and staring through the homemade telescope mounted on the roof of his neighbor's garage. As a teenager, Neil became obsessed with the idea of flight, working odd jobs to pay for flying lessons at a nearby airport. He earned his student's flying license on his sixteenth birthday.

But who was to know that this shy boy who also loved books and music would become the first person to set foot on the moon, on July 20, 1969? This is the inspiring story of one boy's dream, a dream of flying that landed him more than 200,000 miles away in space, gazing upon the awesome sight of a tiny Earth hanging suspended in a perfectly black sky. This story reveals the achievement of this American legend, Neil Armstrong, reminding us that all heroes were once children.

Activities

A. Questions to ponder:

1. What are the qualities of a hero? Did Neil Armstrong show any of these qualities as a child?

2. Was hard work a fair exchange for Neil's airplane magazines and models? Why do you think so?

3. Do you think a shy person can be a hero? Explain.

4. Would you work 25 hours to get to fly a plane for 1 hour? Why do you think Neil did this?

5. Buzz Aldrin and Mike Collins were the other astronauts who flew on the moon mission with Neil. Which of Neil's qualities do you think they shared?

6. Is team work important in space travel? Why or why not?

7. Why might Neil's footprints remain on the moon for a million years?

B. A Web site too good to miss: In the Gallery of Achievers you can read about individuals who have shaped the twentienth century by their accomplishments. Visit the Halls of Arts, Business, Public Service, Science and Explorations, Sports, and The American Dream at: http:www.achievement.org.

HEROES: NOVELS

Harry Potter and the Sorcerer's Stone, by J. K. Rowling. Arthur A. Levine Books/Scholastic Press, 1997.

Harry Potter has never been the start of a Quidditch team, scoring points while riding a broom far above the ground. He knows no spells, has never helped to hatch a dragon, and has never worn a cloak of invisibility. All he knows is a miserable life with the Dursleys, his horrible aunt and uncle, and their abominable son, Dudley, a great big swollen spoiled bully. Harry's room is a tiny closet at the foot of the stairs, and he hasn't had a birthday party in 11 years. Harry is small and his glasses are held together with scotch tape.

But Harry's life changes when a mysterious letter arrives by owl messenger. The letter is an invitation to Hogwarts School of Witchcraft and Wizardry, where Harry finds not only friends aerial sports, and magic in everything from classes to meals, but also a great destiny that has been waiting for him, if he can survive the encounter. Hogwarts School is threatened by an evil force and Harry must meet the challenge and save the school, not by using magic, but by calling on his own reserves of courage and determination.

Activities

A.   Questions to think about:

1.   Why do you think Harry was treated so badly by the Dursleys?

2.   What clues did the author give to show that Harry had unusual powers before he found out he was eligible to attend Hogwarts School?

3.   Why did the Dursleys try to prevent Harry from seeing the letters that arrived for him?

4.   What role did Hagrid play in the story? How would the story change if Hagrid had not been one of the characters?

5.   Cite specific instances where the author blends the real world with Harry's fantasy world. Why do you think she places the characters in two very different worlds?

6.   Although Professor Snape did not turn out to be the villain of the story, what incidents led you to believe that he was? Why do you think the author kept pointing the finger of suspicion at him?

7.   What abilities did Harry have that allowed him to become the star of the Quidditch team? Do you think the author is saying that we all have special abilities that enable us to star at something? Why or why not?

8.   Was it the cloak of invisibility, Harry's magic powers, or Harry's determination not to give up that saved the stone? Why do you think so?

9.   What role did Hagrid's dragon play in the story?

10.   What lessons about life did Harry learn outside the classrooms at Hogwarts?

B.   Creating mental pictures: The author uses descriptive words to create the mental picture she wants the reader to see. Use the most descriptive words possible to create a mental picture for your reader, using the form below. More than one word can go on a line.

The long hallway was as dark as _____. Professor Snape

crept cautiously along the corridor, reaching out to find his way with hands that were

_____. A faint light from the very end of the hall cast shadows of

_____ before him. Professor Snape stopped, afraid of what he

would find around the corner. Slowly, slowly he stretched his _____ neck until

his eyes locked in horror on a _____. It was guarding

the door that led to the room where the Sorcerer's Stone lay.

The creature sensed a foreign presence and let out an eerie _____ that

made the hairs on the Professor's neck stand on end. And then the creature saw Snape! With a

terrible _____ the monster _____.

Snape reacted quickly and _____, leaving the monster

_____ and the Stone untouched.

C.   A rewrite challenge! Rewrite the following sentences, keeping the same meaning. Do
     not use any word in your sentences that contains the letter "A."

1.   Harry awoke so early that it was still dark.

     _____

     _____

2.   He felt a cold breeze on the back of his neck and sat upright.

     _____

     _____

3.   Peeves blew hard and zoomed backwards, cackling.

     _____

     _____

4.   The rain pounded against the castle walls.

     _____

     _____

5.   The Quidditch players had to battle the heavy rain.

_____

_____

6.   Harry grabbed the cat by the end of its tail.

_____

_____

7.   They staggered as they walked out onto the field.

_____

_____

D.   A quotation to think about: On December 8, 1941, in a speech to Congress and the American people, President Franklin Delano Roosevelt said: "The only thing we have to fear is fear itself."

How is this quotation like the theme of *Harry Potter and the Sorcerer's Stone?*

Can you name other real people who have shown great courage when facing danger?

Watch your newspaper and bring to class any stories you find about ordinary people performing courageous acts. Create a bulletin board display of these true stories.

Call It Courage, by Armstrong Sperry. Macmillan, 1968.

I have always hated my name: "Mafatu"—Stout Heart—What a name for a coward such as I! And I have always been afraid of the sea … for as long as I can remember. "So what?" you say! "A lot of people are afraid of the water." You must understand, it is different here in the South Seas, in my time. The Polynesian people worship courage. There is no place here for a gutless boy.

It all began when I was three. A hurricane swept through Hikueru, knocking down trees and capsizing boats. My mother had taken me in an outrigger to gather sea urchins. I'll never forget her cries, as the waves tore apart our boat. Poor Mama! She seized me before the boat went down, and refused to die until she had gotten me safely over the sharp coral onto the shore.

Now I cannot bear to go out into the water. Of course everyone laughs at me and teases me. Here I am, son of the Chief, and I cannot even go spear fishing with the other boys. It's not that I haven't tried. Suddenly a picture flashes into mind—I'm clinging to my mother's neck as the sharp-toothed mao circle around and I am so terrified that I drop my spear.

I can't take it anymore. Today even my best friend made fun of me. All I have left are my animal friends—my little dog and my bird, an albatross whose life I once saved. To die would be better than to feel such a coward; I will face my fear and sail alone. I will face creatures of the deep and those on the islands. If the wild boar charges me I will face it and be killed or return with a necklace made from its tusks.

If the feke reaches from the depths to grab me with her eight arms, I will fight her. If Moana the Sea God draws me down to her dark heart, then so it will be!

Activities

A. Pre-reading activity: Suppose you found yourself marooned on a desert island. Rank the following problems in the order of importance to you, with "1" being the problem you would need to solve first.

___ no shelter	___ hunger
___ a leg wound made by coral	___ no human company
___ thirst	___ no fire
___ not knowing when cannibals will arrive	___ no canoe for getting off the island
___ no food and water for dog	___ no knife
___ no trap for catching fish	

As you read the book, think about how Mafatu would probably rank these items.

B. Introducing vocabulary: Following are some words used in the story; some may be new to you. Work with a partner to decide if a word is a person, place, animal or object. Listen to the description to support or disprove your guesses. Put a "P" for person, "PL" for place, "A" for animal, "O" for Object:

____ albatross	____ boar	____ Polynesian	____ coral
____ feke	____ mao	____ outrigger	____ Hikueru
____ sea urchins	____ tusks	____ Moana	

C. Questions to ponder:

1. Why was the boy afraid of the sea? What finally gave him the courage to face it?

2. How does the author build suspense? What were the questions in your mind that drove you to keep on reading for answers? At what point was the tension greatest?

3. How did Mafatu change? What did he learn?

4. What were the conflicts between Mafatu and nature? What conflicts did Mafatu have with other people? What inner conflicts did he have?

5. Name another story about survival. In how many ways is *Call It Courage* like that story?

D. Post-reading activity: Use the following poetry model to tell how Mafatu went from feeling that he is a coward to feeling that he is a hero.

Diamante

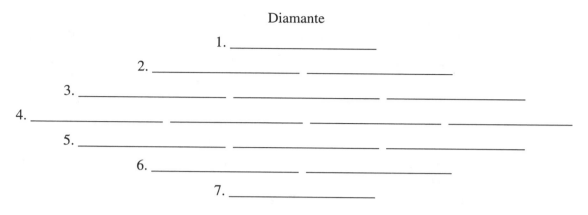

1.   one word—subject noun

2.   two words—adjectives

3.   three words—participles

4.   four words—nouns related to the subject

5.   three words—participles

6.   two words—adjectives

7.   one word—noun, opposite of the subject

The Haymeadow, by Gary Paulsen. Delacorte, 1992.

At fourteen John Barron is asked, like his father and his father's father before him, to spend the summer taking care of their six thousand sheep in the haymeadow. John will be alone, except for two horses, four dogs, and all those sheep.

John doesn't feel up to the task but he hopes against hope that if he can accomplish it, he will finally please his undemonstrative father. But John finds that the adage "things just happen to sheep" is true when the river floods, coyotes attack, and one dog's feet get cut. Through it all John relies on his own resourcefulness, ingenuity, and talents to try to get through.

Activities

A.   Questions to ponder:

1.   Why do you think John admired the great grandfather he had never known more than his father, who was a good man?

2.   Tink said that the sheep, the dogs, and the mountains were all the companionship a man needed. Do you agree or disagree? Why?

3.   List and rank order the many dangers John faced. Defend your ranking.

4.   Why do you think John's father waited so long to tell the boy the truth about his great grandfather?

5.   Compare this novel to Gary Paulsen's *Hatchet*. How are the two novels alike?

B. Vocabulary activities: What can you do with a word?

The words below appear in the novel. Work with a partner. Cut the words apart.

1. Group the words. No group should have fewer than three words. Label the group.

2. Construct a sentence using as many of the words as you can. Add other words as needed. The sentence might describe the cover of the book or tell what you think the novel will be about.

3. Turn the words face down. Choose three words. Use all three words correctly in one sentence.

4. Working with a group, develop a "Concentration" game using the words and their definitions.

5. Divide into teams. Choose five words from the list for a game of "Charades."

6. Match as many words as you can by placing two words together that are related. Identify the words and explain the relationship to the class.

Cawley	John	Wyoming
mountains	chuckwagon	roundup
haymeadow	timberline	vague
persistent	ammonia	resemblance
uncanny	provisions	granary
contraption	farrier	stragglers
intersection	sinkhole	hobble
rebellious	frustrated	stubborn
altitude	ewe	encouragement
momentarily	intensity	canyon
coyotes	poisoned	binoculars
slaughter	disaster	flash flood
rattlesnake	accustomed	disturbance
doubletree	crosspiece	lariat

C. John and Cawley, the hired hand, make ready for the trip to the haymeadow. They set out with the wagon, horses, dogs, and sheep. Cawley lets John come up with a solution about how to get the sheep across the highway. John made a list of things he thought he would need for the-three month stay in the meadow:

Gun
Food
Sleeping gear
Four pairs of socks
Four pairs of underwear
Two shirts
Three pairs of jeans
Toothbrush

Think about the experience John is about to have. What should he have added to his list?

D.   Point of view:

John's first day alone with the sheep is filled with disasters. A lamb is bitten by a rattlesnake, a skunk sprays John and one of the dogs, another dog has an injured paw, and a bobcat stampedes the sheep. Write a sentence describing:

1.   A bobcat from the point of view of a zoo curator.

_____

2.   A bobcat from John Barron's point of view.

_____

3.   A sheep ranch from the point of view of the corporation that owns it.

_____

4.   A sheep ranch from John's father's point of view.

_____

5.   A rattlesnake from the point of view of a herpetologist.

_____

6.   A rattlesnake from John's point of view.

_____

E.   It's all in a word:

Cawley and John reach the haymeadow. During the ride, Cawley talks to John about the extraordinary inborn abilities of the dogs. Cawley heads back to the ranch, leaving John on his own.

1.   The word that best describes John alone in the haymeadow is:

A) forlorn   B) scared   C) weak   D) helpless

because _____

2.   The word that best describes a summer storm is:

A) mystical   B) magnificent C) malevolent   D) eerie

because _____

3.   The word that best describes a flock of 6000 sheep is:

A) overwhelming   B) ambitious   C) dumb   D) immense

because _____

4.   The word that best describes John's great grandfather is:

A) free   B) lonely   C) adventurous   D) ambitious

because _____

5. The word that best describes the haymeadow is:

A) vast   B) forlorn   C) awesome   D) frightening

because _____

6. The word that best describes John's feeling for his great-grandfather is:

A) revulsion   B) admiration   C) kinship   D) curiosity

because _____

7. Which word best describe risking your life to save an animal?

A) ridiculous   B) responsible   C) mandatory   D) daring

because _____

8. The word that best describes Cawley is:

A) unhappy   B) confused   C) courageous   D) taciturn

because _____

Stone Fox, by John Gardiner. HarperCollins, 1980.

Little Willy was worried. Not just a little bit worried like when he overslept that one morning and found the chickens had eaten his breakfast, but a lot worried. The worry began the morning grandfather would not get out of bed. Grandfather was usually the first one up and had half the farm chores done before Willy stirred. On the morning grandfather did not get up, Willy was so worried that he ran to get the doctor. She gave grandfather a real thorough examination but could find nothing wrong with him. "Some folks just decide to stop living," she said, "and there is not much anyone can do about it until they change their minds."

Willy was determined to get grandfather to change his mind! The potato crop was ready for harvest and Willy managed it alone by hitching up his dog, Searchlight, to the plow. But when the tax man came Willy didn't know *what* to do.

The tax man talked about selling the farm for back taxes. "But we always pay the bills on time," Willy protested. "Not the tax bills," the tax man replied. "You owe ten years' back taxes. That comes to about five hundred dollars."

Five hundred dollars! Willy had never seen so much money. Grandfather couldn't help. He just lay in bed and stared at the ceiling. How was Willy going to raise five hundred dollars? He watched the taxman's retreating back. "You can't take our farm!" Willy screamed.

The tax man turned around and smiled through his yellow-stained teeth. "Oh, yes we can," he said.

Activities

A. Willy has a very large problem for a very small boy. On the grid that follows, decide what facts are important and what the major problem is. List many ways that Willy might deal with the problem. Place these ideas on the decision grid. Add one more criterion for judging the ideas and evaluate each idea by giving it a rating of 1 (poor) to 5 (good). Total the score for each idea. What will be the best solution to the problem?

State the problem_____

Ideas	Fast	Safe	Possible	Will Work

B. Pattern report: Read about Wyoming (the setting of *Stone Fox*) and complete the following song by filling in the blank spaces. Find the capital and a large city. Now find some things that are manufactured there and some crops that are grown there. Fill in the blanks. Sing the song to your class to the tune of "She'll Be Coming Around the Mountain." Pattern and example:

State _____

Capital _____

Large city _____

Manufactured goods _____

Crops _____

She'll be coming from _____ when she comes,
                              Capital

She'll be coming from _____ when she comes,
                            Large city

She'll bring _____ (three products)

She'll bring _____(three crops)

She'll be coming from _____ when she comes.
                              State

Your turn:

She'll be coming from _____ when she comes,

She'll be coming from _____ when she comes,

She'll bring _____ and _____ and _____

She'll bring _____ and _____ and _____

She'll be coming from _____ when she comes.

C. Questions:

1. In what way is the setting of this story essential to the events that took place?

2. Could the story have taken place in any other setting?

Titanic Crossing, by Barbara Williams. Scholastic, 1995.

In 1912 Albert Trask, the young boy in this novel, embarks on the *Titanic* for a homeward journey to the United States. He is accompanied by his mother, his sister, and his uncle. Albert's father has recently passed away. Before Albert boards the magnificent ship he has read everything he could about the marvelous floating palace. The ship was widely advertised as the safest vessel on the sea and was guaranteed to be unsinkable.

Upon boarding the ship Albert is amazed by its size and beauty. Albert and his family meet many people, listen to wonderful music, enjoy delicious food, and generally have a pleasant voyage. Then, on the fateful evening of April 15th, the ship hits an iceberg, tearing a huge gash in its side. What was supposed to be the safest vessel on the high seas begins to sink. Albert is then faced with one of the toughest decisions he will ever have to make. To see if you agree with his decision, join 13-year-old Albert, his family, and the other passengers on board the *Titanic* in the spring of 1912.

Activities

A. Questions to ponder:

1. How did Albert's feelings change from the beginning to the end of the novel?

2. Of all the parts of the ship that Albert explored, which do you think he found most fascinating? Tell why.

3. What other ideas could you give Albert for acquiring enough money to buy the lace tablecloth for his mother?

4. Albert was accused of meanness to his sister when she broke his father's watch. What should Albert have done?

5. Why do you think Albert turned down the chance to get in a lifeboat?

6. List all the words you can to describe Albert. Which one word from your list best describes him? Why?

7. What if Albert's mother had survived? How might the story have changed?

8. List reasons Albert had difficulty in dealing with his grandmother's personality.

B.   Chapter projects:

Chapters One through Three

   The setting is London, England. We meet the Trask family: 13-year-old Albert, his sister, Virginia, his widowed mother, and his Uncle Claybourne. They are about to embark on the *Titanic* for their home in the United States.

   Activity: Research a famous sight in London (examples: Buckingham Palace, the Tower of London, Westminster Cathedral) and include facts about the sight in the riddle poem below.

Let us go to London's places

And see the city's various faces

We will find: (List 4–6 things one would see.)

_____

_____

_____

_____

_____

_____

(List 6 more specific details in phrases.)

But that's not all: _____

_____

_____

_____

_____

_____

Do you know where we are?

Chapters Four through Nine

   The Trask family is now on board the *Titanic,* which has left port for the journey to America. Six-year-old Virginia claims that she is ill and Mrs. Trask appears to be very protective of her. The family finds that their table companions at dinner and breakfast are the Brewer family, a mother and three children. Virginia takes Albert's watch, given to him by his father, and breaks it. Albert and Emily Brewer become friends. Albert goes to Uncle Claybourne for money because he wants to purchase an Irish tablecloth for his mother.

Activity: Albert wanted to be an architect but his mother did not approve, so he had to re-think his career choice. People often have to change their goals in life when other people or events interfere. Think about the goals of the many characters you have met in this novel. How many sentences can you complete following the pattern given?

Somebody	Wanted	But	So
ALBERT	WANTED to be an architect	BUT his mother objected	SO he changed his plans.

Chapters Ten through Fifteen

The action takes place on April 11–14. Albert talks about wanting to be an architect but his mother wants him to be a lawyer like his father and uncle. Emily and Albert talk to a seaman about the purpose of the lifeboats and ask how many people a lifeboat can hold. Albert also re-alizes how much fun the passengers in third class have compared to those traveling in first or second class. It is Sunday, April 14th. Albert wants to introduce his mother to the theatrical producer, Harry Gordon, so he attempts to have them meet when they go to worship service. We also meet some of the other first class passengers. In chapter fifteen the *Titanic* hits an ice-berg. Albert is one of the witnesses to the accident and realizes that things are about to get much worse.

Activity: Salvaging the *Titanic*. During the 1980s efforts were made to explore the *Titanic* and retrieve artifacts from the underwater ship. Find the main heading in the table below. Place it in the first box that follows the table. Fill in the subheadings in the four boxes below the main heading. Place the details that fit in the box below each subheading.

Answers: Main heading, 4. Subheadings: 10, with 2, 11, and 15 under it; 1, with 7, 12, and 14 under it; 6, with 3 and 13 under it; and 8, with 5 and 9 under it.

Chapters Sixteen through Twenty-Five

Disaster strikes the *Titanic* when it hits an iceberg. Albert has trouble finding his mother and his Uncle Claybourne so he gets Virginia ready and tells her they are going to play a game. The passengers of the *Titanic* begin to board the lifeboats. Albert has not been able to find his mother or uncle. The lifeboats are taking only women and children first. Virginia is put in a lifeboat but Albert is not allowed to go with her because he is considered to be a man. Albert finds himself alone and not sure of what to do. Albert is thrown overboard during the sinking of the ship and awakens to find himself on another ship that had rescued passengers. Albert and Virginia are reunited and face the reality of the deaths of their mother and uncle. We see them at the end of the novel living with their grandmother, coping with their new lives and trying to leave the past behind them.

Activity: Literary style: Following is a list of literary devices used by writers to make their writing more exciting:

Alliteration: Repeating beginning sounds (Peter Piper picked.)

Hyperbole: Absurd exaggeration.

Imagery: Use of the five senses in describing.

Metaphor: Comparing without using like or as. (The sea was a bathtub.)

Personification: Giving life to non living things. (Fingers of wind plucked the clothes.)

Repetition: Repeating phrases or words for emphasis (His right foot, his enormous right foot, lifted up and out.)

Simile: Comparing using like or as.

Summarize the novel, *Titanic Crossing*, in seven sentences, each sentence using one of the literary devices above.

1. ALLITERATION _____

    _____

2. HYPERBOLE _____

    _____

3. IMAGERY _____

    _____

4. METAPHOR _____

    _____

5. PEERSONIFICATION _____

    _____

6. REPETITION _____

    _____

7. SIMILE _____

    _____

Bearstone, by Will Hobbs. Macmillan, 1989.

Cloyd pulled the blue stone from his pocket and set the little bear on a flat rock at the very top of the mountain. "Lone Bear," he said aloud, "we're not so alone anymore."

Cloyd hasn't gone to school in four years. He's grown up without his parents, half-wild and alone, leading his grandmother's goats into remote Utah canyons. Sent away by his tribe to a group home in Colorado, he fails in school and runs away in search of his father, whom he has never known. Disappointed, he returns to the group home, alone.

When summer comes, Cloyd is sent to work for an old rancher who tells fascinating tales about a gold mine in the nearby mountains. Above the ranch, Cloyd finds a small turquoise bear and forges a new identity as "Lone Bear." He battles the old man over the never-ending ranch work, longs to ride off to the mountains, and makes an enemy of a bear hunter he will meet again. Finally reconciled, Cloyd and the old man ride into the high country together.

In *Bearstone*, a classic rite of passage story, myth and reality merge as a boy tracks his own dreams in a desperate attempt to save the last grizzly in the mountains. Lightning crackles, a blue horse tumbles down the mountainside, and an old man cries out in the darkness of a gold mine. Cloyd leaves behind his loneliness and learns to love and be loved.

Activities

A. Questions to ponder:

1. At the beginning of the novel Cloyd is an angry boy. List as many causes of his anger as you can. Rank order your list from the greatest to the least cause.

2. What is the significance of the turquoise bear? Why do you think this small stone meant so much to Cloyd?

3. Why do you think Cloyd gave himself a secret name? Did having a secret name help Cloyd in any way?

4. What was the role of Rusty in the story? Do you believe Rusty was basically a good person? Why or why not?

5. Did Rusty really not know he was killing a grizzly bear, which was a protected species? Explain why you think so. Why did Cloyd not tell what he saw?

B. The story setting: As Cloyd explores the mountains above Durango, he uses all of his powers of observation. Wildlife that might be unseen by the unobservant catches Cloyd's eye. Complete the observation report that follows as if you were Cloyd telling Walter the things that you saw on your mountain trek.

The Observation Report

Come with me to the _____

Listen for the _____

Follow the _____ as it _____

into the _____ . See the _____

hunt for _____ . The _____

flies into a _____ that looks just right for a

_____ . And _____

gather _____ for the _____ . And

when night comes, the _____

sleep in their _____ .

C. Wildlife in trouble:

In *Bearstone* Rusty kills a grizzly bear: "Suddenly the tall man stood out in the open in front of the bear with the bow pulled all the way back and the arrow aimed. Sensing something, the bear stood up as if to have a better look and took the arrow in its neck." As members of his party congratulate him on the kill, Rusty tells them that he is in big trouble because killing a grizzly is illegal. "They're protected. Hundred thousand dollar fine and a year in jail."

Guess which of the following animals is endangered right now:

_____ lemurs	_____ Mountain Gorillas	_____ tiger
_____ cheetah	_____ Peregrine falcon	_____ leopard
_____ rhino	_____ grizzly bear	_____ elephant

The correct answer is that ALL of these animals are endangered.

Choose an endangered animal to write about. Find out where it lives, what it looks like, and how it moves. Use the information in the pattern poem below. Example:

Animal name: Elephant
How it moves: Lumbering, plodding
Where: In Asian teak forests
Where: In the African grasslands
Describe: Gray Giant!

Animal name: _____

How it moves: _____ _____

Where: _____

Where: _____

Describe: _____

Beardance, by Will Hobbs. Atheneum, 1993. Grades 5–9.

When a novel is popular, readers want to know more about the characters and often write to authors asking for a *sequel,* another novel with the same characters. Will Hobbs wrote this sequel to *Bearstone,* titled *Beardance.*

This is a story of survival, both physical and spiritual. Cloyd Atcitty, who has named himself Lone Bear in the manner of his Ute heritage, takes an expedition into the mountains with his friend and guardian, Walter. Each has something on his mind: Walter dreams of unearthing a legendary gold treasure; Cloyd hopes to see another grizzly, although it is widely assumed that no grizzlies exist as far south as Colorado, certainly not since Rusty shot the one that Cloyd had seen the year before. Cloyd still can't forgive Rusty—or himself—for causing the bear's death. But he can't stop hoping for a miracle. The miracle comes in the form of a scientist who also seeks the grizzly. She and Cloyd have much to teach one another, but ultimately it is Cloyd—Lone Bear—who must risk life itself to save two grizzly cubs.

Activities

A.   You can tell from the description that two grizzly cubs are going to be in some sort of danger and that in rescuing them Cloyd will find himself in danger. Choose one of these situations:

1. Unscrupulous trappers have cornered the cubs in a small cave. They are about to enter the cave and kill the cubs for their fur, which they can sell at a high price.

2. A rock avalanche has buried one of the cubs up to its neck. The other cub stands beside the buried cub to protect it from anyone who would come near. The cub must be dug out before it dies.

3. It is spring and the mountain river goes crazy, overflowing its banks and taking everything in its path with it, including a small bear cub who is struggling helplessly against the current.

On a piece of paper tell how Cloyd saves the cub(s).

Read *Beardance* to see what the dangerous situation really is and how Cloyd deals with it.

Kneeknock Rise, by Natalie Babbitt. Farrar, 1970.

The Mammoth Mountains were not high enough to have their slopes and summits topped by a glacier. But they were high enough to cast a dark shadow over the little village of Instep, which served as a proscenium or stage for the fearful events that happened. One would never want to climb *these* mountains, for if you did you might meet the Megrimum! No one had ever seen this awful creature but everyone had heard it. On any stormy night its anguished and despairing howls rolled down the mountain, striking fear in the hearts of brave men and women alike. Even the animals cowered in fear and for this reason visitors did not stay long in the village.

Traveling merchants like the chandler (candle maker) did not tarry to gossip with the housewives. One look at the darkened rise of the mountain was enough to make them scurry. Yet the creature had for so long been a part of village life that the people would have missed it had it disappeared. So to keep it happy they held a fair each year and invited brave visitors to come and hear the creature's howls. Life might have gone on the way it always had if Egan, a reluctant hero, had not come to visit his aunt and uncle. When he dared to poke fun at the idea of a monster on the mountain, he received a dare to climb the mountain and take a look. To find out what Egan discovers on the mountain that will change lives in Instep forever, read *Kneeknock Rise*.

Activities

A.   Look at the following words. If you think a word is a person, put the letter "P" on the line in front of the word. If you think a word is a feeling, put the letter "F" on the line. If you think it is a nonliving thing that you can touch, put the letter "T" on the line. Guess if you do not know. Then listen to the description to prove or disprove your guesses.

____ glacier	____ slope	____ summit
____ anguish	____ despair	____ rise
____ Megrimum	____ mournful	____ chandler
____ fear	____ Egan	____ proscenium

B.   Questions to ponder:

1.   Explain this famous quote from Franklin D. Roosevelt. "The only thing we have to fear is fear itself."

2.   Did the villagers really want the Megrimum destroyed? Defend your answer.

3.   Why do you suppose no one in the village believed Egan's explanation of the Megrimum?

4.   How did the author build suspense in the story? Why did you want to go on reading?

5.   Could there really have been a creature in the cave? Why or why not?

6.   Egan is described as a reluctant hero. Does this mean he was not really a heroic person? Why or why not?

C.   Perform a "Megrimum Rap!"

Complete the missing words and perform the rap!

Oh, once there was a town sat below some hills,

They were called the (1) M _____ Mountains and they gave folks

(2) c _____.

For somewhere from the mists on a cold and stormy night.

A (3) M _____ raised its voice and gave the folks a

(4) f _____ .

CHORUS (Repeat)

Moan, creature, moan,

In the thunder and the lightning,

Like a wild and anguished beast,

Your cries are truly frightening.

Then there came to the town a lad so brave,

Who went up on the (5) m _____ to the mouth of the

(6) c _____ ,

And found that the sound was from a very hot (7) s _____

And that's how the mountain pretended to sing.

(Repeat Chorus)

Then back to the town went the boy with the news,

But the people wouldn't listen, they just refused

'Cause they loved the old (8) M _____ with its moans in the night,

And relished all their shivers and their shakes and their (9) f _____.

They said, "Boy, doesn't matter, what you think you saw or think you heard,

There is a (10) M _____

Just take our word!"

The authors and titles included in this index are those
that appear in text or in the annotations.